Introducing Communication Research

Introducing Communication Research

Paths of Inquiry

Donald Treadwell

Westfield State College

Los Angeles | London | New Delhi
Singapore | Washington DC

For information:

SAGE Publications, Inc.
2455 Teller Road
Thousand Oaks, California 91320
E-mail: order@sagepub.com

SAGE Publications India Pvt. Ltd.
B 1/I 1 Mohan Cooperative
   Industrial Area
Mathura Road, New Delhi 110 044
India

SAGE Publications Ltd.
1 Oliver's Yard
55 City Road
London EC1Y 1SP
United Kingdom

SAGE Publications
   Asia-Pacific Pte. Ltd.
33 Pekin Street #02-01
Far East Square
Singapore 048763

Printed in the United States of America

Library of Congress Cataloging-in-Publication Data

Treadwell, Donald.
Introducing communication research: Paths of inquiry / Donald Treadwell.
      p. cm.
Includes bibliographical references and index.
ISBN 978-1-4129-4457-1 (pbk.)
   1. Communication—Research—Methodology.   I. Title.

P91.3.T76 2011
302.207′2—dc22   2009043899

Printed on acid-free paper.

10   11   12   13   14   10   9   8   7   6   5   4   3   2   1

Acquiring Editor:	Todd R. Armstrong
Associate Editor:	Deya Saoud
Assistant Editor:	Aja Baker
Editorial Assistant:	Nathan Davidson
Production Editor:	Astrid Virding
Copy Editor:	Melinda Masson
Proofreader:	Dennis W. Webb
Indexer:	Kathleen Paparchontis
Typesetter:	C&M Digitals (P) Ltd.
Cover Designer:	Janet Kiesel
Marketing Manager:	Helen Salmon

Brief Contents

Detailed Contents

List of Exhibits

Preface

Congratulations! You have just finished a tough academic year (let's assume). Now it's time for that trip you have been dreaming about. Two inescapable questions come to mind immediately: Where will you go, and how will you get there?

Generally, you will have some goal in mind. Perhaps, as a lover of art, music, or history, you will be thinking of the great museums or concert halls of the world. Or perhaps you have always been intrigued by the cultures of Asia and think of Asia as a destination. Or perhaps you really want to spend time with Great-Aunt Minerva, who is an endless source of funny stories and whom you have not seen in years. Your trip is triggered by some basic interest, but interest alone is not enough to make it happen. To get to your destination, you must have a specific address, and you must decide whether you will get there by plane, train, car, ship, bicycle, walking, or any combination of these. Two further questions have answers that will shape the nature of your trip: What is my budget, and how much time do I have? Then there's the question of how you will experience your destination when you get there. Some of us like to "put down roots" and stay in one area to experience it as fully as possible. Others are movers—every day a new attraction. The first approach gives you an in-depth experience; the second gives you a broad experience.

Of course you will want to record events and perhaps let others know about your trip, and so questions of recording and communication arise. How will you document your trip—video, audio, photography, notepad, or all of the above? What will you record when you do record, for example, a memorable dining experience—the details of that great meal you had in the restaurant with the harbor view, photographs of the harbor view, or names and addresses of the interesting people you met at the restaurant? Most journeys are fun, interesting, and intellectually and emotionally satisfying. But you cannot undertake two journeys simultaneously, and you had better know where and how you are going or you won't get there.

Researching human communication is very similar. At heart, it is simply a journey from not knowing something to knowing something or knowing something more about human communication. Certainly it is interesting and intellectually rewarding. Broadcast news, love affairs, employee morale, social networking, Web "chat," soap operas, family dynamics, podcasts, advertising, "tweets," and group decision making are just a few manifestations of the complex interactions that we call human communication and that we can research.

Other travel analogies apply. It is difficult to take two journeys simultaneously, so most researchers opt to study one area at a time. They also have a specific "travel plan" in the form of decisions about the phenomena they will study, the method(s) they will use, and the people they will invite to be in their study. And they will undoubtedly seek the advice of those who have been there before to help them avoid the pitfalls and to maximize the return on the time, effort, and intellectual energy that good research demands. As with any journey, time and funding will also shape a research project.

Just as travel agents, Web sites, and guidebooks are your guides to satisfying travel experiences, this book is in a sense your travel guide to satisfying communication research experiences.

Chapters 1–3 examine some of the basic assumptions and disagreements about human communication and how best to understand it, as well as the ethical implications of becoming involved in people's lives as you study them. These chapters give you the language and customs of the territory you will be visiting—scholarly research in communication.

Chapter 4 will help you identify your specific areas of interest and how to find out more about them. It will help you identify the detailed reading you will need to do to get comfortable with the specific area you will be visiting.

Chapters 5–11 discuss mainstream research methods, statistics, and sampling. Metaphorically, these discussions of methods, sampling, and statistics will help you with your mode-of-travel decision. Automobiles can stop anytime you need them to; trucks consume more fuel but carry more weight. Planes are fast and provide a wonderful overview of the territory, weather permitting, but may not take you exactly where you want to go. So it is with research methods. There is no such thing as one best method, only a most appropriate method for your voyage of discovery.

We finish with a chapter on writing your research results so that others can get a good picture of where you went and how you went there, what you discovered, and how you have chosen to interpret it.

Each chapter has starter questions to get you thinking about your research, a chapter summary of key ideas, and an ethics panel to help you think about the implications of your research. Terminology that may be new to you is shown in boldface **like this** the first time it appears in the book. The glossary at the end of the book briefly defines each highlighted term.

Chapters 8–12 have a "Research in Practice" page, written by an industry professional, that shows you an example of communication research methods in practice. You will find additional study resources at www .sagepub.com/treadwellicr.

Communication research is almost inescapable in a communication career. If you are not involved in designing or initiating research at some level, you will almost certainly be in the position of having to interpret the research of others. Therefore, I suggest that you keep this book and find a place for it on your office bookshelf. The ideas and questions that you run into in your research courses will almost certainly come back to visit you in your professional career.

Welcome to that most fascinating of journeys—research in human communication.

For Faculty

Thank you for adopting this text. I have long wanted to write a summary text that gives students a sense of why scholars find human communication research so interesting and to set out some of the assumptions, questions, and methods behind research practice. I hope that this book will give students an enthusiasm for advanced research in communication and give those heading into professional careers a sense of the relevance of research to their careers.

The book aims to be affordable for students and to cover what I consider to be the basics. As noted in the student preface, the text begins with the theoretical bases, followed by mainstream research methods and a final chapter on writing research. The 12 chapters allow instructors to cover one topic a week and to expand their preferred topics while still covering all topics in the typical 15-week semester.

As noted, support for student learning includes chapter starter questions, a chapter summary, ethics panels, organizing examples, highlighted vocabulary words, and a glossary. Chapters 8–12 have a "Research in Practice" page, to show some applications of communication research outside of academia.

You will find additional resources and ideas in the online instructor's site at www.sagepub.com/treadwellicr.

Any faculty member teaching communication research is likely doing so because he or she shares my curiosity about how and why people communicate and my enthusiasm for the methods that give us insight on human communication. I hope you will find that this text makes a useful contribution to your research courses, and I welcome your thoughts on it.

Introducing Communication Research is accompanied by the following supplements, tailored to match the content of the book:

Student Study Site

The open access Student Study Site features a variety of useful resources including e-flashcards, web links, and study questions. Visit the study site at www.sagepub.com/treadwellicr.

Instructor Resources Website

This set of instructor's resources provides a number of helpful teaching aids for professors new to teaching the course and to using **Introducing Communication Research.** Included on the website are PowerPoint slides, a test bank, lecture notes, discussion questions, web resources, suggested in-class assignments and additional exhibits. Visit the instructor site at www.sagepub.com/treadwellicr.

If you are a qualified adopter and have your e-mail address and password on file with SAGE, you may log in to the site and begin accessing the instructor materials immediately. If you are not yet a qualified adopter with SAGE, you will need to register on the site.

Acknowledgments

This book has benefited enormously from the input of many talented people.

I thank Margaret Seawell for her confidence and support at the project proposal stage. Thanks go to Deya Saoud and Alison Mudditt of SAGE for energizing the project, and to Melinda Masson, Sarah Quesenberry, Astrid Virding, and the SAGE production team for making the book a reality.

Every text benefits from rigorous and informed criticism, and I have benefited from all of the thoughtful input provided by Lawrence S. Albert (Morehead State University); Betty Attaway-Fink (late of Southeastern Louisiana University); Berrin A. Beasley (University of North Florida); Mary E. Harnett Schiller (Roosevelt University); Laurel Hellerstein (Endicott College); Jenepher Lennox Terrion (University of Ottawa); J. Drew McGukin (California University of Pennsylvania); Gregg A. Payne (Chapman University); Jeff Shires (Purdue University North Central); Thomas J. Socha (Old Dominion University); and Barbara S. Spies (Cardinal Stritch University). I thank them for their time and patience and hope that they will see the results of their advice in this final product.

Thanks go to my students who thoughtfully critiqued the text as it evolved in both print and online versions.

I am indebted to the communication professionals who set aside time to distill their professional experiences into the "Research in Practice" case studies: Richard Earle, Alfonso González Herrero, Brandi Horton, and Julie Pokela. I thank them for their patience with the academic publication process, for their tolerance of my "picky" questions of wording and detail, and most of all for their ability to distill the concepts and methods in the text into such lucid examples of communication research in practice.

Special thanks go to Qala and its special citizen, Gonzi, for relaxation and inspiration.

Above all, thanks go to Jill Treadwell—muse, creative force, critic, and sounding board during the multiple iterations of this text. Without her input—conceptual and culinary—the text would be a lesser work.

—Donald Treadwell

Introduction

Welcome to Communication Research:
Finding Your Path

Let's drop in on an everyday campus event so we can see where some ideas about communication research might come from. It's Friday afternoon, the end of a long, hard week or possibly the beginning of a long, hard weekend. People are winding down (or possibly up) over their favorite brews at a campus coffee shop. As a casual observer you notice the ambience—carpet, comfortable chairs, cable news running silently on television, new indie fusion rock on the sound system, a continuing traffic of people lined up for coffee and snacks, the hiss of espresso machines, and the overall buzz of conversation.

You decide to listen in on one group more specifically. You discover the names of individuals as they talk to each other, and you hear the following conversation.

Caroline: Am I happy the week's over! I've got three courses I don't like, group assignments in a group that's just about nonfunctional, and more assignments than I can handle. I'll be working all weekend; the only thing that's good about the weekend is that it isn't class. Tell them, Chris. You're in the same group.

Chris: Oh yeah. You should have seen Caroline when we got that group project. You could just about see her blood pressure building up. And then the rest of the group won't even make a decision about how to get organized. Caro and I finally just divided the project across each person in the group, announced that we'd meet here on Monday night to pull it all together, and now I suppose the other three in our group hate us.

Elizabeth: Maybe they just wanted someone to make a decision. Not everybody likes to make decisions.

Caroline: Well, I don't think it's that difficult. You need a decision; you make one. My whole family works that way. Maybe it's genetic, but I just don't think it is that difficult.

Elizabeth: I bet your group's happy you did that. We don't all want to be leaders, and Caroline looks like a leader—doesn't she? I bet they were all just waiting for you to lead.

Caroline: What do you mean, I look like a leader?

Lee: Well, you just sort of do. You look confident; you speak well.

Caroline: I don't, and even if I did that doesn't make me a leader. Anyway, we'd be better off putting our efforts into cutting our workload; then we wouldn't have a problem in the first place.

Lee: How can you cut your workload? The class instructor makes that call, not us.

Caroline: I suppose we get could get up a petition for a reduction in workload.

Chris: Won't work. She'll just see the petition as a bunch of students trying to get out of work. What she needs is a good, reasoned argument.

Lee: But if the whole class signs . . .

Caroline: It just means a whole bunch of people signed. It doesn't mean they have a good idea.

Chris: That's democracy for you! I think decisions should be made by experts, by people who know what they're doing.

Chris: Well, anyway, our instructor won't be persuaded by any number of signatures on a petition. We need a good argument.

Caroline: Like what?

Chris: Like reasoned, relevant, objective, and defensible. Like, for example, we all have to go to a visiting speaker.

Caroline: Maybe—if it's one our instructor approves of. She's the referee in this game.

Elizabeth: Well, at least we can get assignment work done online and get around the hassle of meetings.

Lee: Yeah! You could do your assignment right here! We'll help. And then you can take the weekend off. Chris will buy you another latte to get you pumped up. Right, Chris?

Chris: Only if she does my share of the work as well.

Caroline: Forget it. This isn't a workplace for me. I come here to avoid work. I work best on my own, in my room—no distractions. Just me and my music.

Lee: She's right, you know. I'm just not comfortable with all online. I don't like it that the only real person I ever meet is myself. I can't drink coffee with a virtual group.

Chris: Speaking of coffee, did you see that great computer-animated new coffee ad?

Elizabeth: Chris is a foodie. Remembers every food ad. But can't remember anything else at all. Like what was on cable news last night.

Chris: OK, so I don't watch ads for cars and home equity loans. Why should I? I'm not into cars or banking. And who watches cable news? I can pick up news anytime, anywhere.

Caroline: I've watched you—and I don't think the Web sites you use for news are very credible.

Chris: So television is better? Why should I trust that? It's all just someone's version of the news. That's why I watch all over the place. You can't get informed by just one source.

Lee: But good news sources have trained journalists, more journalists, dedicated newsrooms, professional standards—all that stuff.

Chris: Doesn't matter. It's still just all corporate spin. You know they all accept advertising, and they're not going to say anything that will turn an advertiser off. They might not be politically biased, but they're corporately biased. They're all pushing consumerism. You can't trust them.

Elizabeth: So who do you trust?

Chris: You—to buy me another mocha latte!

Elizabeth: Generic or brand name?

Chris: Brand name, of course.

[laughter]

Lee: Behold—the power of advertising!

Chris: No! It's the other way around. Manufacturers know they need to reach people like me to keep me buying their product. I influence them!

Elizabeth: Well, I have to start work. I hate to have you thinking that Caro was the only one with an academic workload. I'm lucky, though. This weekend I have only two quizzes—both online.

Caroline: Wow! Is that all you ever have to do?

Elizabeth: Yes. Every week. Multiple-choice tests.

Lee: We have to write every week. Our instructor says it's the only way she can assess our learning, opinions, and ability to argue.

Caroline: I thought they were all supposed to be measuring our education or IQ or some such.

Elizabeth: Well, faculty think differently about how to teach and how to test. They're all trained differently, I guess. You'd think by now they'd have figured out one best way, but I haven't seen it. Their thinking is like the coffee here—lots of flavors.

Comments on a Conversation

Dear Reader:

You were invited to listen in on the conversation recorded on the previous pages.

First, you have a decision. Should you do so? Observing people unobtrusively is a research method, but one with ethical implications. If you regard your conversations as private, wouldn't you want to respect the privacy of others and seek their permission before recording their conversations? A big "getting started" decision is what standards of behavior you will adopt as a researcher. We discuss this more fully in Chapter 3, "Ethics: Your Responsibilities as a Researcher."

Some information is missing from the above conversation because it is recorded only as printed words. We can infer that some parts of it are less serious because they are punctuated by laughter, but in the above transcript we can see no facial expressions or body language, nor can we hear any voices. All of these would give us a fuller understanding of this conversation. To get a full understanding we would need to become a part of the group, but then of course the conversation would be different because we would have become a part of it. So another big "getting started" decision is what your level of involvement with your research participants should be.

Questions About Communication

Let's now consider this conversation from a communication research perspective. The following bullet points highlight just some of the many questions that communication researchers might be interested in getting answered.

The conversation starts with a discussion of group projects. A researcher focusing on group and organizational communication could find many questions here as she listens to the discussion. For example:

- What communication behaviors help or harm productivity and member satisfaction in groups?
- What communication behaviors lead (or don't lead) to successful decisions?
- What is leadership?
- How do successful leaders communicate?
- How does face-to-face communication differ from online communication?

The group discusses how best to approach an instructor for a reduction in workload. From a communication perspective the students are discussing the important areas of rhetoric and persuasion. For example:

- What makes messages persuasive?
- What makes a source credible?
- How is communication used to maintain or to challenge power in organizations and groups?
- What role does language play in shaping our understanding of an organization?

Lee's proposal to do an entire project online raises questions about communication technology and its impact on human interaction. For example:

- Do people behave differently on such sites as MySpace, Facebook, Second Life, or online class sites than they do in the "real world" (and what is it that defines any world as "real")?
- Do the rules governing face-to-face communication change when the communication takes place online?

Chris's love of food ads and seeming willingness to rate most sources of information equally raise questions related to media effects. One big question with effects research is causality. For example, are all-powerful advertisements brainwashing Chris into becoming a mindless food junkie, or is Chris an intelligent, discriminating individual who voluntarily and thoughtfully selects relevant sources of information, such as food ads? Some researchers are interested in the "hidden agendas" of the media. For example, news coverage may inform us but also simply by its emphases tell us that some stories are more important than others. For example, science rarely makes front-page news, and some parts of the world routinely receive more coverage than others. Similarly, entertainment programs may give us a needed diversion but also cultivate a particular view of ethnicities or occupations.

Questions that media researchers might ask include:

- What effects, if any, do news and entertainment have on viewers, listeners, and readers?
- How powerful are those effects?
- How can we find out if any observed effects are caused by the exposure to media and not by something else?
- Why cannot news be studied as entertainment or advertising be studied as news?
- Do people who use different information sources develop different views of the world?

Chris changes the conversation by raising a new topic—coffee advertising. Researchers interested in conversational behaviors and small-group dynamics might want to know:

- How do individuals establish that it is their turn to speak?
- How do we know whether a statement is a joke or serious?
- How are verbal messages affected by gesture, intonation, and interpersonal space?
- What rules govern conversation?

The conversation ends on the topic of testing. Can we in fact measure those elusive things called class participation, IQ, and ability, and if so, how? How do we define them in the first place? Communication researchers face similar questions about their research, as noted below.

Questions About Communication Research

How can we define such concepts as "attitude," "communication," and "influence" so that we all agree on them and recognize them when we see them? We discuss such questions in Chapter 2, "First Decisions," and Chapter 5, "Measurement."

Can we arrive at defensible conclusions from studying one person, or do we need to study hundreds of people to be confident in our results? This question is addressed in Chapter 7, "Sampling."

Which captures communication behavior best: words or numbers–or do we need both? This question is addressed in Chapter 2, "First Decisions"; Chapter 10, "Observation"; and Chapter 12, "Writing Research."

Can we generalize about communication, or is all communication situational? This question is discussed further in Chapter 2, "First Decisions."

Generalizations About Communication Research

Generalizations that we can make about communication research are

- communication research inescapably involves ethical decisions

- communication research observations are inevitably selective and incomplete

- communication research results are affected by the methods you choose to use

Closing Thought

How many males and females are in the group we listened in on? We can guess two females perhaps, but do we really know?

This question suggests that we be critical of our assumptions and those of other researchers. Just as a name may or may not predict gender, researchers' labels and descriptions may or may not accurately capture communication phenomena. One of your responsibilities as a researcher is to examine how well descriptions and reports, including your own, capture the events they are describing.

I hope this prologue has stimulated your thinking about human communication research and that this book will help you get answers to the many questions that you might want to ask about human communication.

Getting Started
Possibilities and Decisions

"What should I research and why?"
Beginning researchers cry.
The answer's elusive,
But little's exclusive
When scholars assess, probe, and pry.

Chapter Overview

Welcome to communication research. This chapter introduces some of the different ways communication scholars think about research, their main interest areas, and some of their research methods.

Starter Questions

What kind of study would you design to discover

- if there is political bias in a student newspaper?
- if people's vocabularies change when they are with an intimate partner?
- if regular communication from the boss improves employee morale?
- the communication behaviors that hinder or help decision making in a committee?
- the level of violence in society, as shown in television content?
- how news editors decide what news will or will not be published?
- how people communicate dissent in organizations?

Communication researchers have interests ranging from communication between intimate partners to the level of mass media reaching millions of people. Researchers tend to specialize in areas defined by the numbers of people they are studying, as in interpersonal communication, groups, organizations, or mass media. But many research interests transcend such categories. For example, rhetoricians, those who study the use of language and argumentation, may do so in all four of these areas. Whatever the focus, researchers face decisions about how best to ask and answer questions. Every research question has assumptions behind it that reflect the researcher's view of communication and how best to measure it. By way of example, let's take a look at the many ways a typical pharmaceutical advertisement could be studied.

Some Research Possibilities: What Can We Do With an Ad?

Let's explore the following hypothetical advertisement for "Product X." This "pitch" sells a variety of products for a variety of lifestyles. (Just replace "doctors," "headaches," and "life's daily stresses" with alternate terms to see how many products it can sell.)

> *Nine out of 10 doctors recommend Product X for those headaches that come from life's daily stresses.*

Advertisements are targeted communications designed specifically to have consumers or institutions purchase (usually) an advertised product or service. Communication researchers could be interested in answering a number of questions about this process. Does this advertisement work or doesn't it? How or why does it work? Whose interests are being advanced by the ad? Does the medium itself (radio, magazine, television, newspaper, or Internet) have an effect on how the content is understood?

DOES THE ADVERTISEMENT WORK?

Applied communication researchers, and certainly advertising executives, want to know how many people purchased Product X as a result of exposure to this ad. The question is not that readily answered. Clearly the manufacturer will know how many units were sold after the advertising campaign started. If sales went up, we could assume that the advertisement was effective. Correct? Not necessarily. Many other explanations for a spike in sales are also possible and would need to be ruled out before we could conclude that the ad had a significant effect.

A scientific approach to research is one of several ways to assess this advertisement's effectiveness. Two characteristics of **scientific method** are observation or **empiricism** and the attempt to rule out alternate explanations. From a scientific point of view, we might measure how much advertising time or space we purchased and the sales results and then look for a relationship between the two. We would hope to discover that as the amount of advertising increased so did sales. But we also need to be sure that any observed sales spike is related to our advertising and not to a widespread outbreak of stress headaches, to retailers putting the product on sale, or to a new ad that we launched before assessing whether the old one was working effectively. All possible causes for a sales increase would need to be identified and ruled out before we could assume that the advertisement and only the advertisement caused the sales spike.

WHAT CAN READERS AND VIEWERS TELL US?

Establishing that the advertisement did increase sales provides no insight on why it increased sales. How to answer this question? You could construct a **survey**, asking consumers questions based on what you suspect made the advertisement effective—the celebrity spokesperson, the animation showing how the product is kinder and gentler to the stomach, or the physician recommendation for example.

It is likely that an advertising agency would ask such questions before the advertisement was released in order to know in advance that the ad was going to be as effective as possible. Of course consumers may have totally different perceptions of what is important about the ad; for example, they may decide that the catchy soundtrack is really what is grabbing their attention. It is important therefore to capture what people have to say in their own words as well as to ask the questions that you think are important.

For such public opinion research, surveys are typically used to ask questions the researcher thinks are important, and **focus groups** are used to capture opinions that consumers think are important. Surveys use mail, phone, the Internet, or interviews to present a series of specific, predetermined questions to a predetermined group of respondents. Focus groups involve bringing together maybe 6 to 12 people and asking them to discuss their reaction to an advertisement, issue, or product. The essential focus group strategy is listening to people in order to capture their responses in their own words. Surveys generally produce **quantitative** results (48% did not like the spokesperson); focus groups generally produce **qualitative** results in that they capture people talking ("I really did not like the spokesperson because . . ."). Both surveys and focus groups have their advantages and limitations, as we will see in later chapters.

WHAT CAN THE CONTENT TELL US?

So far we have analyzed the Product X advertisement largely in terms of consumer response, but what could we learn from the ad content itself? There are many angles from which to study media content, including rhetoric, content analysis, and critical theory. These approaches share an interest in media content but take different perspectives for different reasons.

Rhetoricians are essentially interested in the **appeals** the advertisement uses to persuade consumers to use the product. For example, in our hypothetical ad two appeals are apparent—the appeal of physicians as authority figures and the appeal of numbers—with "Nine out of 10" implying that nearly all physicians endorse this product. As this type of ad often shows a "typical" consumer using the product in a "typical" setting of work or home, we might identify a further appeal that "people just like us" use this product and that if "thousands of people are using this product" it must be OK.

Rhetoricians using theory developed by Aristotle (384–322 BCE) might search for appeals based on **logos** (logic), in this case the logic of "pain + pill = problem solved"; **ethos** (character), in this case the credibility of physicians; or **pathos** (emotion), in this case the joy and relief of not having headaches any longer.

Kenneth Burke, a 20th-century theorist who analyzed human communication in terms of drama (**dramatism**), offered a set of analytical questions that ask, essentially, "What is the act, the scene, the people, and the purpose of the act?" We could analyze our ad at two levels using Burke's questions. Looking at the ad content we could describe the domestic setting, the people in it, and the minidrama of a person being restored to health by Product X. Or in a broader context we could argue that the scene is media advertising; the parties are consumers, pharmaceutical companies, and advertisers; the drama is one of consumers becoming loyal users of Product X; and the purpose is the financial health of Product X's manufacturers.

Rhetorical approaches to advertising content are essentially qualitative; they analyze language.

Content analysis, by contrast, is a quantitative method for assessing media content, based on counting. For example, looking at a series of ads for pharmaceuticals, a content analyst might set up categories of content based on her research interests. Two such interests might be representations of gender and of illness in advertising. In the first case, categories for women and men might be defined occupationally such as physician, housekeeper, athlete, secretary, salesclerk, scientist, and so on. Then the analyst might count the number of occurrences of each occupation for both men and women and compare them. She could also compare her results to a known distribution of occupations from census data. She might then be able to conclude that the advertisements overrepresent women as salesclerks and underrepresent them as physicians, not only with respect to men in pharmaceutical advertisements but also with respect to what we know about the distribution of occupations by gender in the workforce.

Similarly, if the analyst counted all the references to specific health problems she found, she might rank these mentions by **frequency** and conclude that in the world according to advertising, most people have lower back pain, a few have toothache or irregularity, and a large majority have "stress." She could then compare advertising's world with what we know of the real world from national health statistics.

Critical analysis works from a basic assumption that communication maintains and promotes power structures in society. With that as a basis, the critic asks, "Whose interests are being served by advertising and, more specifically, how exactly do language and representations maintain the interests of such entities as corporations, colleges, or governments?" Unlike the content analyst, who looks for what is explicit and observable, the critic may look as much for what is implicit or not said.

Example? The critic may discover that advertising for Product X and its real-world relatives portray women more frequently than men as afflicted with day-to-day health problems. This is a conclusion that our content analyst might also have arrived at. But the critic's question becomes "Whose interests are advanced by these portrayals?"

There may be several answers to that question. Obviously there is a financial return to the pharmaceutical company if the advertisement has people buying the product. But the critic's interest is in the deeper messages underlying the obvious advertising appeals. What might be some of these messages?

If women are represented as less healthy than men, is a message being subtly propagated that women are less able than men to function in society? Furthermore, by portraying women primarily as salesclerks (as our imaginary content analyst discovered), is a form of "ideological reproduction" taking place, in which women are influenced into such occupations because they come to understand from the media that this is primarily what most women do?

A different interpretation might be that because women have backache, toothache, and "stress" (or so the advertisements would have us believe) and these problems can be fixed with Product X, it is acceptable for women to turn to such products as a "fix" for such problems.

But what causes such problems in the first place? The critic might argue that pharmaceutical advertisements represent a superficial approach to a deeper problem. If women had a status in society that allowed them to live stress free, this particular product would not be necessary. From a critical perspective then, such advertising packs a double punch. It portrays high-stress situations for women as normal and then provides the solution to a problem that it has subtly created in the first place.

WHAT CAN THE CREATORS OF THE AD TELL US?

Our understanding of the advertisement would of course be enhanced if we could talk with the client and with the producers, directors, and writers in the agency that produced the ad. In this case we would probably be interested in finding out how and why decisions about content and production were made. Researchers interested in organizational dynamics and decision making might want to know whether the basic creative approach was worked out over the course of extended meetings involving large numbers of people or if it came about as a directive from a client or creative director. Researchers interested in decision making would want to interview members of the creative team individually so that each person feels free to talk. They also might want to interview the team as a group and probably would want to get permission to videotape the creative meetings as they are taking place. Such research could give us insight on how communication facilitates or discourages creativity, decision making, client-agency relationships, or how professional communicators build an image of the consumers they are trying to reach.

A Series of Unavoidable Decisions

Communication researchers have different agendas, methods, and assumptions behind what they do. One reason for this is the complexity of human communication. Because it is almost impossible to examine and explain a communication event in its totality, researchers focus on a part of that totality and choose a method for investigating it with which they have a comfort level, be it methodological or ideological. Following are some of the decisions that are almost inevitable for any researcher.

THE FIELD OF STUDY—WIDE OR NARROW?

Time is short, the topic is vast, and we must research the available and the achievable. Methodological preferences aside, communication scholars typically divide communication studies into a number of specific interest areas such as those shown in Exhibit 1.1. This list is compiled from listings of divisions and interest groups of the National Communication Association and the International Communication Association.

EXHIBIT 1.1   Communication Research Interest Areas

Applied Communication	Communication Apprehension and Avoidance
Argumentation and Forensics	
Children, Adolescents, and the Media	Communication Ethics
	Communication History
Communication and Technology	Communication Law and Policy
Communication and the Future	Critical and Cultural Studies

(Continued)

EXHIBIT 1.1 *(Continued)*

Environmental Communication	Journalism Studies
Ethnicity and Race	Language and Social Interaction
Family Communication	Mass Communication
Feminist Scholarship	Nonverbal Communication
Freedom of Expression	Organizational Communication
Game Studies	Peace and Conflict Communication
Gay, Lesbian, Bisexual, and Transgender Studies	Performance Studies
	Philosophy of Communication
Global Communication and Social Change	Political Communication
	Popular Communication
Group Communication	Public Address
Health Communication	Public Relations
Information Systems	Rhetoric
Instructional/Developmental Communication	Semiotics
	Spiritual Communication
Intergroup Communication	Theater
International and Intercultural Communication	Training and Development
Interpersonal Communication	Visual Communication Studies

As we will see in Chapter 2, communication researchers "cluster" on the basis of a few deep beliefs about the world. These beliefs can be neither proven nor disproven but require a choice among them. The major choices follow.

THE RESEARCHER—DISPASSIONATE OR INVOLVED?

To what extent should researchers get involved with their human "subjects"? The scientific tradition values objectivity and dispassionate observation. The "reward" to the researcher is the satisfaction of a new finding, the development of a new theory, or the confirmation or disconfirmation of an existing theory.

By contrast, **action research** involves engaging in research specifically to improve people's lives. Whereas the scientific tradition is to remain detached from one's subjects, the action tradition is to be closely involved with them in order to better lives. One school sees research as a quest for knowledge, and the other sees research as an engaged contribution to engineering a better society. In both cases, the researcher's behavior has ethical implications, as we shall see in Chapter 3.

THE APPROACH—OBJECTIVE OR SUBJECTIVE?

Can research be objective? Scientific approaches generally subscribe to the concept of an external "real" world that can be observed, understood, and agreed on among scholars. **Social scientists** bring this assumption to the study of human interaction. For example, they assume that concepts such as intelligence or loyalty can be found across all people and measured objectively with an "instrument" that will apply universally and perhaps predict human behavior.

By contrast **phenomenologists** and **ethnographers** try to understand people's subjective worlds. They have an **interpretive perspective** in that they seek to understand how humans interpret or make sense of events in their lives. They assume that concepts such as intelligence or loyalty are indeed just concepts and that such concepts are defined subjectively by the people they are researching. Such concepts vary from culture to culture and from individual to individual. For example, simple interpersonal behaviors such as holding hands, kissing, or embracing may have widely different interpretations from culture to culture. The phenomenologist can observe a behavior such as kissing but really wants to know what that action means for the individuals involved. There is no assumption that such behavior has a universal meaning.

THE SAMPLE—LARGE OR SMALL?

How many people do you need to talk to in order to know that you have "a good picture" of a communication phenomenon? Public opinion researchers can answer that question. For an accurate view of adult public opinion in the United States you need about 1,200 randomly selected people—as long as you can live with something like plus or minus 3% error.

"True enough," the small-sample people might reply, "but counting gives you only numbers and knowledge, not understanding. Will a survey of the thousands of people affected by hurricanes or AIDS give us any more understanding of how people respond to such events than an in-depth interview with one family? You know what's going on but you don't know why or how people feel about·it or explain it. That is why one solid series of interviews with a few people can give a better grasp on a situation than all the thousand-people surveys the big-sample people can conduct."

THE DATA—QUANTITATIVE OR QUALITATIVE?

Are humans storytelling animals, counting animals, or both?

Numbers are important; they are after all how democracies and committees make decisions. Count the vote; majority wins. While the ultimate truth may never be known, many researchers accept that the current "best" truth of a phenomenon may be what a majority of researchers currently believe it to be. Numbers and counting are important to scientific methods. Not only are counting and statistical methods an important part of such methods, but the number of researchers in agreement on a particular finding also helps suggest the "truth" of a finding.

Researchers with interests in human subjectivity, motivation, and aesthetics respond that the complexities and subtleties of interpersonal attraction, the responses to modern art, or the critical approaches to understanding media cannot be captured in mere numbers. The "truth" can best be understood by listening to the stories that research participants and researchers themselves have to tell us.

Few of the above "either/or" distinctions are clear-cut. For example, a passionately involved action researcher may use objective scientific methods to study a problem. The above ideas have been presented as "either/or" to help you think about where you stand on such issues. In practice, many of the seeming opposites blend together. The most obvious blending is in the approach called **triangulation** in which a researcher uses multiple methods providing multiple perspectives to ensure that she has a good "fix" on a problem.

For example, in trying to understand how family life interacts with television viewing a researcher might survey several families on their use of and attitudes toward television, interview a few family members in depth, live with a family as they watch television, and conduct a content analysis of television content to determine how content shapes the family's interactions and vice versa. Advertising executives will frequently **pilot** a commercial with a focus group before running the advertisement and then assessing results with a large-scale survey.

Approaches such as **Q Methodology** assume that it is **respondents'** subjective views of the world that are of interest but combine that research focus with quantitative, computational approaches to recording and assessing these views.

THE REPORT—SUBJECTIVE OR OBJECTIVE?

Just as there are different ways of doing research, there are different ways of writing research. Researchers interested in interpreting the subjective world of their informants may use the primarily qualitative languages of ethnomethodology and phenomenology. In most cases, they will report what their informants have to tell them in their informants' own words. By contrast, social science researchers will typically use statistics to report and interpret the data they have collected.

The involved researcher may unabashedly use "I" writing as in "I lived with Thomas and his two children for 3 months and we formed a warm social bond that had us eating together, watching movies together, and exchanging seasonal gifts." Dispassionate researchers will report in a language that strives for neutrality and that removes them from the narrative altogether. Thus "Subjects were recorded on video and their facial expressions subsequently analyzed for changes as visual stimuli were presented to them by the researcher."

The subjectively involved researcher believes that credibility and reporting are enhanced by including personal experiences and reactions. We are getting "the truth, the whole truth, and nothing but the truth." The dispassionate researcher believes that credibility is maximized by objective reporting "uncontaminated" by sentiment and value judgments (ignoring perhaps the idea that to adopt this style of writing is in itself a value judgment).

Both research and research reporting are communication activities framed by disciplinary standards and expectations, ethical decisions, and personal motivations. As critical theorists would point out, published and topical research carries a "metamessage" about what research topics are "hot," what approaches are in vogue, and who the current "stars" are.

The fact that research has an argumentative component does not necessarily mean it is adversarial. The academic journals in which research is published reflect ongoing discussions about research. A research study may be followed by responses, critiques, and other studies that change our thinking about it. You can think of articles in the scholarly communication journals (some listed at the end of this chapter) as a considered, continuing worldwide conversation among researchers regarding how best to understand human communication.

Problem Posing, Problem Solving, Peer Persuasion

Borrowing a model from the biological sciences, communication research can be regarded as having three main components—problem posing, problem solving, and peer persuasion (BioQUEST Curriculum Consortium, n.d.).

PROBLEM POSING

Research questions do not arrive "preposed." You have to decide what the question is. This can be the hardest part of the research process. Once you have clearly defined the question, the rest of your research often seems to fall into place. Defining "the question" is a very human process involving personal interest in the topic, the feasibility of doing a study, and the rewards, tangible and intangible, of completing it.

PROBLEM SOLVING

Having posed a question, we face the problem of how best to answer it. In many respects, this is what this book is primarily about. But problem solving is more than selecting a research method and using it. It can involve amending your methods as they prove to be inappropriate, discovering other questions that must be answered before your "real" question can be answered, finding new questions opening up, or changing your research altogether when someone publishes a "breakthrough" study that gives you a whole set of new ideas about your research.

PEER PERSUASION

Research has no value to the world unless the world knows about it. Research must be published (literally, be made public) if others are to benefit from it. Academic publication is a process of persuasion. Journal and book editors and reviewers must be persuaded that yours is a worthwhile project with worthwhile results, and readers must be similarly convinced if your research is to gain recognition. Publication is a process of persuasion and argumentation even though it is couched in the language of scholarship and conducted via the printed or electronic page.

For most academic journals, your research report will go through a process of **peer review** in which scholars in your field assess your work and suggest ways you could improve your report before it is accepted for publication. This process can be painful to the ego and time-consuming, but research progresses on challenges and rigorous examination of ideas and these challenges are simply another part of "research as conversation." Assertions about communication must be defensible if they are to be accepted. Publication in particular gets you into the cut and thrust of debate about communication and how best to study it.

As the news from time to time reminds us, researchers can be prone to error and to ethical lapses. Publication and peer review are also ways of monitoring the ethics of research, a topic addressed in Chapter 3.

One proposition raised at the beginning of this book was that communication research inescapably involves ethical decisions. This ethics panel, and the ones in following chapters, will give you a sense of the ethical decisions you may face as a researcher. You should try to reason through to a decision for each of the ethics problems as they are typical of the decisions you may face when doing your own research. For help with these ethics panels read Chapter 3, "Ethics: Your Responsibilities as a Researcher."

Ethics Panel: A Health Communication Dilemma

Diabetes is a looming public health crisis (Kleinfield, 2006). A public health agency wants to determine the best way to help people identify the problem so they can take preventive measures and better deal with the condition if they are diagnosed as diabetic.

> To do this, the agency hires your research firm to find out how best to get messages about diabetes to the public. You decide to run an experiment in which people in County A will receive messages about diabetes by traditional mass media (newspapers, television, and radio). People in County B will receive intensive interpersonal communication about diabetes through neighborhood meetings, counseling, and their workplaces. People in County C will receive no messages because you need a "baseline" against which to measure whether your interventions in Counties A and B have any effect. As a result of this study you will be able to develop effective communication programs for your region.
>
> What are the ethical implications, if any, of leaving people in County C out of your study?

Chapter Summary

This chapter introduced the different ways scholars think about communication research, their main areas of research, and the methods they use. In summary:

- Communication research is a systematic process of posing questions about human communication, answering those questions, and then persuading others that your results are valid.

- Communication researchers typically specialize in one aspect of communication.

- Researchers may use qualitative methods, quantitative methods, or both.

- Researchers have empirical, interpretive, or critical perspectives on communication.

Research Example:
Three Views of Pharmaceutical Advertising

We started this chapter with a discussion of the different ways an advertisement for a hypothetical pharmaceutical product might be studied. The following studies from a large selection of research literature on pharmaceutical advertising show three different approaches to research. Notice that while the method, content analysis, is the same across all three studies their purposes are different. Examine these studies for differences in purpose and in the assumptions behind them.

The first (Main, Argo, & Huhmann, 2004) examines pharmaceutical advertising to determine the ratio of informative to persuasive content. The second (Chapman, 1979) takes an essentially critical view in arguing that pharmaceutical advertising has the effect of producing stereotypes, specifically of women as housewives. The third (Bell, Wilkes, & Kravitz, 2000) uses the results of content analysis research to argue for a policy change—increased informational content for pharmaceutical advertisements, mandated if necessary.

CONTENT ANALYSIS: A DESCRIPTIVE PERSPECTIVE

Main, K. J., Argo, J. J., & Huhmann, B. A. (2004). Pharmaceutical advertising in the USA: Information or influence? *International Journal of Advertising, 23*(1), 119–142.

In this study, the authors focused on the promotional part of pharmaceutical advertisements, the part that does not have a required content regulated by statutory agencies. Their purpose was to see if factual information and rational arguments were being provided to inform consumers of health problems, treatment options, and medical science advances. They used content analysis to compare direct-to-consumer (DTC) advertisements for prescription drugs with advertisements for over-the-counter (OTC) remedies and dietary supplements. They found that the DTC advertisements for prescription drugs did not solely rely on rational appeals; instead, they used more emotional appeals than did the advertisements for OTC remedies or dietary supplements. They also found that DTC advertisements feature fewer women, more characters under the age of 18, and primarily Caucasian models.

CONTENT ANALYSIS: A CRITICAL PERSPECTIVE

Chapman, S. (1979). Advertising and psychotropic drugs: The place of myth in ideological reproduction. *Social Science and Medicine, 13A*(6), 751–764.

Chapman too analyzed advertising content but with an essentially critical view. He argues that the limited time and space available for advertisements means that ads "concentrate" symbolism and imagery. They truncate or cut off the full range of information that might otherwise be available on a product or idea. This has the effect not only of producing stereotypes but also of reducing the range of alternative information being offered to the public. His study of pharmaceutical advertising shows women in a narrow range of "housewifely" possibilities, perpetuating the stereotype of woman as housewife.

CONTENT ANALYSIS: A POLICY PERSPECTIVE

Bell, R. A., Wilkes, M. S., & Kravitz, R. L. (2000). The educational value of consumer-targeted prescription drug print advertising. *Journal of Family Practice, 49*(12), 1092–1098. Retrieved February 25, 2006, from Health Reference Center Academic database.

The case for direct-to-consumer (DTC) prescription drug advertising is often based on the argument that it can educate the public about medical conditions and associated treatments. Bell et al. content analyzed DTC advertising to see if this was true.

They collected advertisements in 18 popular magazines from 1989 through 1998. Two coders independently evaluated 320 advertisements for 101 drug brands to see if information appeared about specific aspects of the medical conditions for which the drug was promoted and about the treatment.

They found that virtually all the advertisements gave the name of the condition treated by the promoted drug and provided information about the symptoms. However, few reported details about the condition's precursors or its prevalence or clarified misconceptions about the condition. The advertisements seldom provided information about the drug's mechanism, its success rate, treatment duration, alternative treatments, or behavioral changes that could affect patients.

The authors concluded that DTC advertising in general is not serving the information needs of consumers. From their study they were able to propose strategies for improving the educational value of DTC advertisements and to argue that the medical community should pressure the pharmaceutical industry, via legislation if necessary, to incorporate more information about conditions and treatments in its advertising.

Recommended Reading

There are many books and journals available on communication research, as a visit to your campus library catalogs will indicate. Many journals on topics ranging from administrative theory to women's studies may focus on human communication. A few key journal titles are listed below. Chapter 4, "Reading Research," will move us on to developing more relevant, targeted lists of readings.

GENERAL

Communication Monographs
Communication Research Reports
Human Communication Research
Journal of Applied Communication Research
Quarterly Journal of Speech

MASS COMMUNICATION

Critical Studies in Media Communication
Journal of Public Relations Research
Journalism and Mass Communication Quarterly
Quarterly Review of Film and Video

ORGANIZATIONAL COMMUNICATION

Academy of Management Review
Administrative Science Quarterly
Business Communication Quarterly
Management Communication Quarterly

GROUP COMMUNICATION

Group and Organization Management
Small Group Research

INTERPERSONAL COMMUNICATION

Human Relations
Journal of Applied Psychology
Journal of Family Communication
Journal of Research in Personality
Journal of Social and Personal Relationships

Recommended Web Resources

Association for Education in Journalism and Mass Communication (AEJMC): www.aejmc.org

Canadian Communication Association: www.acc-cca.ca

Human Communication Research Centre: www.hcrc.ed.ac.uk

International Communication Association (ICA): www.icahdq.org

National Communication Association (NCA): www.natcom.org

Defining the boundaries of human communication studies is difficult and a debate in its own right. The AEJMC, Canadian Communication Association, ICA, and NCA are four of several North American academic associations devoted to the study of communication. Looking at their Web sites (provided above) will give you an idea of the many areas of research specialization under the "communication umbrella." By contrast, the Human Communication Research Centre site above shows how the Universities of Edinburgh and Glasgow are reconceptualizing human communication studies by bringing together such fields as computing, philosophy, psychology, and language studies.

References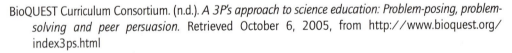

BioQUEST Curriculum Consortium. (n.d.). *A 3P's approach to science education: Problem-posing, problem-solving and peer persuasion.* Retrieved October 6, 2005, from http://www.bioquest.org/index3ps.html

Kleinfield, N. R. (2006, January 9). Bad blood: Diabetes and its awful toll quietly emerge as a crisis. *New York Times.* Retrieved January 9, 2006, from http://www.nytimes.com

Student Study Site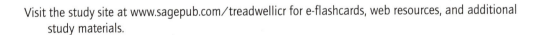

Visit the study site at www.sagepub.com/treadwellicr for e-flashcards, web resources, and additional study materials.

2

First Decisions

What, Why, How?

Getting started can be hard to do
If you want good research to pursue.
You can start with something to show
Or assume that you really don't know.
But most induct or deduct; it's true.

Chapter Overview

"How do I get started?" may be the most difficult question of all for the beginning researcher. The problem, and the good news, is that there are many possible starting points. However, behind every research project are assumptions and decisions that you cannot escape about the nature of human communication and of research. You must ensure that there is a defensible link between these assumptions and the research methods you choose to study them.

This chapter discusses some basic starting points and assumptions that underpin communication research and finishes with a discussion of how we write the questions we hope to get answers to.

Starter Questions

- Can I start a research project without knowing what I'm looking for?

- Do I have to have a theory about what I'm researching?

- Are some research methods better than others?

- Could my presence as a researcher alter what I am studying?

- Can we really make generalizations about human communication?

- Can research findings ever be certain?

Starting With the "What" Question:
Ideas and Observations

The most obvious starting question is "What shall I study?"

Listening to the Rolling Stones' "Start Me Up" probably won't help a lot unless you have a specific interest in rock lyrics. But communication phenomena in the form of rock lyrics, interpersonal behavior, group dynamics, advertising, news coverage, and virtual realities are all around us. So a good starting point is to observe communication phenomena you are interested in.

"Communication" is a large umbrella under which many research interests find a home. As noted in Chapter 1, many researchers specialize at the level of mass, organizational, group, or interpersonal communication, but others have interests such as rhetoric and argumentation that transcend these interest areas. Your career interests and academic electives likely already have you heading toward a general interest area. You may find a more specific focus by looking at the Web sites of the scholarly communication associations listed at the end of this chapter and revisiting the communication research interest areas shown in Chapter 1, Exhibit 1.1.

Reading relevant scholarly articles is a "must." See Chapter 4, "Reading Research," for discussion of one of your most important starting points—your academic library.

A theory or generalization about communication is weak if not supported by evidence, so researchers move between theory and observation. They may start with a theory that needs testing with observations, or they may have observations that lead them to construct or reconstruct a theory. Three thought processes that link observations with theories are induction, deduction, and abduction.

INDUCTION

Induction is reasoning from observations to a theory that might explain your observations. Let's go back to our prologue, which focused on a group of students drinking coffee and wrestling with their individual and collective academic workloads. As an observer, you might see communication behaviors such as the following:

- Gender clustering—males are more likely to sit with males and females to sit with females.

- Class distinction—upper-class students are more likely to be found socializing in the coffee bar than first- or second-year students.

What theories might explain these observations? You might think of several. For your gender-clustering observation, you might theorize:

- Students have a greater comfort level with same-sex than with opposite-sex conversations.

- Male students have more classes in common with each other than they do with female students, and vice versa.

- Male and female students have already formed separate social groups by virtue of being in separate campus housing units.

For your class-distinction observation, you might theorize:

- Upper-class students are more likely to have jobs, grants, and fellowships and can afford to socialize.

- Upper-class students are more likely to live off campus, and meeting on campus is the only way to get group projects done.

- Upper-class students are more stressed as graduation approaches and feel a greater need to "unwind" by socializing with friends.

Having generated several such theories, you would then design a study that will help you decide which theory offers the best explanation of the phenomenon.

DEDUCTION

Deduction, by contrast, moves from a theory to defining the observations you will make to test the theory. For example, you might have some reason to theorize that women are more likely than men to discuss grades and academic performance. You would then design a study to capture the observations that would test this idea. In this case, your research might involve recording the conversations of both men and women and counting for each group the number of times words such as "grade" or "GPA" occur. If you could then show that the frequency of these words is greater for women than for men, your theory would be supported—except for two big "ifs."

First, if you want to make a general statement about women discussing their academic performance more frequently than men do, you will want to be confident that your statement is true for all students, not just the small group of communication majors you have observed. Second, you will want to know that this pattern you observed is true at all times, not just for the one discussion you happened to observe, perhaps as final examinations were approaching. This is where appropriate sampling (Chapter 7) can help us.

Deduction is in a sense more efficient than induction in that it leads to a specific observation that will test your hypothesis or statement about the relationships you expect to find. Having done so, you can then move on to another test. With induction you have a further step, which is finding a way to decide which of the many possible theories you induced from your observations are correct. Induction requires the confidence that you have enough observations to support your conclusion and that you can rule out all the other conclusions that might also be derived from your observations.

ABDUCTION

In the context of research, **abduction** refers not to being kidnapped by aliens from the planet Zog but rather to reasoning from an effect to possible causes. For example, a large group of grade-schoolers in the campus coffee bar would be an unusual sight but a perfectly reasonable one if the university's employees were participating in a "bring your children to work" day. With abduction, your starting point is an effect from which you reason back to possible causes. In this example, your research project would be to find out if there is such an event on campus that explains your observation or if other events would explain the observation better.

Starting With the "Why" Question: Goals and Values

"*Why* do research?" is perhaps a more philosophical starting point. The whys of research can be as varied as human motivations more generally. Peer pressure, ego, financial incentives, or simple curiosity may motivate researchers. Every research study starts with a purpose, be it interest in testing a sophisticated theoretical concept or attempting to get an A in a research course. Most scholars are motivated by curiosity and, more specifically, by the desire to understand human communication.

Generally, research has several purposes—exploration, description, explanation, prediction, control, interpretation, and criticism.

EXPLORATION

Exploration is curiosity-based research. You start down a path that may lead who-knows-where, but that's OK. You have a commendable curiosity to learn more. Good starting points here will be targeted library research, discussions with those who share your interests, and your initial observations.

"I wonder why the residents of two dorms have such different lifestyles" or "Students don't watch TV nearly as much as they used to" may be the beginning of your research career in organizational culture or media use respectively.

DESCRIPTION

Exploratory research typically results in **descriptions** of what you are interested in. The description may be quantitative or qualitative. For example, based on observations and surveys of our group of students we might summarize them statistically in terms of gender, major, class year, choice of drink, topic of conversation, or campus address. But the study could also be qualitative as we interview each person and report, in his or her own words, what it means to be a student, what it means to socialize with others, or how the ambience of a preferred coffee bar helps students socialize or get work done.

Description, especially rich descriptions of people's lives, can be compelling reading. Indeed, one test of a good description of human behavior is that it is compelling reading. But description does tend to leave us wanting more and in particular an answer to the "why" question. For example, reporting that women are more likely than men to discuss their grades or prefer to work in groups is informative but does leave us wondering why.

EXPLANATION

Studies focused on **explanation** attempt to answer the "why" question. For example, your observations might indicate that women are more likely than men to socialize over coffee after class. Your interviews with them lead you to the discovery that more women than men live off campus and that socializing after class is the easiest way to get group projects organized. Thus what was observed to be a primarily female behavior is explained in terms of housing status and "face-to-face" as a preferred way of getting work organized.

PREDICTION

Generally, our explanations have greater credibility if they are capable of **prediction**. The conclusion we arrived at in the previous paragraph about women drinking coffee is reasoned, based on observation, and verifiable, but our theory would be even more impressive if it could predict this behavior. In principle, this is easily done. We could devise an **experiment** in which we give the same group project to equal numbers of on- and off-campus students. If our theory is correct, we should see more off-campus students in the coffee bar, discussing how to get the project done. Note though that this design is weak because it does not rule out other explanations. For example, we cannot rule out the possibility that the students we see meeting have bad Internet access and it is this rather than housing status per se that explains their need to meet in person. We discuss how to strengthen such experimental designs in Chapter 9, "Experiments."

CONTROL

Another goal of research may be **control**. In the physical world, control means researching with a view to being able to predict and manipulate physical processes such as digital recording, combustion, or space flights. In the case of human communication, advertisers, for example, want to be able to control audience responses to advertising, broadcasting, or direct mail. Their interest is in knowing how best to motivate viewers to watch a particular program, purchase a product, or open a piece of direct mail. Industry journals such as *Advertising Age, Broadcasting & Cable,* and *Adweek* contain such advice on how to "control" audiences, frequently in the form of "if . . . then" ideas. "If you make your direct mail piece an unusual shape, then it will attract more readers" is the generic nature of this advice.

INTERPRETATION

Interpretive studies are best understood as attempts to place oneself "in the other person's shoes." In other words, the researcher attempts to understand human communication from the point of view of the people doing it. For example, what does meeting with student colleagues to get coffee really mean for those doing it? Is this an opportunity to set up dates for the weekend, to engage in intimate conversation with significant others, to clarify a difficult concept in the communication theory, to get work organized, or some combination of these? Our interest as researchers is not to impose our own interpretation but to capture the interpretations of those involved in a way that our readers will get an accurate understanding. Almost by definition, this means reporting the results of your research in the language of your research participants.

CRITICISM

The basic quest of critical theorists is to understand and explain the way in which communication is used to exercise and maintain power in groups, organizations, and societies. To this end, critical researchers might look at the way in which organizational structures and processes prevent or facilitate the progress of certain groups within the organization. For example, in the case of our campus coffee bar, do coffee drinking rituals perpetuate and reinforce class or gender distinctions? Can males join a female discussion group? Are there informal rules that say first-year students cannot mix with senior students? Does an individual's language define him or her as a member of an "in-group" or an "out-group"?

The above starting points may mix to a greater or lesser degree. As Kaplan (1964) points out, it is possible to have explanation without prediction and vice versa. For example, we may have a very good understanding of the dynamics of small groups but be unable to predict whether a new group will be a success or not. Or, we may be able to predict the changes in language that two people use as they become more intimate without necessarily understanding why this change is taking place in the first place.

Starting With the "How" Question: Methods and Epistemologies

Many researchers start with a method preference. For example, a political communication consultant may know from experience that telephone surveys of a random national sample of voters are the only way to accurately track rapid changes in voter preferences and to make some generalizations about them. Or a brand consultant consulting on what a new product should be named may know that focus groups offer the best chance of capturing all the (mis)understandings that a new product name is capable of generating.

As such, this "method-start" is really not intellectually defensible. It is the equivalent of saying you will video-record human behavior because you know how to video. For experienced researchers, though, a method-start is grounded in a concept of what it is about human communication that is important to know and how best to know it. It is the track record of the method and its "fit" to the researcher's interests that make the method-start defensible.

Method decisions are rooted in **epistemology**—the question of how it is we know what we know. We might know as a result of **tenacity**—we've always done it or understood it that way, **intuition**—the hunch or gut instinct, **authority**—because a credible source said so, **rationalism**—logical reasoning, or **empiricism**—observation.

Scientific methods typically combine empiricism, rationalism, and **positivism** (the idea that phenomena are governed by, and can be explained by, rules based on objective observation and generalizations from those observations). Two strengths of this approach are openness and self-correction. Openness means that a researcher's methods and data are open to inspection by other researchers, most typically in peer-reviewed publications. Self-correction means that other researchers can replicate a study. If a second study supports the first, researchers can have increased confidence in the findings.

Starting With a Worldview: Basic Beliefs

What do we really believe about human behavior? Are people basically all alike or fundamentally different, predictable or unpredictable, predisposed to cooperation or to conflict, or living in a shared, tangible world or their own internal, subjective worlds?

As evidence supports any and all these views, we ultimately are obliged to decide on the basic beliefs that will inform our research, and to live with them, based on our own best judgment. From a research point of view, basic assumptions about human behavior coalesce into broad **worldviews**.

Worldview I is that human behavior is predictable, objectively measurable, and generalizable. Worldview I researchers aim to make generalizations about human communication that will hold true across space and time. This emphasis on measurement and generalization is called a **nomothetic** approach.

Advertising and audience research subscribe to Worldview I. Researchers seek to find rules that will predict advertising, direct-marketing, or broadcast success, such as how to increase sales or hold a television audience. Television infomercials, for example, are presumably based on research indicating that using a particular type of spokesperson plus showing the product plus repeated exposure of the 1-800 phone number to call predicts that the number of consumer call-ins will be maximized. In principle, such a generalization would apply to most products and most television audiences.

Worldview II, by contrast, sees human behavior as individualistic, unpredictable, and subjective. This view assumes that knowledge is socially constructed out of interaction between people and is subjective. Research based on these assumptions attempts to describe and assess the subjectivity and individuality of human communication, rather than aiming to discover universal laws. This emphasis on individual understanding is called an **idiographic** approach.

For example, researchers who are interested in how consumers respond subjectively to media content will spend time listening to individuals, with a view to capturing this subjectivity. Their goal might be, for example, to understand why some television viewers develop a close relationship to soap opera characters and how they describe those relationships. Researchers make no assumption that their findings will be generalizable and typically reject counting or measuring in favor of reporting what their interviewees said. Their overall goal is understanding more than generalization or prediction.

The research method you select must logically follow from the basic assumptions you have made about human behavior. For example, a Worldview I researcher who believes that people's thinking can be measured and that careful sampling will allow her to generalize results from a small sample to a large number of people may ask, "What type of survey can I run?" A researcher interested in hearing people's subjective experiences in their own words is more likely to ask, "What focus groups or interviews will I need?" The first researcher will use quantitative methods by virtue of her worldview; the second will need to prefer qualitative measures.

These foundational beliefs and arguments about human behavior are issues ultimately of **ontology**, which addresses the nature of what we study.

Ontological questions deal with the nature of existence and what it is that language actually refers to. In communication studies, ontology wrestles with assumptions about the nature of human communication and what it is we "really" observe when we observe it.

For example, have you ever seen someone's attitude? You might answer, "Yes, many times." But what have you really seen? What you have really seen is someone behaving in a particular way, being verbally aggressive perhaps. Or perhaps all you saw was checkmarks on an attitude rating scale, from which you inferred an attitude. Where was the attitude itself? Is there in fact such a thing as an attitude?

Ontological questions for communication scholars include "To what extent do we make real choices? For example, is your decision to attend class voluntary or not?" "Is human experience primarily individual or societal—what would you know of the world and of yourself if you had no interaction with other people?" and "Is communication contextual or universal—does a smile always mean the same thing, or does the meaning depend on who is smiling and under what conditions?"

Starting From the Work of Others

Starting a research project without regard to the work of others is risky business. You run the risk of doing research that has already been done and therefore making no new contribution to knowledge. You will also miss out on knowing about especially relevant research methods and findings that might help you. Most important, perhaps, you will miss out on knowing about "good research"—the research that most scholars agree is well designed, is professionally executed, and makes a significant contribution to knowledge.

The easiest way to join the community of scholars who share your interests is to use your academic libraries regularly. Academic journals (**serials**) record in the form of articles and letters ongoing conversations among researchers. They are admittedly conversations punctuated by lengthy periods of silence as we wait for the next issue of a journal to come out, but browsing communication journals regularly will keep you up to speed with current research and ideas in your interest area.

Chapter 4, "Reading Research," discusses this essential starting point in more detail.

Firming Up Questions

In the Worldview I framework especially, getting started requires that you identify key **constructs** and **operationalize** them. Constructs are ideas or concepts. Operationalizing them means to define them in such a way that they can be measured.

For example, let's suppose that you are interested in the relationship between playing video games and academic performance. You observe individuals who are heavily involved in such games. You conclude inductively that such people keep weird hours and some have peculiar personal habits, but that could be true for any group of people, gamers or not.

Deductively, you reason through to two contrary conclusions. First, time spent on gaming must detract from time spent on studying. Therefore gaming must be detrimental to academic performance. On the other hand, gaming appears to need mental agility, the ability to think fast and to make decisions, and imagination. Deductively, it seems that gaming ought to have a positive effect on academic performance.

You have identified two important ideas or constructs—involvement in gaming and academic performance. You think that there is a relationship between them; you're just not sure what that relationship is.

To operationalize these constructs means to define them in a way that other researchers could replicate your study. Now comes a question of professional judgment: How could we operationalize these constructs—that is, define what they mean in practice?

Exhibit 2.1 shows some of the ways the two constructs could be operationalized or made measurable. We have taken ideas (mental constructions or "constructs") and translated them into observable operations that can be measured.

Exhibit 2.1   Operationalizing Constructs

Construct	
Involvement in Gaming	**Academic Performance**
Operationalizing the Constructs	
Time spent on gaming	Class rank
Money spent on gaming	Number of academic awards
Number of memberships in gaming clubs	Current grade point average
Number of online "personas" or avatars	Cumulative grade point average
Percent of time spent with other gamers	Class participation as rated by faculty
Number of gaming software titles owned	Class attendance as recorded by faculty
Percentage of gaming terms used in conversation	Number of memberships in academic honor societies

At the heart of many studies is a decision as to what measures will be used. Intuitively, some of the measures shown in Exhibit 2.1 appear to do a better job than others. Grade point average for example is a widely, though not totally, accepted measure of academic performance. On the other hand, membership in a gaming club or amount of money spent on games may have little or no relationship to whether an individual is an active game player. Of all the options, a best guess might be that time spent on gaming is the best measure of involvement as long as we can measure it accurately.

These constructs or concepts have now been operationalized into **variables**. Variables are the aspects of a construct that are capable of being measured or taking on a value. In other words, they can "vary." The constructs "gaming" or "academic performance" cannot be measured; the variables "time spent on gaming" and "grade point average" can.

HYPOTHESES: MAKING PREDICTIONS

A statement about the relationship that we expect to find between variables is a **hypothesis**. Hypotheses can state simply that there will be a relationship, specify the direction of the relationship, or state that no relationship is expected. In research writing, the shorthand "H" is used to designate a hypothesis.

Two-tailed hypotheses state that there is a relationship between two variables but do not specify the direction of the relationship. For example:

> H_1: There is a relationship between involvement in video gaming and academic performance.

One-tailed hypotheses require extra confidence because you commit to predicting the direction of the relationship between the variables. For example:

> H_2: As time spent in video gaming increases, academic performance decreases.

Null hypotheses, usually symbolized as H_0, specify that there is no relationship between variables. For example:

> H_0: There is no relationship between involvement in video gaming and academic performance.

RESEARCH QUESTIONS: LESS CERTAINTY, MORE ROOM TO MOVE

Hypotheses specify the results you expect to find from your research. But suppose that your preliminary research does not give you the certainty to make a prediction. In that case you are left with not a prediction but a **research question**. The shorthand "*RQ*" is used to designate a research question.

Open-ended research questions ask simply whether there is a relationship between variables. For example:

> *RQ₁:* Is there a relationship between involvement in video gaming and academic performance?

Closed-ended research questions focus on a direction of relationship. For example:

> *RQ₂:* Does academic performance decline as involvement in video gaming increases?

Starting with an open-ended research question such as *RQ₁* above is appropriate for the exploratory study you would conduct when you don't have a lot of evidence as to what might be going on. With additional evidence you can question the direction of the relationship between variables as in *RQ₂* above. With even more evidence, you may be able to predict a relationship and to write that prediction in the form of a hypothesis.

Preferring a hypothesis over a research question gives you the advantage of focusing your study because you have said in effect, "I know what's going on." Your study then simply becomes an exercise in determining whether or not your hypothesis is supported.

A research question on the other hand is more speculative. You sense that something is going on but you may need to be more open-minded in your research design in order to capture relationships you had not anticipated.

Questioning the Questions

Hypotheses have the advantage of focusing your research, but you may not be able to focus your research initially, or indeed want to. For some researchers the specificity of hypothesis testing is its own weakness. Researchers out of the ethnomethodology and phenomenology traditions especially would argue that complex human behavior cannot be simplified into variables as we did with our hypothetical video game study. They may further argue that finding a relationship between two variables provides no explanation of why the relationship exists and oversimplifies complex relationships by focusing on a few variables rather than on the multitude of influences on human behavior. Fundamentally, they are interested in rich description that provides understanding rather than a simple "yes; there is a relationship" answer to their questions. We will examine such approaches to communication more fully in Chapter 10, "Observation: Watching and Listening for In-Depth Understanding."

Starting With No Questions

A specific question or hypothesis focuses your study and helps define your research priorities and methods, but it may blind you to relevant phenomena outside your immediate focus. Another approach therefore is to begin your study with no prior assumptions (in itself an assumption that you have selected an appropriate starting point). For example, as organization culture researchers Evered and Reis (1981, p. 387) describe their process of finding out about a new organization, "We were 'probing in the dark' into the hidden organizational realities around us, in many directions simultaneously. . . . We did not form and test explicit hypotheses, we did not do a literature search, we had no elaborate instruments, and we did not use sample statistics or draw inferences at the '.05 level of significance.' In comparison to the idealized scientific method, the process we used to make sense of our organization was a messy, iterative groping through which we gradually, though quite rapidly, built up a picture of the organizational system of which we were a part."

This approach is the complete reverse of designing a study to test a specific idea. It is an approach that builds a picture of human communication impression by impression until the researchers have enough information to confidently make statements about the topic that interests them.

"My method beats your method" arguments can take place repeatedly and heatedly in research circles, but your reading of this chapter should have you thinking that one method never "beats" another method. The real question is "Is your research method theoretically and practically appropriate for the research you want to do?"

Ethics Panel: Do Some Research Methods Require More Ethical Decisions Than Others?

The subjectivity in human communication requires that you explore the subjective life of individuals as they report it. Typically, this means interviewing people and "probing" as to why they see things the way they do. To facilitate this process, you assure your interviewees that their confidences will be respected and that nothing you report will identify them.

As you explore the complexities of organizational culture in a major corporation, one informant, based on your assurances of confidentiality, "lets loose." You hear all about his unsatisfactory working conditions, personal life, and prospects in general. The veiled threats that emerge from the informant's interview suggest that he may become a danger to his colleagues, if not himself. What do you do?

(Continued)

(Continued)

As you walk away with a voice recorder full of statements that you have chosen to interpret as veiled threats, you contemplate the fact that had you asked simple "yes/no" multiple–choice-type questions the troubling information you now have may never have surfaced.

Could it be that some research methods raise more ethical problems than others?

What is your obligation to those who may be harmed in some way if the threats you detect were to translate into action?

What is your obligation to the individual you interviewed?

What is your obligation to the research process in general? For example, should you stay away from such research because of its potential complications or be prepared to break your assurances of confidentiality when you detect potential danger to your participants or others?

Chapter Summary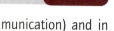

- Communication researchers differ in ontology (how to define communication) and in epistemology (how best to understand communication).

- Generally, researchers assume either that human communication is objectively measurable and can be summarized in rules and generalizations or that communication is subjective, is individualistic, and must be described as such.

- The processes of induction, deduction, and abduction link observations to theory.

- Ways of understanding communication include tenacity, intuition, authority, and empiricism.

- The general purposes of research are exploration, description, explanation, prediction, control, interpretation, and criticism.

- Research may begin with specific hypotheses, with general research questions, or with no specific questions at all.

- Credible research must have a logical link between the methods chosen and the assumptions that underpin them.

Recommended Reading

Anderson, J. A., & Baym, G. (2004, December). Philosophies and philosophic issues in communication, 1995–2004. *Journal of Communication, 54*(4), 589–615. A review of many of the issues discussed in this chapter.

Becker, H. S. (1997). *Tricks of the trade: How to think about your research while you're doing it.* Chicago: University of Chicago. Discusses ways of thinking about research in practice.

Littlejohn, S. W., & Foss, K. A. (2008). *Theories of human communication* (9th ed.). Belmont, CA: Wadsworth/Thomson Learning. Provides coverage of major communication theories, their intellectual origins, and their relationships.

Lowery, S., & DeFleur, M. L. (1988). *Milestones in mass communication research: Media effects* (2nd ed.). New York: Longman. Summarizes major breakthroughs in conceptualizing and answering major questions about mass communication.

Pirsig, R. M. (1974). *Zen and the art of motorcycle maintenance: An inquiry into values.* New York: Morrow. A best seller that documents one individual's personal journey through the nature of knowing.

Powdermaker, H. (1967). *Stranger and friend.* New York: W. W. Norton and Co. Hortense Powdermaker is known for her ethnographic studies of African Americans in rural America and of Hollywood. Her book title captures the balancing act that communication researchers must often adapt when working with research participants.

Trent, J. S. (1998). *Communication: Views from the helm for the 21st century.* Boston: Allyn & Bacon. An overview of where the field of communication is heading, from the points of view of a diversity of communication scholars.

Recommended Web Resources

Communication Research (SAGE Publications): http://crx.sagepub.com. You can sign up for free content alerts from this journal at this site.

The Idea Monkey: www.cios.org. The Idea Monkey, a creation of the Communication Institute for Online Scholarship (CIOS), works by pairing key concepts identified by the CIOS in its analyses of the communication literature. Concepts with high prominence in the field are paired, and the pairings are rated for originality.

Visual Communication Concept Explorer: www.cios.org. You can use the CIOS "Visual Communication Concept Explorer" (VCCE) to explore related concepts from the communication literature and to learn what communication concepts are related to other concepts.

SCHOLARLY ORGANIZATIONS

Association for Education in Journalism and Mass Communication: www.aejmc.org

International Communication Association: www.icahdq.org

National Communication Association: www.natcom.org

The above sites are for three of the many academic interest groups in communication. Visit them to explore the diversity of academic research areas and method interests.

APPLIED COMMUNICATION RESEARCH

American Association of Advertising Agencies: www.aaaa.org

American Marketing Association: www.marketingpower.com/

Direct Marketing Association: www.the-dma.org

The National Association of Broadcasters: www.nab.org

Public Relations Society of America: www.prsa.org

The above five Web sites are for major communication industry groups. You will not be able to access all aspects of these sites, but you will be able to browse for insights on current research, research issues, and possible careers.

References

Evered, R., & Reis, M. (1981). Alternative perspectives in the organizational sciences: "Inquiry from the Inside" and "Inquiry from the Outside." *Academy of Management Review, 6*(3), 385–396.

Kaplan, A. (1964). *The conduct of inquiry: Methodology for behavioral science.* San Francisco: Chandler Publishing.

Student Study Site

Visit the study site at www.sagepub.com/treadwellicr for e-flashcards, web resources, and additional study materials.

CHAPTER

3

Ethics

Your Responsibilities as a Researcher

Ethics are complex, it's true,
With many a rule to think through.
But there's one easy guide;
Keep this by your side—
"Would you do what you're doing to you?"

Chapter Overview

Researching human communication means interacting with people, and there is no escaping the fact that this has ethical implications. Your relationship with research participants will be guided by your personal standard of ethics as well as codes of ethics and laws designed to protect participants from psychological and physical harm. This chapter focuses on some of the ethical issues in human communication research, codes of ethics that govern research on human subjects, and approval procedures for human communication research in a scholarly setting.

Starter Questions

- Is deceit ever a justifiable part of research?

- Is recording people's behavior without their consent ever justifiable?

- What aspects of my research do I really need to get permission for?

- Must I ensure anonymity or confidentiality if my research participants request it?

- Are there any ethical implications in writing a literature review or a final research report?

Some Ethical Decisions

You will recognize the verse at the beginning of this chapter as a loose interpretation of the "do unto others" rule. If only specific ethical decisions in human communication research were that simple. Consider the decisions that might need to be made in the course of designing communication research. For example, would you expose research participants to sexually explicit or violent material? Deliberately deceive participants? Ensure that some people receive important information while denying it to others? Accept research funding from a source that hopes your research results will help promote its products or services? Start false rumors? Monitor people's behavior without their knowledge or consent?

The following paragraphs set out some of the ethical decisions for communication researchers, some of the "classic" ways of resolving ethical dilemmas, and some specific ethical standards and practices that anyone researching human communication should be aware of.

SEX, VIOLENCE, AND DECEPTION

Sex, violence, and deception sound like the ingredients of a soap opera, but each can be the focus of serious research in communication, and each clearly has ethical implications.

Debates, often politically fueled, rage over sexually explicit and violent media content and over the nature of their effects. From a research point of view, there are two major questions: First, what are the effects (if any) of viewing such content? Second, what causes these effects? In other words, can we claim that exposure to such content causes some condition, or is it possible that the condition itself leads to voluntary exposure to such content? Many studies and research designs address these two questions, but suppose there comes a point in your own research where you decide that you need to expose participants to explicit content so that you can assess their response(s) to it. With respect to minors, this may be a legal question, the answer to which is "you can't." For adults you probably can, but should you?

You may be interested in how audience feedback influences a speaker. For example, does a supportive audience improve a speaker's performance; can a hostile audience weaken a speaker's performance? To answer such questions, you decide to expose speakers participating in your study to an audience made up of **confederates.** Confederates are participants in a study who have been briefed to behave in a particular way. In other words they are "faking it" and deceiving the speaker. The speakers then address audiences who are faking a response such as enthusiasm or disinterest. Legal? Sure. Ethical . . . ?

You are interested in how information travels in organizations. The only way you can study this in a controlled fashion is to start a rumor, ask around to find out who heard it, and then backtrack to see from whom individuals first heard the rumor. This allows you to track the speed and the patterns of informal communications in an organization. To begin the experiment, you decide to sit with a couple of strangers in your campus coffee bar and, conversationally, let out the information that your university's trustees are planning a 30% hike in student fees and tuition. You are of course lying. Does the value of your research outweigh the need to deceive people?

Many health communication studies seek to establish the most effective means of getting health information to people. One basic research design is to provide information to one community by interpersonal means, to another by mass media, and to a third by a combination of the two. In order to establish that there have been any effects at all, you need a fourth (control) community that receives no information. As part of your study, then, you deny the control community information that could perhaps save or extend a life. Legal? Sure. Deceptive? Maybe. Ethical . . . ?

MONEY AND RELATIONSHIPS

If sex, violence, and deception can feature in our list of ethical considerations, can money and relationships be far behind?

Let's take a look at the hypothetical ClickAQuiz educational technology company. This company has a keen interest in your research in interactive technologies. In fact, it offers to write a check to support your research. The company makes software that allows multiple-choice quizzes to be downloaded to cell phones for students to answer in their own time and space and then to upload their answers wirelessly for grading. Your interest is in how such technology affects academic performance, and you have designed survey questions that focus on technology and academic performance. In return for its check, ClickAQuiz wants you to include a large number of additional questions about how and where students might use this technology, what they would be willing to pay for the service, and how they feel about banner advertising on their phones. Do you incorporate these questions into your research or reject them as an unnecessary commercial "intrusion" unrelated to the focus of your research? Could the ClickAQuiz questions, if used, affect student responses to the questions you want answered by, for example, "framing" the technology as "user pays" rather than free? On what basis might you change or drop any of ClickAQuiz's questions?

In the "relationships" department, researchers may engage with their research participants in ways that range from dispassionate observation to psychologically intimate contact.

For example, you are interested in what attracts visitors to an Internet site other than content; that is, you are interested in Web interface design. This is an important area of research because results from your research could help improve online education, increase the ease with which people can read news online, and perhaps lead to more accessible Web sites for the visually and hearing impaired. You find a number of Web sites that have similar content—for example university home pages. You solicit access to the server logs of these institutions, explaining that you need information only on how much time visitors spend on these sites, where they come from, and how they navigate their way through the sites. The institutions will refuse of course, though they may well have to comply with similar requests from government agencies. Your relationship with the Internet users you would be tracking is quite disinterested and impersonal, but how defensible is your request?

Monitoring Internet behavior is one example of **unobtrusive measures**, an approach that by definition observes people's behavior without their being aware of it. It is often used to check on the reliability of information people provide about their personal behaviors. For example, most people would probably say when interviewed that they wear seat belts when driving. One unobtrusive measures check on this is simply to observe people driving and to record the percentage you see wearing seat belts.

At the other extreme, as someone researching family dynamics and how parents and siblings interact across generations, you may find that you need in-depth face-to-face interviews to gain an understanding of a particular family's culture and communication patterns. As you question family members in depth you may find that the questions you need to ask are distressing to your interviewees. Or you may find that they are revealing confidences about other members of the family, who would be hurt if they knew that this information was going outside the family to a stranger—you.

Less dramatic decisions such as simply listening in on a conversation also have an ethical component. In the prologue to this book, I invited you to listen in on a discussion among a group of students and asked the question, "Should you?" From a straight research point of view, this might be an interesting thing to do, but it seems intuitive that just as we would ask permission to physically join the group, so also would we ask permission to record, and in due course publish, our report and interpretation of the students' discussions.

Even the study of texts rather than people can have ethical implications related to what is and is not selected for study and reported.

The overriding question in all the hypothetical cases outlined above is "What standards of behavior should apply to my research?" Typical issues in communication research are discussed in the following section. Some relate to your relationship with research participants, some relate to your relationships with the readers who will depend on you for an accurate account of your research, and some relate to both these groups, equally important to your career as a researcher.

Issues in Communication Research

HONESTY

It seems axiomatic that honesty is always the best policy, but honesty in practice can be difficult. We have already established that deception can be part of legitimate and professional research studies. To be honest and reveal the deception "up front" may be to weaken the whole research design. Professional codes of ethics generally address this dilemma by allowing deception in some research designs as long as the participants are made aware of the deception immediately after the study is concluded.

Researchers have an ethical responsibility to their readers as well as to their research participants. In this case this means reporting possible flaws in your research and negative results as well as the good news. Most research papers have a section where the author discusses possible weaknesses in the study. Such a section is helpful, not an embarrassment, because it provides a launch pad for further research. Finding "nothing" or results that are counterintuitive may not do a lot for your research ego, but it does not invalidate your study. Obviously, a significant finding is more likely to be published, but the fact that something you expected to find was not found is still a contribution to knowledge, and you can honestly report that finding.

CONFIDENTIALITY AND ANONYMITY

To protect the individuals who may be giving you personal information, it is customary to assure them of **confidentiality**. This means that you will not release any information that identifies your participants. However, as the researcher you know what information each participant provided.

To fully protect and reassure participants, you may need to offer **anonymity**. Anonymity goes a step further in protecting people in that the data you collect from them absolutely does not identify them. Even you do not know which participants provided the information you collected. Typically you ensure anonymity by instructing respondents not to put their name on any information they provide. Any consent forms that they sign are turned in separately so that there is no link between those documents that identify them and any other document.

Violation of any anonymity or confidentiality agreements when reporting your research results is an ethical issue and may well become a legal one. Researchers usually protect their respondents' anonymity in qualitative studies by referring to them as "Respondent A," "Respondent B," and so on or by using false and typically uncreative names such as "Bob Smith" or "Jane Jones." Quantitative studies typically report average scores and other such statistical summaries for a group of people, so there is no need to identify specific individuals at all.

MAKING GENERALIZATIONS

The professional codes of practice discussed below require that research participants be volunteers. If only willing volunteers are recruited to your study, you will be recruiting a group that has a "bias" toward your study in the sense that they are willing to participate in it. Generalizations from your study, then, can be made only to this type of individual. Because you recruited volunteers for your study, you cannot make statements about the likely effect of these materials on the "non-volunteer" type. Ethically, we cannot force people into a research study, and ethically therefore we cannot generalize our findings to the non-volunteer population.

DEBRIEFING

If your participants have been exposed to deception, you have an ethical obligation after the study is over to ensure that you contact them, explain the deception, and invite any follow-up questions they may have. Failure to do so means that your participants will leave the research assuming that they have been involved in a real event when in fact they have not. The American Psychological Association (APA) Ethical Principles of Psychologists and Code of Conduct calls for any deception to be revealed to participants no later than at the conclusion of data collection and for participants to be given an opportunity to withdraw their data if they wish.

More generally, researchers should promptly respond to partici-pants' requests for information about the nature, results, and conclu-sions of the research. Most researchers need to ask their participants to document their agreement to be in a research study by signing a con-sent form. Consent forms typically describe the nature of the study and emphasize the right of participants to leave the study at any time and to access the results of the study. Because consent forms obviously must be signed in advance of any study, they may not explain any deceptions that are a part of the study. As noted above, participants who have been subject to deception should be made aware of that deception as soon as possible, and readers of your research report will want to know that the results you report were obtained under conditions of deception.

THE LITERATURE REVIEW

A large part of any research project is the literature review. This is your summary and evaluation of what other researchers working on your topic have published. You review this literature to get ideas on how best to do your own research but, more important, to demonstrate to others exactly how your research contributes to the shared body of knowledge.

There is voluminous literature on communication research. You will have to read and report it selectively. This means that your readers' view of the field, and your own, will be shaped by what you choose to write and how you write about it. Following are some of the questions you might have about a literature review.

How far back in time should I review? Can I use secondary (summary) articles rather than primary (original) sources? Should I report articles that do not support my viewpoint?

Can I report research that is relevant but proprietary (i.e., "owned" and I do not have permission to publish it)?

Views about communication change over time, as they should. Just as it is possible to misrepresent the current state of knowledge by selecting only certain authors to review, so it is possible to misrepresent by selecting particular time periods for review. Reviewing summaries of research rather than the original can give you an initial overview of the field, but summarizing summaries may lead to dangerous oversimplifications. Articles that do not support your ideas and methods should be reported because your readers need to be aware of any debates and controversies in your area of interest and you have a responsibility to summarize the debates.

Proprietary information is information that is owned, typically, by corporations and may not be published without their permission. As a researcher you may have access to proprietary information, but publishing that information may be both an ethical and a legal violation.

In summary, what you write and how you write shape readers' understanding of your field. Your writing may accurately represent the work of other researchers or misrepresent it and therefore requires that you be ethically sensitive.

ACKNOWLEDGING OTHERS

It is rare for one individual to be able to take full credit for a research project, especially in the physical and biological sciences where a team of technicians and colleagues may be needed to bring a project to successful completion. Authorship of a published paper implies more than just writing it; it implies taking responsibility for the project reported. To the extent that others contributed to your project it is appropriate to list them as coauthors or at least to acknowledge their contributions.

The basic decision is what constitutes "others." Researchers reporting summary data for hundreds of survey respondents are unlikely to acknowledge any individual specifically. Researchers whose results are based on close collaboration with one or two collaborators may well want to acknowledge those individuals but then may be unable to do so because to do so would identify individuals who have been promised anonymity.

APPROPRIATE LANGUAGE

Seeking permission from participants or communicating results to them needs to be done at their level of understanding if they are to understand your research. The Office of Human Subjects Research of the National Institutes of Health recommends that as a general rule consent documents be written so that they are understandable to people who have not graduated from high school. Consent forms and other materials that are needed to explain research to children, non-English speakers, and people with relatively little concept of what research is all about obviously require special attention to readability levels (Office of Human Subjects Research, 2006).

Communicating information at a level that participants cannot understand is an ethical transgression because your writing may have the effect of misinforming them.

Similarly, members of the research community who share your interests will want a full understanding of the relevant literature as well as your research methods, results, and interpretation. Bias in any of these aspects of your report has ethical implications because, once again, you would have the effect of misinforming your audience.

PLAGIARISM

There are a number of reasons to dislike plagiarism. Primarily of course it is an unethical (and possibly illegal) representation of others' work as your own. From the point of view of your busy research colleagues, however, plagiarism also represents the problem of "used goods." Representing others' work as your own means that readers may end up reading both the original research and the plagiarist's version of that research. It does a disservice to researchers trying to stay current because they may be misled into reading two different versions of the same research. Of course if the plagiarist is publishing proprietary research, the issue also becomes one of copyright violation (at least).

Some Classic Ethical Positions

All the above issues pose questions that must be answered. For many researchers the answers come in the form of specific ethical codes that must be followed, with penalties such as loss of funding if they are not followed.

More generally, researchers may turn to one or more of the following "classic" ethical positions for guidance.

The Judeo-Christian ethic is the basis of the verse at the beginning of this chapter. Its test of ethical behavior is a simple one. Would you be willing to be a participant in your own study? If not, your project as it affects other people may be ethically suspect.

Philosopher Immanuel Kant proposed that a behavior is valid if you are willing to see it applied as a universal rule. For example, if you are willing to use deception as part of a research design, then you ought to be prepared to accept deception as a universal value.

The principle of utilitarianism, associated with philosophers Jeremy Bentham and John Stuart Mill argues for the greatest good for the greatest number. It suggests that research designs that may hurt a minority of people are justified if there is an overall greater good. For example, we might argue in communication research that misinforming a few people via a false rumor is defensible if out of that research emerges a fuller understanding of how best to use informal communication networks in an emergency.

Philosopher John Rawls's "veil of ignorance" approach asks us to take a dispassionate approach, reviewing all sides of a decision equally. We are asked to wear a veil that blinds us to all information about ourselves that might cloud our judgment. For example, suppose our research design has the potential to cause severe psychological distress to our research participants. We need an ethical decision as to whether this is acceptable or not. The "veil of ignorance" blinds us to the role we would be playing in the research; that is, we could be the researcher or we could be participants. Recognizing that psychological distress is undesirable and could happen to us, we would probably decide that our research ought not to cause any distress to our research participants.

Contemporary Codes of Ethics

It is unlikely that any of the above research designs would harm people in the way that an experimental surgery could. However, there is always the possibility of psychological harm, for example as a result of exposure to graphic violence or from requiring participants to behave in a way contrary to their beliefs. Codes of ethics seek to protect research participants from any form of harm by prescribing professional standards of behavior for researchers. Professional concern for human subjects dates back to at least the 4th-century-BCE oath of Hippocrates.

It's a long way from Nazi Germany to monitoring people's behavior on the Internet, but Nazi medical experiments during World War II were the 20th-century impetus for codes of ethics covering research on human subjects. After the war, a number of Nazi physicians and administrators were charged with crimes against humanity, more specifically with conducting medical experiments that caused death and inflicted injury on concentration camp inmates without their consent.

THE NUREMBERG CODE

One outcome of the trials was the 1948 Nuremberg Code, the first international code to emphasize that

- research subjects must consent to the research in which they are involved, and
- the benefits of the research must outweigh the risks.

THE DECLARATION OF HELSINKI

In 1964, the World Medical Association's Declaration of Helsinki established international ethical guidelines for medical professionals researching human subjects. The Declaration of Helsinki continues to be revised and emphasizes that

- research protocols be reviewed by an independent committee prior to the research,
- informed consent be obtained from research participants,
- research be conducted by medically or scientifically qualified individuals, and
- research risks should not exceed the benefits.

THE BELMONT REPORT

The National Commission for the Protection of Human Subjects of Biomedical and Behavioral Research prepared the Belmont Report in 1979. The report outlines three basic ethical principles surrounding research with human subjects. These are respect for persons, beneficence, and justice. The principles and their application in practice are summarized in Exhibit 3.1.

EXHIBIT 3.1   **The Belmont Report Principles and Applications**

Principle	Application
Respect for Persons • Individuals should be treated as autonomous agents. • Persons with diminished autonomy are entitled to protection.	Informed Consent • Subjects must be given the opportunity to choose what shall or shall not happen to them. • The consent process must include three elements: information, comprehension, and voluntariness.
Beneficence • Human subjects should not be harmed, and efforts should be made to secure their well-being. • Research should maximize possible benefits and minimize possible harm.	Assessment of Risks and Benefits • The nature and scope of risks and benefits must be assessed systematically.
Justice • The benefits and risks of research must be distributed fairly.	Selection of Subjects • There must be fair procedures and outcomes in the selection of research subjects. For example, subjects ought not to be recruited simply on the basis of accessibility or manipulability.

Source: Adapted from Office of Human Subjects Research, n.d.

Regulations

Many nations have regulations that implement principles such as those set out above. In the United States, Department of Health and Human Services regulations that implement these principles have been adopted by many other agencies that fund or conduct research on human subjects. These shared standards are known as the Federal Policy for the Protection of Human Subjects, or "Common Rule."

The Common Rule addresses requirements for ensuring compliance by research institutions, requirements for obtaining and documenting **informed consent**, requirements for **institutional review boards** or **IRBs** (see below), and special protections for vulnerable research subjects such as pregnant women, prisoners, minors, and the handicapped.

Peer Review and Institutional Review Boards

Peer review at its simplest consists of qualified researchers with similar interests assessing each other's work. Formal and informal peer review of your research design should influence how you think about your research and its ethical implications.

Informally, researchers brainstorm over coffee cups, swap ideas at conferences, and put together research teams for major projects. Such interactions can provide an informal check on ethics and research design more generally before any project is launched. This of course can be a hit-or-miss operation, depending on how actively the researcher networks.

Formal review is required when researchers undertake any human subjects research for the federal government or are employed by any institution that receives federal funding.

The most typical method of formal peer review with respect to ethics and treatment of human participants is the institutional review board or IRB. The IRB is a panel established to review research proposals specifically for their impact on any human participants. There is an IRB in some form on almost every college and university campus where human subjects research is conducted.

The fact that most communication research does not involve physical impact on participants does not exempt it from IRB review. Protection involves psychological protection as much as physical protection. As you saw from some of the examples at the beginning of this chapter, subjects could potentially suffer psychological distress from exposure to explicit materials or from having been deceived.

What Should I Call You? The Ethics of Involvement

The student-professor relationship is often described, if not predicted, by whether it is a "Professor," "Dr.," "Ms.," or "call me Fred" relationship. "Dr." implies a formal student-faculty relationship; "Fred" an informal one. Similarly, the labels used to describe the people involved in research vary along with the nature of the relationship the researcher has with them. While researchers are generally known as researchers or investigators, the individuals participating in the research may be known as "subjects," "informants," "participants," or "collaborators."

Traditionally, researchers used the term *subjects*, with the connotation of a white-coated professional observing a subservient group of humans for the cause of a greater good. The term *informants* better recognizes that researchers would be nowhere without the information provided by participants. *Participants* and *collaborators* are more recent terms recognizing the active and voluntary role that participants play in making research projects possible.

As you can see from Exhibit 3.2, terminology, research design, and the nature of the relationship with research participants are closely related. All researchers are bound by relevant regulations and professional codes, but as our participants move from being subjects to being collaborators, the ethical dilemmas can increase. It is unlikely that a researcher out of the "let's survey 1,200 people" school of thought would need to be professionally concerned with her subjects' private lives. At the other extreme, a researcher working with a small group of collaborators is much more likely to assume an ethical responsibility for their well-being because they are part of the team that has decided on the nature of the research from the beginning and that continues to shape its progress.

EXHIBIT 3.2   Varieties of Involvement in Communication Research

Researcher's Involvement With Participants		
Researcher's Orientation to Participants	**Low**	**High**
Dispassionate observer "Stranger"	Measure people objectively Not involved Behavior motivated by regulations and ethical codes People: "Subjects"	Explore people's subjective views Involved in order to elicit subjective information Behavior motivated by regulations, ethical codes, and need to establish trusting relationship People: "Informants"
Involved in participants' condition "Friend"	Involved in lives only as a means of observing them Behavior motivated by regulations, ethical codes, and need to successfully access participants People: "Participants"	Involved, with participants' views driving research design and implementation Behavior motivated by regulations, ethical codes, and research goals important to participants People: "Collaborators"

Ethics Panel: Tainted Data and Deception

I: The Use of Tainted Data

Tainted data are data that have been obtained illegally or unethically but may in themselves be useful. Examples include information that has been stolen, released without authorization, or obtained under duress. The general question is "Should a researcher use information that has been obtained illegally or unethically?" For example, a researcher may be interested in how different personality types communicate under conditions of stress. Such information may be available from records of police or military interrogations. There are two problems with using such information. Obtaining it may be illegal, and there may be a further ethical dilemma if the results of the interrogations were obtained under degrading or inhuman conditions. Would you recommend the use of a "data are data" approach or argue that to use the data is to endorse the conditions under which they were obtained?

II: The Stanley Milgram Experiments

In a series of experiments at Yale University in the 1960s, researcher Stanley Milgram found that a majority of his subjects were willing to give apparently harmful electric shocks to another person simply because a scientific "authority" told them to do so. Even though the other person was apparently in pain, many, though not all, participants continued to increase the level of shock at the command of the researcher.

The overall objective of these experiments was to explain the conditions of obedience to authority. The "victim" was, in fact, an actor; the "pain" was simulated; and this information was revealed to participants at the end of the experiment.

To what extent do you feel the psychological stress that many participants felt was justified by the goals of the experiment?

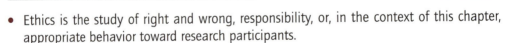

Chapter Summary

- Ethics is the study of right and wrong, responsibility, or, in the context of this chapter, appropriate behavior toward research participants.

- Communication research ethics share with medical and psychological ethics a basic concern to protect the well-being of human participants.

- The formal mechanism for reviewing the protections for human subjects at most institutions is an IRB—institutional review board.

- Peer review and publication also provide a check on the ethics of research.

- Ethical decisions are involved in treatment of human participants, in research design, and in research reporting.

- Formal codes of ethics include the Nuremberg Code, the Declaration of Helsinki, the Belmont Report, the "Common Rule," and the American Psychological Association's Ethical Principles of Psychologists and Code of Conduct.

Recommended Reading

Hamilton, A. (2005). The development and operation of IRBs: Medical regulations and social science. *Journal of Applied Communication Research, 33*(3), 189–203. An overview of institutional review boards (IRBs), the most common means of reviewing research on human subjects.

Recommended Viewing

Milgram, S., & Johnson, C. (1965). *Obedience.* University Park: Pennsylvania State University Audio-Visual Services. A documentary film created by Stanley Milgram, showing the obedience experiment referenced in this chapter and its results.

Recommended Web Resources

FORMAL ETHICS AND CODES OF PRACTICE

American Association for Public Opinion Research Code of Professional Ethics and Practices: http://www.aapor.org/AAPOR_Code.htm

The Direct Marketing Association Ethical Guidelines: http://www.dmaresponsibility.org

The above two Web sites provide the codes of ethics for two areas of applied communication—public opinion research and direct marketing.

American Psychological Association Ethical Principles of Psychologists and Code of Conduct: http://www.apa.org/ethics/code2002.html. Many of the ethical principles set out by the American Psychological Association (APA) apply to communication research. APA style is the publication style used to format many communication research papers.

Illinois Institute of Technology Center for the Study of Ethics in the Professions: http://www.iit.edu/departments/csep/codes/. This site has hundreds of codes of ethics from a variety of disciplines, including communication. In addition to the codes, you can find discussion on the value of having such codes and guidelines on constructing a code for your own organization.

National Communication Association Code of Professional Ethics for the Communication Scholar/Teacher: http://www.natcom.org/index.asp?bid=13592. The above code of professional ethics is for one of the major U.S. academic communication associations. It sets out professional standards for research and also teaching and community service.

GENERAL

Dr. Thomas Blass's Stanley Milgram Web site: http://www.stanleymilgram.com. This site provides information on the social psychologist Stanley Milgram and his controversial studies. See the ethics panel in this chapter.

The National Institutes of Health Bioethics Resources: http://bioethics.od.nih.gov/IRB.html

U.S. Department of Health and Human Services, Office for Human Research Protections: http://www.hhs.gov/ohrp/

These are two central sites for information related to research on human subjects in the United States. You will find information, regulations, and an online tutorial.

The President's Council on Bioethics: http://www.bioethics.gov. This site provides information on human subjects research and research ethics.

References

Office of Human Subjects Research. (2006, December 28). *Sheet 6: Guidelines for writing informed consent documents.* National Institutes of Health. Retrieved February 12, 2007, from http://ohsr.od.nih.gov/info/sheet6.html

Office of Human Subjects Research. (n.d.). *Regulations and ethical guidelines: The Belmont Report.* National Institutes of Health. Retrieved October 14, 2009, from http://ohsr.od.nih.gov/guidelines/belmont.html

Student Study Site

Visit the study site at www.sagepub.com/treadwellicr for e-flashcards, web resources, and additional study materials.

4

Reading Research

To Boldly Go Where Others Have Gone Before

In his student days, he had won several retrieval championships racing against the clock while digging out obscure items of information on lists prepared by ingeniously sadistic judges. ("What was the rainfall in the capital of the world's smallest national state on the day when the second-largest number of home runs was scored in college baseball?" was one that he recalled with particular affection.)

(Clarke, 1984, p. 136)

Chapter Overview

All good research is built on a foundation of previous research. Reviewing and synthesizing this research is an essential start to any scholarly paper. Your review of the research literature should suggest research topics, ways of doing research, and most important how your proposed research will contribute to our collective understanding of human communication. Finding relevant information may be easy, but scholarly research requires that you prefer relevant and credible sources of information. This chapter will help you identify the most credible sources of information and discusses how to search for them in a way that gets you the most relevant and credible results.

Starter Questions

- Why do I need to read other people's research?
- Where do I find relevant research?
- Are some sources better than others?
- Is there one best way to find relevant research?
- How can I identify high-quality research?

Library Research: Why Bother?

*If I have seen further than other men it is by
standing upon the shoulders of giants.*

This quote attributed to Sir Isaac Newton (1642–1727), the British physicist and mathematician, refers to his dependency on Galileo's and Kepler's previous work in physics and astronomy.

The purpose of any research is to add to knowledge. The operative word is *add*. Unless you know what has gone before, you cannot know if your research will add to knowledge or merely replicate what others have already done. You must know the past if you are to contribute to the future.

Knowing the scholarly research in your area—or, in research jargon, "the literature"—will stimulate your own research, give you a broader vision of your field, suggest appropriate research methods, and show where your own research fits into the broader body of knowledge.

Once you know what has been researched you will be able to assess what needs to be researched and be confident that you will be making a contribution to knowledge. You will also be able to identify other people working in your area of interest, the research methods used, and the debates surrounding your interest area and how best to research it. By synthesizing and thinking about previous and current research in your field you will be able to see much farther than you ever would have on your own.

The place to find published relevant literature is in most cases your academic library. Academic libraries are the one-stop shop for scholarly research reports. They will also have other material such as newspaper and video archives of potential relevance to communication researchers. You may want to look at such material to identify the breadth of material that may be relevant to you. Ultimately, though, you will want to focus on "the literature," the published scholarly research that has been done to academic standards and is available most typically through the databases in academic libraries.

A good literature review will help you in the following specific areas.

METHODS

Focus group or field interview? Ethnography or experiment? Your readings of the literature will identify accepted methods of research in your area of interest. A good literature review should also reveal methods that challenge conventional wisdom and the debates about how best to do the research that interests you.

ETHICS

Most communication research is research on human subjects. How people are recruited, treated, and debriefed is important to them psychologically and to you professionally. The research literature can suggest how to deal with, for example, minors; how to manage issues of deception that may be necessary as part of a study; or how to handle confidential information in a way that protects informants.

LANGUAGE AND STYLE

Each research specialization is a community defined by its own language and way of writing. From your readings you will see the somewhat formulaic format that most research papers have, the language that typifies each subfield, and its specific style for citations, abbreviations, and use of tables and graphics. Just as reading generally is a good way to develop your general vocabulary, reading research is a good way to develop your research vocabulary and writing skills.

INSPIRATION

An unpredictable but joyous outcome of a thorough literature search is discovering that "breakthrough" paper that suddenly makes a difficult concept clear, shows precisely how to use a specific method, or takes you off in a whole new direction. You will know it when you see it. You may find it out of a random search, but a systematic, thorough search will maximize your chances of finding it.

In summary, a targeted, systematic search for relevant articles and books will have you "standing upon the shoulders of giants" and able to envisage your research project, how to go about it, and the contribution it will make to our collective understanding of human communication.

Finding Relevance, Finding Quality

We want two things from a literature search—relevance and quality. The two are not the same.

Relevant information is information that is immediately useful to you. Quality information is information that is credible, can be relied on, and in the case of scholarly research meets the standards of the research community. Information can be highly relevant but not of any academic quality, or it can be highly credible but irrelevant. For example, you may find that the *National Enquirer* has information about communication with extraterrestrials that is highly relevant to your interests but not of any scholarly merit. The *New England Journal of Medicine* publishes research that is highly credible but probably irrelevant to your interest in corporate rhetoric. The art and science of a good literature search is finding out how to overlap relevance and quality.

HOW DO I FIND RELEVANT INFORMATION?

"Out there" is a lot of information that will be highly relevant. There is also a significantly larger volume of information that is irrelevant. Example? Use "communication" as a **search term** and you will get material on mass, group, interpersonal, and organizational communication. You will also get information on telecommunications, animal communication, and communication with extraterrestrials. If your interest is in, say, rhetoric and public address, you will drown in information you don't need even though it all relates to communication.

The strategy of the search for relevance is diagrammed in Exhibit 4.1. What you want to find is all relevant information—only. You do not want to find irrelevant information, and you do not want to miss relevant information. In the communication field this can be difficult because so many other fields ranging from evolutionary psychology to Web site design or marketing can be relevant to communication research. One key to obtaining relevant information is to develop a good vocabulary and to appreciate the difference in results that different search terms may bring. For example, "groups" and "teams" though similar may produce quite different results when used as search terms.

EXHIBIT 4.1   The Search for Relevance

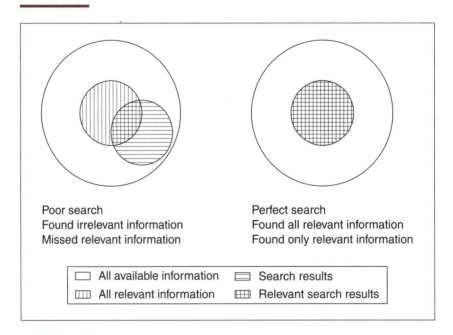

Poor search
Found irrelevant information
Missed relevant information

Perfect search
Found all relevant information
Found only relevant information

| ☐ All available information | ▤ Search results |
| ▥ All relevant information | ▦ Relevant search results |

HOW DO I FIND QUALITY INFORMATION?

Quality information means information that has been obtained in a way that meets scholarly standards. These standards include a clear, defensible, ethical research design; data analyses that logically fit the research design; and results and conclusions that make an original contribution to our understanding of communication. Academic journals put all the research reports they receive through a process of peer review or **refereeing**. A refereed article is one that has been reviewed or refereed by other researchers in the author's field (peers) before being accepted for publication. Academic journals by definition contain refereed articles that meet scholarly standards. Most other journals do not.

Databases Versus Search Engines

The place to find academic journals is academic **databases**. Do not confuse databases with **search engines** such as Google, Yahoo, or Dogpile—a search engine that combines many search engines.

Search engines are popular if for no other reason than their elegantly simple interfaces. A one-line box allows you to type in search terms and get results, usually far more than you can cope with. For example, a Google search for "communication" as I was writing this chapter resulted in 636 million "hits." The ease of use of search engines and easy access to them are their two pluses. The minuses are, typically, the unmanageable number of search results and the questionable quality of the results.

If you use search engines in your research, think about what you are not getting. It is a fair bet that articles from the *Canadian Journal of Communication,* for example, will not be among them. Search engines can be useful in giving you a sense of what's "out there" and what is popular. For example, the Web resources listed at the end of this chapter include the Yahoo, Lycos, and Google sites that rank each engine's most popular search terms. These can be one way of accessing what is of current interest to Internet users, but any understanding based on these rankings will obviously be superficial.

Databases, on the other hand, have a defined number of entries, and many databases consist of scholarly articles that have been peer reviewed. You will not get millions of irrelevant "hits" as the result of a search, and your research results should have a high level of credibility. Therefore, you can automatically improve the quality of your search results simply by preferring databases to search engines.

Databases are similar to phone directories in that you have to know how to access them. You must enter the correct spelling of a name in order to find the correct entry. A wrong search term will give you the "wrong" results.

Library databases have a more sophisticated interface than search engines. Their multiple search windows allow you to search for an article by author, date of publication, title, subject matter, or any combination thereof, resulting in a much more targeted search. A well-executed database search should give you the results you want and none of the results you don't want.

Because different databases contain different content, you can make your search for relevant literature even more focused by selecting the most relevant database. For example, the EBSCO database *Communication and Mass Media Complete* might be a good starting point for a literature review unless you are specifically interested in business communication, in which case *Business Source Premier* may be preferable.

Don't forget CIOS, the Communication Institute for Online Scholarship, introduced in Chapter 2. You can use a keyword system, the Visual Communication Concept Explorer, or the Idea Monkey to get started on your research project.

By combining relevant academic databases with a focus on refereed articles, you can maximize your chances of getting relevant, quality search results. Two cautions are in order though. First, you should not restrict yourself to refereed journals exclusively. Books, news media, and Web sites may all be relevant. Second, communication studies are wide ranging. You may find the article you need in political science, international affairs, psychology, journalism, or business databases. Your initial searches will require both a broad vision and a narrow focus.

Scholarly, Popular, and Trade Publications: What Is the Difference?

What is the difference between scholarly and popular material? **Scholarly articles**, as noted, go through a process of peer review before publication. Peer review means that before a journal editor will accept an article for publication, she will seek the opinion of other scholars doing the same kind of research. These reviewers read the article to determine whether the research has been done to professional standards, that the article makes a contribution to knowledge, and that there are no apparent ethical violations such as plagiarism.

HOW WILL I KNOW A SCHOLARLY ARTICLE WHEN I SEE ONE?

The title *Journal of . . .* is a clue but does not automatically flag a journal as refereed. Another clue is the format of the article. If you see headings titled "Abstract," "Method," and "Literature Review" and a list of references at the end of the article, there is a good chance that the article is refereed. Frequency of publication is also a clue. Refereed publications are typically quarterly, perhaps monthly, but not daily or weekly.

By contrast, **popular articles** are published without a refereeing process, typically in daily or weekly media, and are targeted to a lay audience. They do not have the formal subheadings noted above or a list of references as scholarly articles do. Newspaper and magazine stories are typical examples of popular articles.

Between these two extremes are the so-called **trade publications**. Trade publication articles, like academic articles, are written by experts, but the experts are more likely to be practitioners than academics and their articles are not usually peer reviewed or refereed.

Articles in the trade press are more topical than academic articles because they appear daily, weekly, or monthly and do not get held up by a review process. However, information important to you as a researcher, such as a literature review, a method description, and references, will not be included.

Primary Versus Secondary Sources

One reason to prefer scholarly, refereed journals and books is that they give you access to primary (original) research. Popular and trade articles may give you a summary of other authors, but you will need to go to scholarly sources to read what the original author wrote. Only scholarly articles provide **citations** ("cites") at the end of the article to let you find out what their sources wrote. Popular and trade articles do not do this; you have to accept what one author is telling you about other authors.

The Champagne Glass Model of Bibliographic Research

In overview, your bibliographic research should take the profile of a champagne glass. You start with a wide-ranging search and a large number of search results. You then narrow your findings down to a few very relevant results. Sometimes, there is just one "breakthrough" article that summarizes the history of a topic, explains how to research it, and inspires you to research it further. From the citations in such very focused findings, you will be able to generate a bigger set of highly relevant readings, as shown in Exhibit 4.2.

EXHIBIT 4.2   **The Champagne Glass Model of Bibliographic Research**

(1) Wide-ranging findings from your initial search
should lead you to
(2) very specific
citations,
which
generate
(3) still more highly relevant readings.

Here's an example.

- A search of the EBSCO *Communication and Mass Media* database using the term "communication" resulted in 112,619 "hits" (compared with 636 million hits on Google).
- A search using "communication in organizations" resulted in 1,070 hits.
- A search using "communication in nonprofit organizations" resulted in 2 hits. One of these was a magazine; the other an academic journal. That one journal, cited below, lists 61 references. If you have a specific interest in nonprofit communications, this search should give you 61 immediately relevant references, at least according to Lewis, Richardson, and Hamel in:

When the "Stakes" are Communicative. By: Lewis, Laurie K.; Richardson, Brian K.; Hamel, Stephanie A. Human Communication Research, Jul. 2003, Vol. 29 Issue 3, p400, 31p, 6 charts; (AN 10718624)

Cited References (61)

(Note that this citation is reproduced from the original search result. It is not formatted in the APA style frequently used for citations in communication research.)

How Can the Library of Congress Help My Literature Search?

The answer is subject headings. You will want to be familiar with Library of Congress Subject Headings. The specific subject headings—and there are many of them—are a standard reference item in academic libraries. The subject headings show you how information is categorized by the Library of Congress (LOC), but more to the point they give you alternate search terms and perhaps a reminder of how your own vocabulary can limit or expand your search. To use the LOC's own example (*The General Collections*, n.d.),

If you search the Library's online catalog for the keywords "battered women," you find more than one hundred entries and may be perfectly satisfied. But by not identifying the Library's correct subject headings, "Abused women," "Abused wives," and "Wife abuse," you may miss the best materials for your topic. A search combining these three terms yields more than one thousand records.

In other words, thinking of alternate words to *women* and to *battered* can substantially multiply the number of relevant "hits" you get.

Other Resources

Journals, books, and databases are not the only resources available. Other resources include catalogs, dictionaries, encyclopedias, indexes, annuals, yearbooks, handbooks, and abstracts. Some of these are listed as resources at the end of this chapter.

How to Be Skeptical About Information, Especially Web Information

Your initial search results may vary in quality between refereed journal articles and Web sources of extremely variable quality. When anyone with a Web site can post to the world the "fact" that his or her parents were Martians, a touch of skepticism is required in evaluating Web sites. The following questions will help you identify good scholarship in print and Web formats.

STAGE 1: THINK BOOK OR JOURNAL

Ask of the Web site the same questions you would ask of a book or journal.

- Author's credentials (e.g., Prof., Dr., PhD, MD).

- Author's affiliation (e.g., university, college, corporation, "think tank").

- Date of publication and edition or revision. Remember that a book that has been frequently reprinted and is now into its 20th edition may have scholarly credibility or it may simply be popular.

- Publisher. University presses and academic associations are academically respectable, as are academic publishers. This does not mean that their books and journals are unbiased; it means merely that there is a level of good scholarship behind them.

- Title. "Lost Tribes of Israel Found at South Pole" versus "Conceptualizing and Assessing Organizational Image: Model Images, Commitment, and Communication" will give you some clue as to academic credibility.

- Intended audience. From the style of writing (word and sentence length and language) you will be able to guess at the intended audience and also whether the author's intent is persuasive or informative.

- Objectivity/subjectivity. What biases can you discover?

- Coverage. Is it comprehensive or selective?

- Writing style. Is it popular, technical, or academic?

- Reviews (if any). Use the name of the author or title of the article as search terms; you may pick up reviews of the article that will give you some critical insight on it.

- Citations. What references (credible or otherwise) does the author(s) draw on?

STAGE 2: ADDITIONAL QUESTIONS FOR WEB SITES

- What does the URL tell you? Is it .com, .edu, .org, .mil, .gov, or another domain?

- Does the site tell you the criteria by which information is accepted or rejected? Does it accept all contributions, or is there some review process?

- What people or organization wrote the page? Do they have demonstrable expertise? Note that *expert* does not have to mean unbiased. We expect XYZ Company's Web site to be an authoritative source of information on XYZ products and predictably biased toward them.

- Could the page be a satire or comedic? It doesn't happen often in academia, but it does happen. Check out the *Journal of Irreproducible Results* by way of example (http://www.jir.com/).

- Is contact information provided?

- Can you verify what is said or shown on the Web site? If not, it is academically suspect.

- Are documents in the site dated, and when was the site last updated?

- Comparable sites: If you do a Web search for sites with a similar name, URL, or content, what is the quality of the information you get?

Many library Web sites demonstrate with examples how to distinguish quality sites from the more suspect ones. Some of these are listed at the end of this chapter.

Mr. Boole and the Three Bears

One way to reduce the number of search results to something manageable is to ask the right combination of questions.

George Boole (1815–1864), an English mathematician, invented a type of linguistic algebra, the three most basic operations of which are *and, or,* and *not.* The relevance of these "**Boolean operators**" is this. Suppose you were unwise enough to use the search term "communication" in a search. Even from a database, you would likely drown in the number of largely irrelevant results. You would similarly drown in the results of using the term "Smith" for an author search. But if you search for "communication *and* Smith" you will reduce the number of results significantly. Similarly, "communications *or* telecommunications" will expand your search results if you need to, and "communications *not* telecommunications" will narrow your search.

Exhibit 4.3 demonstrates the use of Boolean operators on a search of the EBSCO *Communication and Mass Media Complete* database. I was interested in feminist approaches to communication study, so I did separate searches for "communication" and "feminist" and then combined the terms using Boolean operators. You can see that combining search terms with the *and* operator can reduce the number of search results significantly.

EXHIBIT 4.3   *Use of Boolean Search Terms*

Search Term	Number of Results
Communication	171,947
Feminist	2,008
Search Term Combinations	
Communication *or* feminist	172,901
Communication *not* feminist	170,893
Communication *and* feminist	1,054

As with the story of Goldilocks and the three bears, literature searches can produce results that are too big, too small, or just right. Mr. Boole's operators can help you fine-tune a search to "just right."

Saving Your Search Results

Ways of recording your search results include good old-fashioned pen and paper, dumping everything to print or a "flash drive," and bookmarking Web sites. Saving search results to CD or a flash drive makes sense because you will record citations accurately and your saved content can be edited as necessary for your literature review. Pen and paper still are helpful because they allow you to visualize what is important in your search and to summarize details that are important to you.

INFORMATION YOU MUST RECORD

Record *full* bibliographic information. For print media this includes the following.

- Author—full name. Note that American Psychological Association (APA) citation style uses author first initials and last name; other styles use the author's full first name. Play it safe and record the full name initially so you have it if you need it.

- Title of book or of article and journal in which it appears.

- Date of publication and volume and issue number if a journal.

- Edition number if a book.

- Page numbers for a journal article and for any direct quotes that you wish to use from a book or journal.

- For Web sites, additionally record the URL (Web address) and the date you downloaded the information. (Someone visiting the site on another date may find it different and will need to understand why the URL he or she is viewing is different from the one you cited.)

INFORMATION YOU SHOULD RECORD

What you should record depends on the purpose of your research, but typically you will want to record the following.

- Method—how the research was conducted.

- Results—what were the results of and conclusions from the research.

- Participants—who or (in the case of critical analyses or content analyses) what was studied.

- Unique aspects of the study—what is so special about it.

Exhibit 4.4 shows one possible design for summarizing and recording the results of your searches. The example is based on an initial interest in searching for research on bias in U.S. news media. When starting your search, you might prefer to use the headings shown on a notepad or index cards until you have a more specific sense of the headings you will need to best summarize your findings. Setting up the form shown or your own version as a word-processing table or a database will allow you to sort your records by author, date, or title and search for words just as you would in an online database search. Many database services of course allow you to build your own portfolio of search results online and format the results of your research to a particular style, such as APA.

Exhibit 4.4   One Way to Summarize Your Bibliographic Research

1

Title	Author(s)	Publication Details
Group Allegiances and Perceptions of Media Bias: Taking Into Account Both the Perceiver and the Source	Ariyanto, Ainarina Hornsey, Matthew J. Gallois, Cindy	Group Processes & Intergroup Relations; Apr. 2007, Vol. 10 Issue 2, p266–279 CMMC database, March 27 2010

Summary

Study assesses interaction of religion of perceived news source and religion of reader.

The same newspaper article was seen to be biased in favor of Muslims when attributed to a Muslim newspaper, in favor of Christians when attributed to a Christian newspaper, and intermediate when the newspaper was not identified.

Perceptions of a "hostile" media bias occurred mostly with individuals who identified strongly with their own religion.

When people have prior beliefs that media are biased against them, they interpret media in line with those beliefs.

Method

Experimental design. Muslims and Christians in Indonesia read an article describing interreligious conflict. The article was the same for all readers but was identified as coming from a Muslim newspaper, a Christian newspaper, or an unidentified newspaper.

My Notes

Interesting (and unique?) design of having people of a specific religion respond to articles supposedly written by people of other religions. Measures perceptions rather than media content, and it's an experimental design. Can I find objective measures of editorial bias? Also, my initial interest is U.S. media; what can I find on U.S. media?

(Continued)

EXHIBIT **4.4** *(Continued)*

2

Title	Author(s)	Publication Details
Objective Evidence on Media Bias: Newspaper Coverage of Congressional Party Switchers	Niven, David	Journalism & Mass Communication Quarterly; Summer 2003, Vol. 80 Issue 2, p311–326 CMMC database, March 28 2010

Summary

Examined newspaper articles on congressional party switchers or members who left their political party in midterm, in order to find objective evidence on media bias. Basically found Democrats and Republicans who leave their parties get very similar coverage.

Method

Looked at newspaper coverage of four members of congress (Democratic and Republican) who switched parties. Examined coverage of the members beginning 7 days before they switched and for 30 days after they switched. Used national newspapers and home-state candidates for each member. Analysis based on coders' estimate of the "tone" (positive or negative) of newspaper paragraphs.

My Notes

Aha! Looks exactly like what I want.

Content analysis good idea—more objective than interviewing journalists. Follow up on the citations in this article. Need to also look for interview studies though to find out *why* editorial or journalistic bias might occur.

Writing Your Search Results: The Literature Review

When you write up your research, your readers will want to know your justification for doing it and how it contributes to existing knowledge. This means summarizing your search results in the form of a literature review.

The literature review is your summary of your library research, but it is more than a summary. It is also your job to evaluate each article and assess its significance. There are two basic ways of structuring a review.

Some reviews may be written as a straight "history." Write up your relevant findings in order from oldest to most recent. This gives the reader a sense of how thinking about your topic has changed over time.

If your review shows no consensus among scholars, you might write up your findings in a "pro–con" structure and then try to come to a conclusion. You could, for example, base your review on method, discussing all the studies that were done as surveys and all those done by experiment, and then come to conclusions about why your proposed method will be the most appropriate for your research.

APA (AMERICAN PSYCHOLOGICAL ASSOCIATION) STYLE

APA is the standard style for many communication scholars when they reference other people's work. It uses an "author (date)" style in the body of the paper and places the full citations, alphabetized by author, at the end of the paper. Exhibit 4.5 shows a brief summary of APA style. More detailed information is available in the *Publication Manual of the American Psychological Association* (2009), on many academic Web sites, and in any academic library.

EXHIBIT 4.5   One-Minute APA Style

The following paragraph shows three common APA citation formats, in order of appearance, a fictitious book, a journal article, and a Web article with no author and no date (n.d.).

You should cite other people's work correctly (Able, 1945). Baker and Charles (2007) say that there is an ethical obligation to identify the work of other people that you are drawing on. There is also an obligation to give your readers accurate information so that they can find the original materials you have summarized for them ("Using Citation Style in a Web-Enabled Millennium," n.d.).

APA style dictates that all citations be provided in a single "references" section at the end of the document. The section will always begin on a new page.

References (center heading on new page)

Able, C. D. (1945). *A philosophy of citation* (2nd ed.). Boston: Fictitious Publishing.

Baker, K., & Charles, F. (2007). Thinking about ethical communications: A guide for the perplexed. *Ethical Communications Quarterly, 45*(2), 10–27.

Using citation style in a Web-enabled millennium. (n.d.) Retrieved November 15, 2010, from http://www.allaboutapa.org

Ethics Panel: Politics and Publication

In July 2009, the *New York Times* revealed that officials at the National Highway Traffic Safety Administration had withheld hundreds of pages of research about the hazards of using cell phones while driving (Richtel, 2009).

Critics say that this decision cost lives and has allowed a culture of driving while multitasking to blossom. (Research suggests that motorists talking on a phone are four times as likely to crash as other drivers.) We could therefore wonder why this research was not released in a more timely fashion.

There appear to be two answers. First, the then-head of the agency was apparently urged to withhold the research to avoid antagonizing members of Congress who did not want the agency lobbying states about legislative solutions to the problem. Second, the research data were considered to be preliminary rather than conclusive.

This story reminds us that not all research data on human communication lie within academic libraries. Such data may also be found in businesses and government agencies. More to the point, the story raises two important ethical questions.

Are there circumstances under which political control of research publication can be justified?

Can research relating to health and safety ever be "final"? For example, in communication research, what kinds of research and how much might be needed for a researcher to recommend with absolute confidence that action video games not be sold to children under a certain age?

Chapter Summary

Library research, well done, will guide you on

- what other researchers in your field have discovered,
- research methods,
- research ethics, and
- language and style.

You should know

- the difference between databases and search engines;
- the difference between primary and secondary sources;
- the difference among scholarly, trade, and popular publications; and
- how to focus your library research by using appropriate databases, search terms, and search techniques.

Recommended Reading

Communication Yearbook (annual). An annual review of communication research, published by the International Communication Association. The series provides in-depth articles on research on such aspects of communication as interpersonal, health, organizational, intercultural, international, technology, politics, and rhetoric.

Cull, N. J., Culbert, C., & Welch, D. (2003). *Propaganda and mass persuasion: A historical encyclopedia, 1500 to the present.* Santa Barbara, CA: ABC-CLIO. Surveys key propaganda campaigns, people, concepts, techniques, and current research.

Danesi, M. (2000). *Encyclopedic dictionary of semiotics, media, & communications.* Toronto: University of Toronto Press. Describes the terms, concepts, personages, schools of thought, and historical movements related to these fields.

Jones, S. (Ed.). (2002). *Encyclopedia of new media.* Thousand Oaks, CA: Sage. Articles in this encyclopedia examine the people, technological innovations, ideas, and legal and social issues connected to new media.

Rubin, R. B., Rubin, A. M., & Haridakis, P. M. (2010). *Communication research: Strategies and sources* (7th ed.). Belmont, CA: Wadsworth. This book will help you learn library research skills, scholarly writing, and the basics of APA style.

The above resources provide an overview of some key areas in communication. Use your own academic library to find more specialized resources such as *Broadcasting and Cable Yearbook* or the *Handbook of Political Communication Research.*

Recommended Web Resources

Academic Serials in Communication: http://www.ascus.info/#. Academic Serials in Communication—Unified System (ASCUS) is a not-for-profit, society-governed, full-text database of academic publications in communication. ASCUS is a collaboration among academics, societies, and publishers in which content is widely distributed at low cost.

American Psychological Association: http://www.apa.org. Provides insights and resources on psychological aspects of human communication and on APA style.

The Electronic Journal of Communication: http://www.cios.org/www/ejcmain.htm. One of the first peer-reviewed and electronically distributed scholarly journals.

Library of Congress Subject Headings: http://www.loc.gov/catdir/cpso/lcco. This site shows the Library of Congress's classification of its holdings. Use it to identify key words that might help you in a literature search.

Media and Communications Studies Site (University of Wales, Aberystwyth): http://www.aber.ac.uk/media. This site provides access to articles, bibliographies, and links related to television, film, news, popular music, and other topics.

Voice of the Shuttle: A Web site for Humanities Research: http://vos.ucsb.edu. This site from Alan Liu of the University of California at Santa Barbara provides annotated links to resources in media theory and theorists, media histories, TV, film/video, new media, popular music, journalism, radio, comics, telecom issues, consumerism and advertising, censorship, journals, departments, programs, and professional associations.

EVALUATING WEB SITES

Cornell University "Evaluating Web Sites: Criteria and Tools": http://www.library.cornell .edu/olinuris/ref/research/webeval.html

New Mexico State University Library "Evaluation Criteria": http://lib.nmsu.edu/instruction/ evalcrit.html

MISCELLANEOUS

Code of Ethics of the American Library Association: http://www.ala.org/ala/aboutala/ offices/oif/statementspols/codeofethics/codeethics.cfm

WHAT IS EVERYBODY ELSE SEARCHING FOR?

You can find out the most popular nonacademic search terms by month, category, or country at the following sites.

http://buzz.yahoo.com/

http://lycos.com/

http://www.google.com/press/zeitgeist.html

References

American Psychological Association. (2009). *Publication manual of the American Psychological Association* (6th ed.). Washington, DC: Author.

Clarke, A. C. (1984). *The fountains of paradise.* New York: Ballantine Books.

Library of Congress. (n.d.). *The general collections.* Retrieved February 18, 2008, from http://memory .loc.gov/ammem/awhhtml/awgc1/lc_subject.html

Richtel, M. (2009, July 20). Driven to distraction: U.S. withheld data on risks of distracted driving. *New York Times.* Retrieved July 25, 2009, from http://www.nytimes.com

Student Study Site

Visit the study site at www.sagepub.com/treadwellicr for e-flashcards, web resources, and additional study materials.

5

Measurement

Research Using Numbers

I often say that when you can measure what you are speaking about, and express it in numbers, you know something about it; but when you cannot measure it, when you cannot express it in numbers, your knowledge is of a meagre and unsatisfactory kind.

(Thomson [Lord Kelvin], 1889, p. 73)

Chapter Overview

This chapter introduces a quantitative approach to human communication. If we are to have faith in research numbers, they must measure what they are supposed to measure (validity) and do so consistently (reliability). This chapter discusses the important notions of validity and reliability, the different levels of measurement, and two "classic" scales used in communication research.

Measures can be nominal—essentially labels; ordinal—allowing rank ordering; interval—allowing statistical calculations; or ratio—allowing more sophisticated statistical operations.

Starter Questions

- How can communication be measured?
- What do we mean by measurement?
- Can all communication phenomena be measured?
- How do I know I'm really measuring what I'm supposed to be measuring?
- How do I measure attributes such as intelligence, loyalty, or intimacy?
- Do numbers describe human communication better than words?

What Do Your Head Size, Attitudes, and Readability Have in Common?

Nineteenth-century **phrenologists** argued that there was a relationship between cranial size and shape and mental attributes such as, perhaps, ability to comprehend language or mathematical concepts. After all, if you have a big head, you must be brainy, right? Twenty-first-century wisdom rejects such a connection, but head size, attitudes, and readability all have one thing in common. They have all been subject to measurement, the focus of this chapter.

As we will see in Chapter 10, the quote from English physicist and mathematician Lord Kelvin (William Thomson, 1st Baron) (1824–1907) at the beginning of this chapter is open to refutation by qualitative researchers, but most of us have an intuitive sense that measuring and assigning numbers to things is a good way to make sense of the world. Think of the numbers in your life. Vehicles are advertised on the basis of miles per gallon. Committees make decisions on a "six for–two against" basis. Academic careers and financial aid are predicated on such numbers as grade point average, GRE (Graduate Record Examinations) score, and SAT score. Broadcast programs live or die on audience share and ratings. Politicians live or die on approval ratings, opinion polls, and of course votes. Web advertisers count "click-throughs." You buy clothes and shoes based on a measurable body size. And then there's hang time, yardage, runs batted in, assists, and handicaps.

Assigning numbers to things seems to lend precision to an imprecise world and is of course the basis of all statistical analysis.

This chapter discusses **measurement** as it is understood in communication research. To begin with, a couple of definitions:

- **Numerals** are labels. On their own, "13," "2010," and "64" are not numbers but simply labels for phenomena. They could be street addresses, a brand name, a new commuter jet, or a cologne.

- **Numbers** assign value and relativity to phenomena. For example, the numbers 1 through 5 indicate increasing levels of agreement with a statement where people are asked to rate their agreement on a scale where 1 = strongly disagree and 5 = strongly agree. "64" as an age signifies that someone has been on this earth longer than someone who is "13."

The advantages of numbers to researchers are the ability to make accurate discriminations and the ability to generalize.

The ability to make accurate discriminations is important when trying to decide if there are "real" differences between groups. For example, a survey shows that 48% of a group of women and 52% of a group of men prefer candidate X. Can we assume that in the wider voting population candidate X would win the male vote and lose the female vote, or is there a probability that both groups are much the same in their attitudes?

Numbers and statistical methods can allow us to generalize with varying levels of confidence. Intuitively, if the above groups consisted of 10 men and 10 women, we would have some difficulty predicting the outcome of a national election. If the groups were each 100 people, we would feel more confident, and if each comprised 1,000 people perhaps we would feel more confident still. Statistical calculations, as we will see, allow us an ability to generalize based on numbers and tell us the level of confidence that we are entitled to in those generalizations.

One major advantage of numbers in applied communication fields such as marketing, political communication, advertising, employee communication, and public opinion tracking is the ease of processing the answers. If 2,000 people each write one page explaining their views on television violence, you are in for a lot of reading. If the same 2,000 people each position themselves on scale between 1 (strongly disagree) and 5 (strongly agree), their responses can be readily collected by e-mail, phone, Web site, or optical scanners and, once collected, computer-analyzed in seconds.

Of course those who disagree with Lord Kelvin would argue that adopting a "numbers only" approach ignores qualitative information and therefore loses a great deal of information and the potential for in-depth understanding of human communication. They are correct. We will explore the advantages of qualitative methods more fully in Chapter 10.

An Introduction to Scales

Measurement is essentially the process of finding out whether our focus of interest (be it individuals or media content) has more or less of an attribute we are interested in. For example, we might be interested in whether people watch 5 hours or 50 hours of television a week, whether they score high or low on a measure of religious intolerance, or whether they are rich or poor. It is clear that each of these questions can be answered with a greater or lesser degree of accuracy and judgment. For example, it is relatively easy to measure how much time a person spends watching television. You could simply time his or her television viewing and get an answer. If two independent observers did this and agreed on their results, we could have even more confidence in the measurement.

On the other hand, measuring whether someone is rich or poor is problematic. We could measure a person's wealth, but that raises two questions. First, how do we measure wealth precisely? Second, assuming we have a good measure of wealth in, say, dollars, how do we decide what counts as rich and what counts as poor?

Measurement constantly poses two questions. First, "What in practice shall we measure and record?" Second, "Does the measure capture what we're interested in?" For example, communication researchers often record demographic information such as political affiliation, level of education, or sex. These are legitimate "measurements," but what precisely is it that Republicans have more of than Democrats, seniors more than sophomores, and females more than males? The questions are not that readily answered, and some of these demographic variables often are little more than labels—a very low level of measurement, as we will see.

Research NOIR

We don't cover film noir in this book, but research NOIR is a handy acronym to help you remember the basic levels of measurement. NOIR stands for four basic levels of measurement—**nominal**, **ordinal**, **interval**, and **ratio**.

NOMINAL MEASUREMENT

Examples: New York, Nevada, Idaho, California, Ontario, Quebec
            Male, female
            Press, radio, television

Nominal measurement is really nothing more than labeling or classification. For example, "male, female"; "Buddhist, Christian, Muslim, Hindu"; and "413, 508, 415, 775" are all sets of nominal "measures." Even when the first two examples are **coded**, or transformed into numbers for computer processing, they remain nominal. Coding *male* into "1" and *female* into "2" does no more than substitute labels because in this instance "1" and "2" are numerals, not numbers. Similarly, 413, 508, 415, and 775 are area codes. They also are numerals, not numbers. They don't "measure" anything. You can't add them up or come up with an "average area code." The 775 area code is not inherently bigger or better than the 413 area code (except perhaps to those who live in Nevada).

The only numbers we can really generate from nominal variables are percentages, as in "30% of respondents were male; 70% percent were female."

ORDINAL MEASUREMENT

Examples: Freshman, sophomore, junior, senior
            First, second, third place
            BS, MS, PhD
            Private, corporal, sergeant

Ordinal measures indicate some level of progression. One category has "more" of something than another in some sense. School records for example indicate that second graders have "more" education than first graders. Sophomores have "more" education than freshmen. Generally, parents, faculty, and students are comfortable with such a status ranking, but it is imprecise. Is the difference between freshmen and sophomores time at school, number of credits, or a combination of the two? If the difference is credits, how many credits make a difference—one, three, six, nine? The distinction is not a clear one. We cannot say that a sophomore has X times more education than a freshman; we can say only in some less-than-precise way that a sophomore has been at school "longer" and/or has "more" credits.

In public opinion polling, rank order questions are an example of ordinal measurement. If you rank order restaurants on some attribute such as value for money, convenience, or hygiene, you are telling the researcher that you believe that your top-ranked restaurant has "more of" but not "how much more of." As researchers, we get a sense of difference or proportion, but we still have no numbers with which we can compute. You cannot determine from such a ranking that restaurant X is twice as good as restaurant Y; you can determine only that it is "better."

INTERVAL MEASUREMENT

The basic characteristic of interval measures is the assumption of equal intervals between points on a scale. In our NOIR hierarchy we finally have instruments to which we can attach numbers rather than numerals and results we can quantitatively analyze.

Two classic interval scales in communication research are the **Likert scale** named after its developer, Rensis Likert, and the **semantic differential** scale pioneered by Osgood, Suci, and Tannenbaum (1957). Examples of both are shown later in this chapter. Interval measurement is common in quantitative communication research. You will almost certainly be familiar with such scales from completing course evaluation forms at the end of each semester.

RATIO MEASUREMENT

Ratio scales contain a "true" zero that captures the absence of the attribute. There are authentic zeros such as zero speed on a speedometer, zero heartbeat or brain activity, and an absolute zero temperature. There are some authentic zeros in human communication as well. Both class attendance and going to the movies for example can be zero, as in they never happened. It is possible to have zero income, zero employment, or zero formal education if you never attended school at all.

Ratio scales are at the top of our NOIR hierarchy because they permit the use of the most sophisticated statistical tools.

NOIR IN ACTION

The following shows how the variable of age might be measured at the four different levels of NOIR:

Nominal: Parent, child (note that *a* child could be older than *a* parent)
Ordinal: Child, adolescent, adult
Interval: Age (years): __ 0–4 __ 5–9 __ 10–14 __ 15–19
Ratio: · Age in years _____

The reason to remember NOIR is that statistical calculations assume a particular type of underlying measurement. To revisit an example, you cannot code men as "1," women as "2," discover that you have seven women and three men in your sample, average the scores, and report that the average sex for the group was 1.3. "Sex" as a variable is nominal. It lends itself to classification but not to computation.

This is not a mistake most people make, but the danger comes with the use of statistical analysis software, which by and large requires information to be coded numerically. While it is possible to code *male* as "M" and *female* as "F," the temptation is to use numbers for everything and code *male* and *female* as "1" and "2" respectively. Computers do exactly what they are told to do and will "average" men and women together and report a "mean" sex of 1.3 if you ask them to do so.

To NOIR Is Not Enough: Reliability and Validity

Credible research results demand the use of credible research instruments. Credible in a general sense means trustworthy or believable. You must use instruments that you and the readers of your research can have confidence in. In research, confidence is maximized, though never ensured, by knowing that your measures have both reliability and validity.

Reliability

Imagine the frustration of having an erratic watch. You arrive in class at 9:59 to discover that the time on everyone else's watch is 10:15. You're late! You set your watch correctly and arrive in class the following day at 10:00 to discover that you are early. Everyone else thinks the time is 9:45. This brings up the epistemological question of whether truth is ultimately that which most of us agree on; perhaps everyone else is wrong. But the important issue for now is that your watch is unreliable; you cannot trust it.

Reliable instruments are a must. Unreliable speedometers can get you into trouble, and so can unreliable measures of communication. A measure of interpersonal intimacy that captures a couple in love on Monday, mutually homicidal on Tuesday, and indifferent on Wednesday may be capturing the natural swings in any relationship, but assuming some level of steadfast mutual regard, it appears that the measure is behaving unreliably.

The easiest way to establish the **reliability** of a measure is to repeat measurements on the same phenomenon and to look for similar results each time. If this does not happen, the reliability of your measure is questionable. The following paragraphs discuss ways of assessing reliability. All reliability measures basically involve repeating measurements and then comparing the extent to which the results are the same.

TEST-RETEST

A common test for reliability is **test-retest**. A test is administered to a group of people and then repeated with the same group a week or two later. Their test scores are then compared using a process called **correlation**. Correlation scores in this particular case are referred to as **reliability coefficients** and range between 0 and 1.0 with 1.0 being perfect and, typically, unobtainable.

The administration, timing, and interpretation of test-retest scores are matters of judgment. Retesting within 24 hours of the first test can result in a high correlation because people probably remember how they replied the first time around and will repeat that. They will also find the retest easier to do because they have already done the same test once. Retesting a month later probably means that a number of people will have changed their minds, will have developed other priorities, or will find the test a challenge because they don't recall how to answer. Thus most test-retests typically take place within a week or two.

INTERCODER OR OBSERVER RELIABILITY

Just as you want a measure to be reliable over time, so you would want different observers to agree that they are observing the same thing and are consistent in their observations. In other words we want observer A and observer B to record the same thing if they are both observing it.

Two typical research scenarios are observing human interaction and content analysis of television programs. Let's say that in both cases you are interested in measuring aggression. As a starting point, you will need to be able to define aggression so that all observers can agree that they have or have not seen it. This is the process called operationalization introduced in Chapter 2. You might then develop two broad categories of aggression, armed and unarmed, and you might want your observers to classify each incident of aggression they see as either armed or unarmed. Armed aggression seems obvious enough. Assertive behavior with firearms or knives would count. But how about a kitchen situation where your observers see aggressive domestic behavior involving a pan full of hot spaghetti sauce? Observers could easily disagree on whether the gesture is armed or unarmed or even whether it is or is not aggressive.

The secret to high **intercoder or observer reliability** is thorough training of observers and clear definitions and classifications of behavior. That done, you will still want to know that your observers are categorizing the same content in the same way, so you will calculate a correlation between the coding of observers to see whether this is happening.

Validity

A 100% reliable instrument that measures the wrong thing is 100% useless. This is obvious in the physical sciences. We do not expect barometers to measure wind direction or thermometers to measure air pressure, but life is not so simple in the social sciences. Take a simple Likert-type question such as the following:

	Strongly Agree	Agree	Neutral	Disagree	Strongly Disagree
I enjoy watching television.	___	___	___	___	___

If respondents reply to this by marking their answers on paper, all that you have recorded literally are marks on paper. Because you have used an interval-level measure, you can make some summary statements such as "13% disagreed or disagreed strongly, 50% were neutral, and 37% either agreed or strongly agreed." But what is it that they have agreed or disagreed with?

"Enjoyment" could mean enjoyment of content. So while 37% agree or strongly agree that they like watching television, in fact some are really telling you that they like watching football, others cooking shows, and others 24-hour news or weather. "Enjoyment" could also mean enjoying the television process in that these viewers don't really care what's showing. Just having another voice and maybe some background music in the house while they are doing something else altogether (maybe even reading a book) counts as their definition of television viewing. Some research suggests that people may be attracted to television by production values such as cuts, zooms, and changes in volume, voices, or lighting. In other words there is a vaguely hypnotic quality to television quite independent of content that attracts some people.

What, then, has the "enjoy watching television" question captured? If the question was intended to capture the television viewing experience and instead captured a content preference, it has little validity. It is in a sense "misreporting" a communication phenomenon.

There are several kinds of **validity**. The literature has somewhat different names for them and ways of classifying them, but we can think basically of three kinds of validity:

- Content validity—looks OK

- Construct validity—theoretically OK

- Criterion validity—tests OK

CONTENT VALIDITY: LOOKS OK

If a measure has **content validity**, it "looks OK."

Face validity means basically that the questions do appear to measure what they measure. An average, non-expert person for example might regard the above question about television viewing as having face validity. However, a group of communication theorists or broadcasters might disagree and decide that "I enjoy watching television" is really measuring the level of desire for escapism and fantasy. A determination by experts gives the questions **expert validity** or **panel validity**.

Expert validity is preferred because it means that your questions have passed the test of peer approval. Other experts in the field agree with what you are doing. However, face validity can be important. A series of questions about people's attitudes toward sex may have no face validity to respondents who think they have been recruited to answer questions about romance; they may not see the two as related. The politics of research may also require face validity. For example, you may suspect that a high level of involvement in online chat rooms negatively affects students' academic performance, and you may want to ask a whole series of questions exploring that aspect of student lifestyle. However, agencies or foundations funding your research may expect to see questions that directly capture classroom activity. Your "chat" questions may have little face value to them and render the relevance of your study suspect to them.

CONSTRUCT VALIDITY: THEORETICALLY OK

Convergent Validity

In organizational communication studies, for example, one would expect employees to show a high correlation among their scores on measures of identification, loyalty, and commitment. This is **convergent validity.** All of these are somewhat different concepts, but all live under one conceptual umbrella called something like "willingness to stay with my organization."

Divergent Validity

We would expect employees who score highly on measures of loyalty to score low on measures of individuality or independence. The theory is that highly individualistic, self-centered individuals are not attracted to the group ethos required of many organizations. If scores on commitment to an organization have a low correlation with scores on individuality, we can argue that we have good **divergent validity.** In other words, valid measures should not only have a close relationship to similar measures (convergent validity); they should not show any relationship to dissimilar measures (divergent validity).

CRITERION VALIDITY: TESTS OK

Criterion validity relates your measures to other specific measures in two ways.

You have high **concurrent validity** if scores on your measure correlate highly with other measures designed to measure exactly the same construct. If you construct a measure of political alienation, for example, you would expect scores on your measure to correlate highly with other measures of political alienation.

You have high **predictive validity** if your measures predict "real world" outcomes. For example, SAT scores should predict success in college, GRE scores should predict success in graduate school, and vocational preference tests should predict comfort if not success in a particular career field. If they do, they have high predictive validity. The personal interests questionnaire you filled out when applying for college or university may have been used to match you with a roommate. If the relationship is still flourishing, the questionnaire had good predictive ability (maybe!).

Frequently the reason for many such tests is to predict outcomes in the workplace and in relationships. Private enterprise, government agencies, schools, career and psychological counselors, dating services, and the military all use tests with presumably high predictive validity to help identify people who will perform in a particular way. Implicitly, there is a second reason for testing, and that is to rank order people on their scores in an attempt to predict who will be most or least successful in a particular job, graduate school, or profession. There are many proprietary tests available, each of them marketed on the basis of its predictive validity.

WHO WINS IN THE RELIABILITY–VALIDITY SHOOTOUT?

An ideal instrument has both reliability and validity. It should measure what it measures well and consistently. But validity has a theoretical priority. It does not matter how reliable an instrument is; if it is measuring something other than what you have in mind, it is, in a sense, capturing irrelevant data and has no value. That said, reliability has a claim also because if an instrument is unreliable you can never properly assess its validity.

Two Common Measurement Scales

There are many ways of capturing human communication behavior that will be discussed in subsequent chapters. In terms of scaled measurements, you should know two scales commonly used in attitude research in academia and industry.

THE LIKERT SCALE

Note, as in the following example, that the Likert scale is not framed as a question; it is a statement. There is a different statement for each scale.

The scale itself may vary between 5 and 7 points. It most commonly has 5 points, and the response options are always the same—"strongly agree" through "strongly disagree." Respondents are asked to check the answer that best describes their level of agreement with the statement. Each answer is given a numerical value between 1 and 5 for a 5-point scale, and the answer from each person for each question is recorded as a score.

Suppose, for example, we are interested in consumers' attitudes toward hybrid vehicles. We might ask Likert-formatted questions such as the following:

	Strongly Agree	Agree	Neutral	Disagree	Strongly Disagree
1. Hybrid vehicles are powerful.	—	—	—	—	—
2. Hybrid vehicles reduce dependency on foreign oil.	—	—	—	—	—
3. I would be willing to pay more for a vehicle with above-average fuel economy.	—	—	—	—	—

THE SEMANTIC DIFFERENTIAL SCALE

The semantic differential scale pairs opposite ideas and invites respondents to decide where between the two opposites their opinion lies. There may be multiple word scales for each concept.

The semantic differential shown below explores attitudes toward hybrid vehicles using similar issues to the Likert example above. It has a 5-point scale, and each point is assigned a value between 1 and 5. Scores for each person for each question are recorded after respondents have marked a position representing their opinion on each scale.

Hybrid Vehicles

Powerful	—	—	—	—	—	Weak
Expensive	—	—	—	—	—	Cheap
Simple	—	—	—	—	—	Complicated

A semantic differential scale is obviously more difficult to construct. Words that form authentic opposites have to be found and pretested for meaning before use. For example, is the opposite of "expensive" "cheap," or should it be "affordable"? Likert-type questions, being simply a series of statements, require no such effort. Of course neither type of question is exempt from the requirement that it have good reliability and validity. Significant pretesting time and effort may be required to establish this.

In summary, Likert-type scales and semantic differential scales allow us to assign numbers to respondents' answers and to then make some summary statements about their responses.

For example, Exhibit 5.1 shows a basic Likert-scale question, the answers from five respondents, and in a sneak preview of Chapter 6,

EXHIBIT 5.1   Example of Likert Question, Responses, and Basic Descriptive Statistics

(Statement)	I would be willing to pay more for a vehicle with above-average fuel economy.				
	Strongly Disagree	**Disagree**	**Neutral**	**Agree**	**Strongly Agree**
Score	1	2	3	4	5
Value assigned to statement by respondents					
Respondent 1		X			
Respondent 2			X		
Respondent 3					X
Respondent 4	X				
Respondent 5					X
Descriptive Statistics					

Sample size   5
Minimum score   1
Maximum score   5
Range of scores $(5 - 1) = 4$
Mode (most frequent score)   5
Average score (sum of   3.2
scores/sample size)

"Statistics," the simple **descriptive statistics** that summarize those answers. Looking at the five responses we received, we can say from inspection and some elementary calculations that

- scores ranged between 1 and 5,
- the most frequent score was 5, and
- the average score is 3.2, or $(1 + 2 + 3 + 5 + 5)$ divided by 5.

We can summarize these data by saying that while there is some disagreement with the statement, the average score of 3.2 is closer to agreement than disagreement and therefore that overall our respondents are more likely to agree with the statement.

While we can make statements about the distribution of results with nominal and ordinal variables (e.g., 65% of respondents were male; 35% were female), interval measures allow us for the first time to make summary statements such as "the average score was 3.2."

Note that the assumption of equal distances between points on a Likert or semantic differential scale is just that—an assumption. Mathematically, the distance between any two adjacent points on the scale is the same. Psychologically, however, this may not be the case for respondents. People can be reluctant to take extreme positions and may be likely to favor middle-ground positions such as "agree" more than "strongly agree."

In summary, measuring communication phenomena at the nominal and ordinal levels allows us to classify and rank communication phenomena. Measuring at the interval and ratio levels allows us to use statistics as a reporting and decision-making tool.

The downside of such quantification is the loss of all information that cannot be turned into a number and the danger of **reification** or turning the measure itself into the reality it is supposed to measure. As evolutionary scientist Stephen Jay Gould (1996) pointed out in his excoriating review of attempts to measure human attributes, scales and tests can lead us to assume that the test is the thing. The map is not the territory, but the fact that there is an IQ test leads us to assume, unwisely, that there is a single measurable entity called "intelligence." The second problem is the danger of ranking based on such scales. Given the existence of an IQ scale that is supposed to measure a unitary entity called intelligence, how wise is it to rank people on the basis of a single score?

This question is the focus of this chapter's Ethics Panel.

Ethics Panel: The Ethics of Measurement Scales

Stephen Jay Gould (1996) in his book, *The Mismeasure of Man,* discusses the major problems with the development of measures such as the IQ test: first, the assumption that there is a single unitary human ability called intelligence; second, the related assumption that a test can be devised to assess it; and third, the assumption that individuals can be accurately ranked and their futures perhaps determined on the basis of such a test. A familiar example is SAT scores, intended to predict (academic) success in college. In a general sense, academic success is a product of many factors—the quality of high school preparation, socioeconomic status, personal "drive," study habits and ambition, and of course the college environment itself. On what basis then should a student with high SAT scores be preferred for college admission over another student with lesser scores?

Questions

- How ethical is it to rank or evaluate students based only on the results of a single set of tests such as the SATs?
- More generally, how wise is it to classify people on the basis of any single measure such as authoritarianism, conservatism, or dogmatism?

Chapter Summary

Measures of communication must have

- validity—they must measure what they are supposed to measure, and
- reliability—they must produce the same results consistently.

Measures exist at four different levels:

- nominal—essentially labels,
- ordinal—allow rank ordering,
- interval—allow statistical calculations, and
- ratio—allow more sophisticated statistical operations.

Two frequently used scales in communication research are

- the Likert scale, which ranges between "strongly disagree" and "strongly agree"; and
- the semantic differential scale, which ranges between polar opposites such as "strong" and "weak."

Recommended Reading

Gould, S. J. (1996). *The mismeasure of man.* New York: W. W. Norton & Company. Gould's book discusses the problems with the development and use of unitary measures such as the IQ test.

Rubin, R. B., Palmgreen, P., & Sypher, H. E. (Eds.) (1994). *Communication research measures: A sourcebook.* New York: Guilford Press. This book shows many scales' uses in communication research and discusses scale development. Examples include student motivation, communicative adaptability, and interpersonal attraction scales.

References

Gould, S. J. (1996). *The mismeasure of man.* New York: W. W. Norton & Company.

Osgood, C. E., Suci, G. J., & Tannenbaum, P. H. (1957). *The measurement of meaning.* Urbana: University of Illinois Press.

Thomson, W., Lord Kelvin. (1889). Electrical units of measurement (3 May 1883). In *Popular Lectures and Addresses* (Vol. 1, p. 73). London: Macmillan and Co.

Student Study Site

Visit the study site at www.sagepub.com/treadwellicr for e-flashcards, web resources, and additional study materials.

6 Statistics

Analyzing Your Numbers

Statistics will help you unwind
Questions of numeric kind.
They can help you make sense
Of numbers immense
With tools for that purpose designed.

Chapter Overview

Statistics describe the numbers obtained from quantitative research.

Statistical calculations can help us decide whether there are significant differences among groups of people, whether there are significant relationships among variables, and what level of confidence we can have when we attempt to generalize our findings from a small sample of people to a larger population. In the context of statistics, "significance" has a special meaning. It means that there is a better-than-random chance that a relationship exists.

This chapter sets out the three main uses of statistics: describing data, generalizing from data, and testing the strength of relationships and differences.

Starter Questions

- How will statistical analysis help my research?

- What unique insights do statistical analyses provide?

- What confidence can I have in statistics?

- Can statistics be misinterpreted?

- How credible is statistical evidence?

Why Statistics?

Data sets—the data from a research project—can be big. A 20-question survey of 50 people means 1,000 answers to be analyzed. The same survey administered in a typical national opinion poll of 1,200 people will result in 24,000 answers that have to be analyzed, summarized, and understood. If each question were formatted as a 5-point scale, we would have $1,200 * 20 * 5 = 120,000$ possible answers to be examined.

Fortunately, statistical procedures come to our rescue in a number of ways. Statistics help us

- summarize complex data;
- show how the data vary—for example, whether everyone checked "5" on a 5-point scale or whether "1," "2," "3," and "4" also got votes;
- show the level of confidence we can have in generalizing from a sample to a wider population;
- test whether different groups of people differ significantly in some way; and
- test whether there is a significant relationship among variables we are interested in.

In this chapter we will follow the statistical adventures of 20 people. We have gathered data on their use of the Internet and radio, their political orientation, their knowledge of world affairs, and their gender.

Our research results are shown in Exhibit 6.1. The columns, in order, show the names of respondents, the identifying numbers we have assigned them, the number of hours per week they report spending on the Internet, the percentage of their time they estimate spending on the Internet, their scores on a test of knowledge of world affairs, their gender (male or female), their self-reported political preference (liberal or conservative), and their preferred news source (radio or Internet). Each column also shows a brief variable name, typically used to label data for computer processing.

This data set, apart from the small numbers of both people and variables, is typical for a social science study in which we measure a number of variables and look for the relationships among them. Typically, we would have started with a hypothesis or research questions linking these variables, such as the following:

H_1: Women spend more time using the Internet than men.

H_2: People who use the Internet as their primary news source will score higher on a test of world affairs knowledge than those who use commercial radio as their primary news source.

In conducting such a study our first step would be to gather data from each respondent and to record them in the form shown in Exhibit 6.1. We would then input the data into a computer for statistical analysis. Normally, letters such as *M* and *F* for male and female or *I* and *R* for Internet and radio would be replaced by numbers in the coding process. We would also be dealing with thousands of data points rather than the few shown here.

Exhibit 6.1 **Survey Results for 20 Respondents**

Name (NAME)	ID Number (ID)	Hours per Week Internet	% Time on Internet (PTI)	Knowledge World Affairs (KWA)	Gender* (GEND)	Political Preference* (POLP)	Preferred News Source* (PREFNEWS)
Helen	01	0	0	04	F	L	R
Kiri	02	100	60	06	F	L	I
Lin	03	20	40	04	F	L	I
Miriama	04	10	20	10	F	C	R
Lakesha	05	10	10	02	F	L	I
Thomas	06	20	40	06	M	L	R
Harry	07	60	60	04	M	L	R
Wiremu	08	40	20	08	M	C	R
Jacques	9	80	80	04	M	C	R
Carlos	10	60	40	08	M	C	I
Marie	11	0	0	06	F	L	R
Fahima	12	100	80	06	F	L	I
Michiko	13	20	60	08	F	L	I
Caroline	14	20	20	10	F	C	R
Elizabeth	15	10	10	02	F	C	I
Gordon	16	20	40	06	M	C	R
Alfonso	17	60	60	04	M	L	R
Rafael	18	20	20	08	M	C	R
Tariq	19	100	80	04	M	C	R
Juan	20	60	40	04	M	C	I

* F = female; M = male: L = liberal; C = conservative; I = Internet, R = commercial radio

Describing Data: Descriptive Statistics

Twenty respondents and eight variables mean 160 answers in our data set, so our first challenge obviously is to summarize the data in a way that gives us a good overall picture of what's going on. We do this with measures of central tendency and frequencies.

MEASURES OF CENTRAL TENDENCY: MEAN, MEDIAN, AND MODE

The three basic statistics used to summarize data are **mean**, **median**, and **mode**. They are called **measures of central tendency** because they describe the central features of a data set rather than its extreme or outlying values.

- Mean is the average score. Calculate it by adding all scores and dividing by the number of scores.

- Median is the midrange score. When all the scores are arranged from lowest to highest, find the score that has an equal number of scores on either side of it. When the number of scores is even, find the score halfway between the two "middle scores" when the scores are ordered from lowest to highest.

- Mode is the most frequent score. It is commonly, but not necessarily, in the midrange of scores.

Let's take the self-reported percentages of time spent on the Internet (PTI) recorded for each person in column 4 of Exhibit 6.1 and stack them in order to show the frequency of each score, as shown in Exhibit 6.2.

EXHIBIT 6.2   **Distribution of Scores for Percentage of Time Spent on the Internet (PTI)**

			40		
		20	40	60	
		20	40	60	80
0	10	20	40	60	80
0	10	20	40	60	80

We can see that there are two "0" scores, two "10s," four "20s," and so on. The mean for this variable is 39 (the sum of all values divided by 20). The most frequent score is 40. The median by inspection is also 40 (the score halfway between the 10 lowest scores and the 10 highest scores).

Generally, we need all three measures of central tendency because any one of them may be misleading.

For example, a group of 10 people that contains one millionaire and nine other people each with an income of $1,000 has a mean income of $100,900. The mean in this case does not portray the group's individual incomes accurately. The median income is $1,000 because half the incomes are over $1,000 and half are under it. We might decide that the best descriptor in this case is the mode, which by definition states that the most frequent income is $1,000. However, we could also get a mode of $1,000 if only two people each had an income of $1,000 and everyone else had a uniquely different income. Obviously, none of these measures on their own summarize the unique characteristics of this group of people well. We need additional measures to do this, and these are discussed below under "Measures of Dispersion."

FREQUENCIES

The term **frequency** refers to the number of times or frequency with which a particular score occurs. To produce **frequency tables**, we construct categories that include all the scores we expect to find on a test or a survey and then report the number of scores that fall in each category.

Frequency distributions in absolute numbers and percentages for the variable use of the Internet in hours per week (HWI) are shown in the first three columns of Exhibit 6.3. Note that columns 4 and 5 summarize the results by gender. We will return to these columns when we discuss contingency tables later in this chapter. For now, we will work only with columns 1 through 3.

Note that the hours-per-week categories represent a judgment call on how best to summarize or reduce data. We could have had only two categories— "0–49" and "50–100" hours—or a larger number of categories such as "0–9,"

EXHIBIT 6.3   **Frequency Table: Hours of Internet Use per Week (HWI)**

Hours per Week Internet (HWI)	Respondents	% Total Respondents	Male	Female
0–19	5	25	0	5
20–39	6	30	3	3
40–59	1	5	1	0
60–79	4	20	4	0
80–100	4	20	2	2
TOTAL	20	100	10	10

"10–19," "20–29," "30–39," and so on. The fewer categories we have, the more **data reduction** or simplification we can do, but the more information is lost in the process.

MEASURES OF DISPERSION: MINIMUM, MAXIMUM, RANGE, VARIANCE, AND STANDARD DEVIATION

Mean, median, and mode summarize the central features of a distribution but do not describe the range of scores. The range and variability of scores are described by **measures of dispersion**. These measures include **minimum**, **maximum**, **range**, **variance**, and **standard deviation**.

Minimum, Maximum, and Range

- Maximum = highest value
- Minimum = lowest value
- Range = maximum value – minimum value

If our values range between 100 and 0, as in hours per week of Internet use, the range is 100 − 0 = 100. If all scores were identical, say 75, the range would be 75 − 75 = 0.

Variance and Standard Deviation: Purpose

Variance and standard deviation standardize different measures so that we can compare them "on a level playing field."

The range statistic, for example, provides no basis for comparing different sets of scores. Suppose a class has test scores ranging between 5 and 48 out of a possible 50. The scores have a range of 43; so do the scores for another class that range between 53 and 96 on a test scored out of 100. Clearly the second class did better because all of its scores are over the 50% mark, but we can't directly compare the two sets of scores and the way in which they vary. Variance, standard deviation, and z-scores help us do this.

Variance, as the term implies, measures the extent to which scores in a data set vary. Standard deviation is the square root of variance. The larger the standard deviation, the wider the range of scores on either side of the mean.

Importantly, the standard deviation also allows us to make generalizations about the wider population from which we have drawn our sample and to calculate the probability that our generalizations are accurate. This is discussed further below under "Generalizing From Data: Inferential Statistics."

Variance and Standard Deviation: Formulae

Computing variance is a four-step process:

1. Subtract each individual score from the mean score for the group.
2. Square each result (to eliminate the problem of dealing with negative numbers).
3. Add the results.
4. Divide the sum of these squares by the number of scores minus one to get an average of the squared variations from the mean.

This is expressed in the following formula.

Formula for Calculating Variance	
$$s^2 = \dfrac{\sum (\overline{X}-X)^2}{(N-1)}$$	s^2 = variance $\overline{X}$ = the mean score for the group X = each individual score N = the number of scores $\sum$ denotes the sum of

Standard deviation (SD) is the square root of the variance. The formula for calculating standard deviation is

$$SD = \sqrt{s^2} = \sqrt{\frac{\sum (\overline{X}-X)^2}{(N-1)}}$$

Variance and Standard Deviation: Example

Let's calculate the variance and standard deviation for the current variable of interest—hours per week on the Internet.

The mean value for the HWI variable is 40.5. Using the 20 values for this variable, we compute the variance and standard deviation for the group as shown in Exhibit 6.4.

Note that the numbers shown in column 4 of Exhibit 6.4—the differences between each individual score and the group mean—always add to 0. The sum of the squared differences is 22,295, which divided by the number of scores minus one (19) gives us a variance of 1,173.42.

The standard deviation, the square root of the variance (1,173.42), is 34.25.

We will revisit this important statistic under "Generalizing From Data: Inferential Statistics" later in this chapter.

EXHIBIT 6.4   Computing Variance and Standard Deviation

ID	Hours Per Week Internet (HWI)	Group Mean (40.5)	(HWI – 40.5) $(X - \bar{X})$	(HWI – 40.5)^2 $(X - \bar{X})^2$
1	0	40.5	−40.5	1640.25
2	100	40.5	59.5	3540.25
3	20	40.5	-20.5	420.25
4	10	40.5	−30.5	930.25
5	10	40.5	−30.5	930.25
6	20	40.5	−20.5	420.25
7	60	40.5	19.5	380.25
8	40	40.5	−0.5	0.25
9	80	40.5	39.5	1560.25
10	60	40.5	19.5	380.25
11	0	40.5	−40.5	1640.25
12	100	40.5	59.5	3540.25
13	20	40.5	−20.5	420.25
14	20	40.5	−20.5	420.25
15	10	40.5	−30.5	930.25
16	20	40.5	−20.5	420.25
17	60	40.5	19.5	380.25
18	20	40.5	−20.5	420.25
19	100	40.5	59.5	3540.25
20	60	40.5	19.5	380.25

Compute sum of column 5. (HWI – 40.5)^2 =		$\Sigma (X - \bar{X})^2 =$	22,295.00
Compute variance.	$\dfrac{\Sigma (\bar{X} - X)^2}{(N - 1)}$	$= \dfrac{22,295}{20 - 1} =$	1173.42
Compute standard deviation.		$\sqrt{1173.42} =$	34.25

Z-Score: The Apples and Oranges Statistic

A **z-score** is the number of units of standard deviation any one score is above or below the mean. In our survey, we asked respondents, "How many hours per week do you spend on the Internet?" Obviously there are other ways of asking the same question. For example, we also asked, "What percentage of your time do you spend on the Internet?" There is no good way to compare the two sets of answers even though they address the same question. The two questions use different **metrics** (units of measurement) and are of a different order of magnitude. The first question uses absolute numbers with a maximum possible answer of 7 days * 24 hours = 168. The second question uses percentages with a maximum possible score of 100. The two sets of answers cannot be compared unless we standardize them in some way.

One standard statistic that allows us to compare results from two or more different measures would be desirable, and this is what the z-score accomplishes. Expressing each individual score in terms of standard deviation allows "apples to oranges" comparisons. The larger a z-score, the further away its value is from the group's mean score; the smaller the z-score, the closer it is to the mean. The z-score is to an individual's score as standard deviation is to a group's scores.

Generalizing From Data: Inferential Statistics

Inferential statistics help us generalize (make inferences) about a wider population from a smaller sample of it. They are based on two assumptions:

- The population sampled has normally distributed characteristics, as described below.
- The sample is randomly selected; that is, every individual in the population has an equal chance of being selected.

In a statistically perfect world, data conform to a symmetrical, so-called **normal curve**, as shown in Exhibit 6.5. When plotted out, scores with a normal distribution form a symmetrical curve from lowest to highest value with the majority of scores "peaking" in the middle. Test results for example often approach this pattern; one or two people may score 0, one or two will achieve that magic 100, and a large number of people will score around the 50 mark, with fewer numbers scoring in the 80s and in the 30s.

In a normal distribution the values for mean, median, and mode are all the same, as is almost the case for the data shown in Exhibit 6.2 (page 91).

EXHIBIT 6.5   The Normal Curve and Standard Deviations

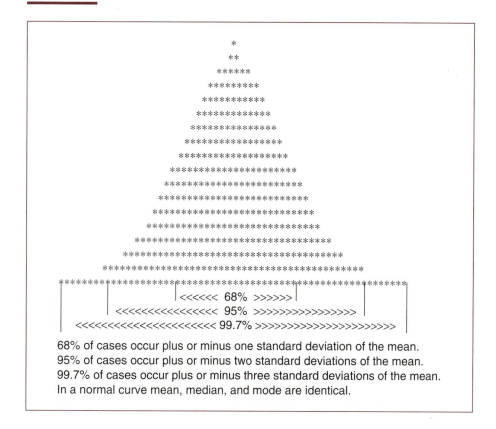

68% of cases occur plus or minus one standard deviation of the mean.
95% of cases occur plus or minus two standard deviations of the mean.
99.7% of cases occur plus or minus three standard deviations of the mean.
In a normal curve mean, median, and mode are identical.

Public opinion polling is one example of sampling and surveying a small number of people and then trying to extrapolate the findings from that sample to the larger **population** from which the sample was drawn. The big question is "How accurately do sample results capture what is going on in the wider population?" Inferential statistics and the normal curve together

- help us calculate our level of certainty when we project results from a sample to a wider population, and

- tell us—conveniently—that as long as we are prepared to accept a known level of uncertainty in our projections, we do not need huge sample sizes.

RETURN OF STANDARD DEVIATION

As you will see from Exhibit 6.5, the properties of a normal curve are such that

- 68% of its values occur plus or minus one standard deviation from the mean. This means that a result greater or less than one standard deviation can be expected in only 32% (100% – 68%) of the samples or has a .32 probability of occurring.

- 95% of its values occur plus or minus two standard deviations from the mean. This means that a result greater or less than two standard deviations can be expected in only 5% (100% – 95%) of the samples or has a .05 probability of occurring.

- 99.7% of its values occur plus or minus three standard deviations from the mean. A result greater or less than three standard deviations from the population mean is likely to occur in fewer than 0.3% (100% – 99.7%) of samples or has a probability of occurring of less than 0.003.

Why would we care? Because we want to know how confident we can be that the results from our small sample are true for the bigger population we sampled from.

Look at Exhibit 6.4 again. For the variable HWI, our sample of 20 people has a mean of 40.5 and a standard deviation of 34.25. We know this is true of the 20 people we sampled, but how likely is it that these numbers represent the population at large? To get a sense of how likely our calculated mean of 40.5 is true for the bigger population, we look at the standard deviation for the sample. Assuming normally distributed scores, we can say that there is

- a 68% probability the true result lies between 40.5 plus 34.25 and 40.5 minus 34.25—that is between 6.25 and 74.75;

- a 95% probability it lies between 40.5 plus 2(34.25) and 40.5 minus 2(34.25)—that is between –28 and 109; and

- a 99% probability it lies between 40.5 plus 3(34.25) and 40.5 minus 3(34.25)—that is between –62.25 and 143.25.

These are rather sweeping ranges and may not give us much confidence in a psychological sense. However, the confidence we are interested in here is statistical confidence. Reporting that the true value of the mean for the wider population lies between –28 and 109 at the 95% **confidence level** at least gives us an estimate of our confidence. We can in a sense be certain about our uncertainties.

Note that we are discussing statistical confidence here. The above results simply state the probability that if we repeated our survey, 95 times out of 100 we would find the mean value lying between –28 and 109. We may decide that we have no professional confidence in our result because, for example, we suspect that a question was badly worded or our survey sample did not really represent the population we were interested in. Also, the probability calculation can produce theoretical results that do not have a "real world" counterpart. For example, the above calculations show that people could be spending a negative amount of time on the Internet. It is difficult to see what in real life this would actually mean.

We do not know the "real" value of the population mean because we have not sampled the whole population. All we have is a calculated range of possibilities. This range of values is called the **confidence interval**. In our example the confidence interval is −28 to 109 at the 95% confidence level.

For a **sampling distribution** (the distribution of our sample results), the standard deviation is called the **standard error**.

When we report results, we report the confidence level and the standard error. For example, media polls of public opinion often print a statement to the effect that in 19 out of 20 cases the sample results will differ by no more than 3% from the results obtained from surveying the entire population. In other words, they are reporting that at the 95% confidence level (19 out of 20 = 95%) the standard error for their results is plus or minus 3% given their sample size of, typically, 1,200. This means that we can be statistically confident that if the survey were repeated 100 times under the same conditions, we would find that the results would vary by no more than 3% 95 times out of 100.

Confidence Level and Sample Size

There is a trade-off among confidence level, standard deviation, and sample size. This is discussed more fully in Chapter 7, but for now let's revisit the formula for standard deviation, shown above under "Variance and Standard Deviation: Formulae."

The square root in the formula indicates that the sample size needs to be quadrupled to halve the standard error. For example, our sample size of 20 would need to be quadrupled to 80 to halve the standard error, would need to be quadrupled again to 320 to further halve the error, and would need to be increased to 1,280 to halve the error again. For a national survey of public opinion, a sample of 20 people intuitively seems too small, 1,280 perhaps reasonable, and 5,120, which would halve the standard error yet again, a lot of work! There is obviously a law of diminishing returns here. You could put time and effort into obtaining a sample of 5,000 people (or in the ultimate to surveying an entire population), but it is usual to settle for the convenience of a smaller size and to accept some level of error (which you will be able to calculate) as a trade-off.

Obviously, larger sample sizes become important where a smaller level of error is needed. Suppose for example your public opinion polling for a candidate in a closely fought political race reveals that 51% of voters, plus or minus 3%, plan to vote for your candidate. This means if the vote were held now, this candidate could get 54% of the vote and win or get 48% of the vote and lose. Clearly we need to get the level of error down to 1% or less, and this means increasing the sample size.

Knowing the level of error and the confidence level we can afford allows us to work back to the sample size we need, a discussion we continue in Chapter 7.

Univariate, Bivariate, and Multivariate Statistics

All of the statistics described so far are **univariate statistics**; that is, they describe one variable such as time spent on the Internet. Statistics that describe the interaction of two variables are **bivariate**. Frequently, our basic research interest is in how two variables interact. **Multivariate statistics** are used where we want to study the interaction of three or more variables. The remainder of this chapter deals with statistical tests used to assess the strength or probability of bivariate relationships.

One way of assessing the interaction between two variables is to set out data in the form of a **contingency table** or "**cross-tabs**" (cross-tabulations), as shown in Exhibit 6.3. They are called contingency tables because the value of one variable is contingent or depends on the value of another. Exhibit 6.3 shows how Internet usage (column 1) varies by gender (columns 4 and 5). The table suggests that males are represented in almost all categories from heavy to light use whereas females tend to be either light or heavy users. Survey researchers often use such tables to show how public opinion on issues breaks down by gender, ethnicity, or income level.

Testing for Differences and Relationships

A frequent question in communication research is "Do two groups differ in a particular way?" One way to answer this question is to measure the variable we are interested in for each of the two groups and then to compare their scores on that variable. The *t*-**test** and the **chi-square** test look for differences in scores between groups and let us calculate the probability that two groups really do differ on a given variable.

t-TEST

The *t*-test compares the mean scores of two groups on the same variable to determine the probability that the groups are different.

Let's return to Exhibit 6.1 and look at two groups—respondents who get their news from the Internet and respondents who get their news from commercial radio. Our hypothesis will be that each group's knowledge of world affairs (KWA) will differ because each uses a different news source.

Column 5 of Exhibit 6.1 lists the KWA scores of the 20 respondents on a 1-to-10 scale. Column 8 shows the preferred source of news (PREFNEWS), commercial radio or Internet, for each of the respondents. We can plot the distribution of scores for individuals who get their news from the Internet and the distribution of scores for those who get their news from commercial radio, as shown in Exhibit 6.6.

You can calculate from the data shown in Exhibit 6.1 that the mean score for knowledge of world affairs for the Internet-preference group is 5.0 (40/8) and for the radio-preference group is 6.2 (74/12).

We might conclude based only on the mean scores for each group that the radio-preference group has a higher knowledge of world affairs than the Internet-preference group, but look at the distribution of the two sets of scores shown in Exhibit 6.6. The Internet group has two unique low "2" scores and the radio group has two unique high "10" scores, but overall the two groups have a number of "4," "6," and "8" scores in common. The two distributions of scores overlap.

EXHIBIT 6.6   **Distribution of Scores on Knowledge of World Affairs (KWA) by Preferred Source of News (PREFNEWS)**

Radio News Source (Mean = 6.2)		4 4 4 4 4	6 6 6	8 8	10 10
Internet News Source (Mean= 5.0)	2 2	4 4	6 6	8 8	

The question becomes "Did *all* of the radio listeners score higher than *all* of the Internet users, suggesting that we have two groups from two different populations?" Or, "If many of the individual scores are the same in both groups, are we basically looking at two groups from one population?" Clearly, the latter appears to be the case in our example.

The question is usually expressed as "Do the means of the two groups differ significantly?" More precisely, what we are asking is "What is the probability that the mean score for one group falls within one, two, or three standard deviations of the mean score for the second group?"

If we conclude that we are looking at samples from two different populations, we can say that the two groups are significantly different. If we conclude that we are looking at one population with two subgroups in it, we can reject the hypothesis that the two groups are significantly different.

The *t*-test is based on the differences in mean scores for a variable common to both groups but also takes into account the range of scores for each group and each group's size.

The *t*-test calculation results in a value that is then compared against a table of values, which shows the probability of your calculated value occurring. Basically, we are calculating whether our observed difference in means, corrected for the number of observations and the range of scores, is of low or high probability.

To use a t-distribution table or to interpret the output that statistical software will give you, it is necessary to understand two concepts— **degrees of freedom** and **one-tailed** versus **two-tailed** distribution of scores.

Degrees of freedom is a measure of "room to move." How many ways could our data be combined and still produce the same t-value? In this case it is calculated as the number of scores in group 1 (minus one) plus the number of scores in group 2 (minus one), or $(12 - 1) + (8 - 1) = 18$.

A one-tailed test means we are proposing that the differences between the groups will be in one direction—for example, that the mean score for the Internet group will be higher than for the radio group. A two-tailed test means proposing simply that the groups will differ (i.e., either group could score higher or lower).

The higher the t-value, the lower the probability that it will occur. As it happens, the result of our calculation for the above groups is $t = 1.11$ for 18 degrees of freedom. This is under the value needed to demonstrate a significant difference between our two groups at the 95% probability level whether we are looking at a one- or a two-tailed test. Therefore we conclude there is a 95% probability that the groups are not different.

CHI-SQUARE TEST

Let's look at another way of measuring group differences. This time we want to know if there is a relationship between gender and political affiliation. In other words, do males and females differ significantly in political philosophy?

We interview 20 people of both sexes and ask them for their political affiliation. The results are shown in Exhibit 6.7.

EXHIBIT 6.7   Political Affiliation by Gender

	Male	**Female**	
Liberal	3	7	
Conservative	7	3	
Expected Distribution for Identical Groups		Expected Distribution for Totally Dissimilar Groups	
5	5	0	10
5	5	10	0

Looking at Exhibit 6.7, it appears that males are more likely to be conservative than females. To get a more precise reading we would want to compare males' scores on a conservatism scale with the scores for females.

But wait! There are no scores. Exhibit 6.7 shows numbers of people, not scores. We cannot calculate an average of male and female or of liberal and conservative. What to do? All we can do is look at the pattern of responses and the difference between the expected pattern of results and the observed pattern.

Remember "NOIR" from Chapter 5? Variables such as "religion," "liberal," and "female" are nominal—that is to say basically labels. We can count them, but we cannot work with them mathematically. We may code *male* as "1" and *female* as "2," but "1" and "2" are simply labels; they do not imply that the two sexes are quantitatively different on some scale that measures "gender."

This is where the chi-square test comes in. It can handle the nominal or ordinal variables that the *t*-test cannot.

Exhibit 6.7 also shows the distributions we would expect if there were no difference between groups and if the groups were completely different. Remember that the figures shown are numbers of respondents, not scores.

The chi-square test is based on computing the difference between the observed result for each cell in the table and the expected result if there was no difference between the groups.

As with the *t*-test, we need to know the degrees of freedom (df). For the chi-square test it is the number of categories (male, female, conservative, liberal) minus one, or $(4 - 1) = 3$. We would go to a table of chi-square values or interpret a computer calculation to make sense of our result.

For the results shown in Exhibit 6.7, our computed value of chi-square = 3.2 at df (3) is under the value needed to demonstrate significance at the 95% (.05) confidence level. In spite of what appears to be a difference between males and females with respect to political leaning, we conclude that if the study were to be repeated, in 95 cases out of 100 we would find no significant relationship between gender and political affiliation.

CORRELATION

A frequent question in communication research is "What is the strength of the relationship between two variables?" For example, does the amount of time spent studying online relate to academic performance? Does the level of antisocial behavior increase with the level of viewing violent television? Statistically, such questions are answered with a procedure called correlation.

One way to visualize correlation is to make a graph in which the horizontal axis represents scores on one variable and the vertical axis represents scores on another. If we plot the individual scores for each individual, we get a so-called **scatterplot**. Exhibit 6.8 shows four typical patterns we might get when we do this.

Exhibit 6.8   Correlation Patterns

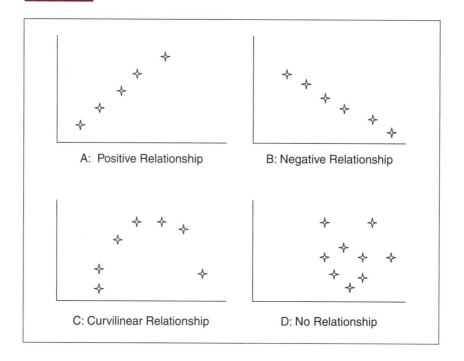

"A" shows a perfect positive correlation. For example, for every unit increase in time spent online, there is a unit increase in grade point average. The two variables are strongly related. "B" shows a perfect negative correlation.

"C" shows a so-called **curvilinear relationship** between two variables. There is no "straight line" relationship between the two variables, but rather there is a relationship that varies depending on whether the variables have a high or low value.

"D" shows a random scatter of results. There is no discernible pattern. (However, it is still possible to calculate the strength of the relationship between the two variables.)

Correlation coefficients express the strength of the relationship between two variables and range between −1.0 and +1.0, indicating a 100% negative and a 100% positive correlation respectively. Social scientists regard a score of around .60 as moderate, consider a score over .80 as strong, and are suspicious of anything under .50.

Note that correlation is not causality. For example, we cannot know from a survey whether time spent online improves knowledge of world affairs or whether having a high knowledge of world affairs predicts that individuals are more likely to spend time online. To get an answer to that question we need the experimental methods outlined in Chapter 9.

Ethics Panel: A Communicative Tension

You might not predict a book titled *Introduction to Statistical Principles* to be a best seller, but *How to Lie With Statistics* by Darrell Huff has been selling since 1954. What explains this? Could it be the title? *How to Lie With Statistics* does trigger a level of curiosity that the first title does not, and therein lies the dilemma of communicating statistics.

Two forces are at work in reporting statistics and research methods—simplification and selectivity.

Simplification occurs most commonly when journalists writing for lay audiences use their professional skills to report scientific research in a way that their audiences will understand. Most people are not familiar with chi-square tests, *t*-tests, or multiple polynomial regression, so there would be little point writing for most audiences in such terms. News writing in most cases has a "get to the point" style, and so journalists understandably focus on a bottom-line "what's in it for the reader?" interpretation of research results.

It is easy to see the nature of this simplification. Just compare a scholarly research paper on media effects with any "newsstand" magazine article on such a topic as "Is watching too much TV bad for your kids?"

Selectivity occurs when statistics are used to bolster an argument. For example, a political party may argue that it has reduced income taxes across the board for everyone by an average of 2%. The opposition will point out that because low-income people by definition are paying little tax, the effect of the tax cut on them is minimal in terms of absolute dollars. People in the top income bracket gain much more in terms of tax cuts. Which party is correct? Both. Neither is lying; both are merely selecting the most relevant statistic to make a point.

Questions

- Could simplifying research data mislead readers and thus violate professional standards of behavior for journalists, science writers, and researchers?

- Do researchers have an ethical responsibility to ensure that all relevant statistics are reported when they publish their research?

- Do researchers have an ethical responsibility to ensure that all relevant statistics are reported when their work is reported by others (e.g., journalists)? How could they go about doing this?

Chapter Summary

- Descriptive statistics describe and summarize data.
- Inferential statistics help with generalizations to a larger population from a smaller sample of that population.
- Statistical analyses summarize data, test for differences between groups, and test for relationships between variables.
- The *t*-test assesses whether groups differ on an interval or a ratio variable.
- The chi-square test assesses whether groups differ on a nominal or an ordinal variable.
- Correlation assesses the strength of the relationship between variables.

Recommended Reading

Huff, D. (1954). *How to lie with statistics.* New York: Norton. A statistical "best seller" since 1954. Be guided by the content, not the title!

Paulos, J. A. (1997). *A mathematician reads the newspaper.* New York: Random House. This book discusses how research results and statistics are reported or misreported in newspapers.

Recommended Web Resources

The many statistical resources on the Web range from easy interactive tutorials on the basic statistics discussed in this chapter to specific routines of interest only to a specific discipline. They range from "click and go" to "installation required" and often come with a "no guarantees" warning.

Because statistics is a language that transcends discipline, you will find statistical help at many different academic and commercial sites.

The following list errs on the side of brevity. To see the vast range of statistical Web sites, do your own search or check out the John Pezzullo Web page below.

Graphpad: http://graphpad.com/quickcalcs/index.cfm. Provides basic statistical calculators online. You will find *t*-test and chi-square calculators here, among others.

John Pezzullo's statpages: http://statpages.org. The starting point for statistical Web sites.

StatSoft: http://www.statsoft.com/textbook/stathome.html. An online textbook/tutorial on statistics.

Reference

Huff, D. (1954). *How to lie with statistics.* New York: Norton.

Student Study Site

Visit the study site at www.sagepub.com/treadwellicr for e-flashcards, web resources, and additional study materials.

CHAPTER 7

Sampling

Who, What, and How Many?

Sampling's basic intent
Is selecting to best represent.
Select randomly
Or judgmentally
For people or published content.

Chapter Overview

We cannot study the entire universe of human communication in one research project, much as we might want to. The universe is too large, and the questions are too numerous.

What we can do, however, is study a small segment of the universe we are interested in, be it political communication or podcasts, and within that select some people or media samples rather than all of them. The process of selecting the individual units for study is called sampling.

This chapter discusses two types of sampling—probability and nonprobability—and the important issue of sample size. Probability sampling strives to obtain representative samples that statistically represent the overall population. Nonprobability sampling is not statistically representative of a wider population but may have greater theoretical relevance and the advantage of convenience.

Sample size, as we will see, depends on the homogeneity of the population and on the level of confidence you want when making generalizations from your data.

Starter Questions

- How many people or media samples should I study to get credible results?
- Will talking to fellow students give me the best insight on students' opinion?
- Are online surveys better than phone surveys for reaching most people?
- How can I know my public opinion survey really has captured public opinion?
- Will a survey of 1,000 people provide more insight on human communication than interviews with 10 people?

Sampling Decisions

A decision to do research is a decision to sample. As soon as you have a research question you automatically have questions of who or what and how many you will study in order to answer it. This is true even for qualitative research methods.

A **population** consists of every individual of a type you want to study. Populations are defined not by size but by the fact that they contain every one of the units the researcher has elected to study, for example every *Rocky* movie ever produced or every U.S. release of a Harry Potter book. Large populations can be difficult to study because their exact size and nature may be unknown. This is one reason we use sampling and the inferential statistics discussed in Chapter 6. They help us make intelligent estimates from a sample when the population's exact size and nature are unknown. Exhibit 7.1 provides an example of a population containing four subgroups.

EXHIBIT 7.1   **Population**

The above diagram shows a population containing four groups. They could be ethnic or occupational groups of a human population or groups of a media population (radio, television, newspapers, magazines for example).

A **census** is a study of every member of a population. A **sample** is a selected segment of a population presumed to represent that population.

Nonprobability sampling is based on a judgment by the researcher; **probability sampling** involves random selection of the sample units. Both approaches have advantages and disadvantages.

We will follow the sampling adventures of one hypothetical student—Elizabeth—as she begins her research as a basis for an on-campus campaign aimed at improving campus food offerings and student eating habits.

Nonprobability Sampling

Nonprobability sampling has the advantages of convenience and providing insight. Statistically, it does not permit generalizations to a wider population, but that does not make it a second-class citizen of the sampling world. To the contrary, there are situations in which it can be the most logical method. For example, a researcher may make a professional judgment that one particular informant or item of text will provide the insights he or she is looking for or that seeking out volunteers is the only way to build a relevant sample of people.

CONVENIENCE SAMPLING

As the name implies, **convenience sampling** is based on convenience to the researcher. You may have been part of a convenience sample when an instructor requested your consent to participate in a survey or an experiment (i.e., you were part of a convenient group). Constraints on time or money may lead researchers to use convenience sampling. Convenience sampling can be useful when pretesting a study or when the results of the research are not intended for scholarly publication. For example, Elizabeth may initially survey her class colleagues about their eating habits and campus food services. She makes no assumption that her survey results will apply to the student body as a whole or that her research will contribute to new theoretical models of human communication. She just wants a basis on which to start her inquiries.

PURPOSIVE OR JUDGMENTAL SAMPLING

Purposive or **judgmental sampling** is based on the idea that a specific person or specific media content will meet specific criteria the researcher has. For example, Elizabeth may decide that the director of campus dining services and only the director of campus dining services can provide the insight on the economic, nutritional, and scheduling decisions that lead to the menu options that students see on a day-to-day basis. She will therefore seek out that individual and no one else.

QUOTA SAMPLING

Quota sampling is one of the first survey designs that attempt to bring a scientific approach to survey research. It attempts to replicate in a sample the features that the researcher thinks are important in the population. Let's suppose that Elizabeth has decided to interview students who live on campus and those who live off campus because she suspects that the attitudes of these two groups will differ with respect to eating and to campus food services.

She knows that 80% of students live on campus, so she decides to interview 8 resident students, plus 2 students who live off campus. She has successfully replicated one important feature of the student community in her sample, but the 10 students she interviews are her choice. They have not been randomly sampled, as discussed below under "probability sampling." Something other than chance has put them in the sample. That something is the researcher's judgment, which may be biased. For example, she may know all of the students she sampled.

NETWORK OR "SNOWBALL" SAMPLING

Network or "**snowball**" **sampling** occurs when you rely on members of a network to introduce you to other members of the network. Let's suppose that one student group Elizabeth is especially interested in researching is vegetarians. In spite of all her homework, she can find no campus listing of vegetarians, nor can she find any links to a local vegetarian group. She decides that the only way to identify such students is to post on campus bulletin boards a request that any vegetarians contact her to discuss possible participation in her research.

One such person contacts her, and Elizabeth realizes that the only way to recruit more vegetarians into her study is to ask this person to identify other vegetarians who might be willing to be interviewed. If she is lucky, the size of her sample will grow exponentially as more and more vegetarians introduce her to more and more vegetarians. Obviously, the quality and size of any such sample depends on the willingness and ability of others to identify other people in their network to you.

VOLUNTEER SAMPLING

Calling for volunteers may be the only way you can obtain research participants. If, for example, Elizabeth is seeking student members for a focus group to discuss possible changes in campus meal services, she has little choice but to use **volunteer sampling**. The focus group method, as we will see in Chapter 10, requires the active participation of people prepared to express opinions.

You may also want volunteers and volunteer enthusiasm if you intend to translate the results of your research into action. For example, the vegetarian volunteers Elizabeth recruited using her "snowball" sampling may provide her not only with the information she needs but also with the volunteer enthusiasm to help her develop educational materials, newsletters, and lobbying efforts in support of changes to the campus food offerings.

Volunteer samples can be problematic because by definition you are recruiting one type of person—volunteers! Research findings from volunteer samples will be biased because you have no idea what nonvolunteers might have said.

Web-based public opinion polls such as those hosted by your local television station are particularly prone to this problem because they attract people willing, by definition, to visit a Web site and volunteer a vote. Other people are not willing to do this, and so these Web polls represent only the opinions of a particular personality type. Unless the Web site has some form of control over access it is also possible that these volunteers can vote more than once, further compounding any bias.

Of course, in a general sense anyone participating in a research project is a volunteer, as our discussion of ethics and institutional review board (IRB) procedures in Chapter 3 should make clear.

Volunteer sampling and network or snowball sampling obviously apply only to human participants. Convenience, judgment, and quota sampling can be used with nonhuman subjects, most typically to select media content for study. In all cases the researcher would be the one deciding what media content goes into a sample. There will inevitably be some bias behind that decision, as shown in Exhibit 7.2 where selecting the first 10 units on the basis of convenience may mean that the sample is not representative.

EXHIBIT 7.2   **Convenience Sample**

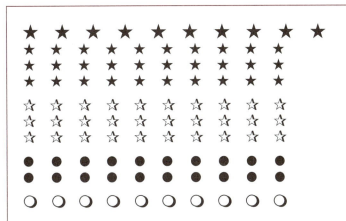

The above diagram represents a convenience sample obtained by arbitrarily selecting the first ten units in the population (the large ★). This may overestimate or underestimate one or more groups in the population. In this case all the ☆, ● and ◯'s have been eliminated from the sample. If ★ represented newspapers, then only newspapers would be included in the sample.

Ideally, we need some mechanism that reduces or eliminates researcher biases in sampling as far as possible. In the context of survey research particularly, that mechanism is probability sampling.

Probability Sampling

All sampling ultimately is based on judgments by the researcher and as a result has an inbuilt bias. For example, a researcher interviewing only her friends is likely to select in people that are similar to her and to select out people who are different. This may be deliberate and defensible, but it is more likely to be a decision of convenience that will bias the sample by reducing its diversity.

Is there a way to reduce such bias in sampling? The answer is yes, in the form of probability sampling. Basically, probability sampling means turning the selection of sampling units over to a mechanism over which the researcher has no control so that every unit has an equal chance of being selected.

Probability sampling permits us to make statistical generalizations from our results. Researchers, especially in such applied fields as political communication, marketing, and broadcasting, want to be able to make generalizations to large audiences or markets and therefore may put considerable effort into probability sampling.

One major contribution of sampling theory to communication research is to tell us that we do not necessarily need huge samples as long as we are prepared to live with a level of uncertainty about the population we are trying to understand. This level of uncertainty can be calculated and known. With probability sampling, statistical formulae can help determine the relationship among such issues as sample size, confidence level, and uniformity of the population being sampled.

Sampling frames are the master lists from which a probability sample is selected, for example a list of graduates held by your college or university's alumni office. In practice, and especially in the case of large populations, we sample from a sampling frame because we cannot identify every member of the population. In our example, the actual population of graduates may not be known, but the alumni records form a sampling frame from which we draw a sample presumed to represent the population.

Sampling units are the units selected for study. Often in communication research the unit will be individuals, but the unit could also be couples, corporations, or comic strips.

RANDOM SAMPLING

Random sampling is the most obvious and perhaps most common example of probability sampling.

Examples of random sampling include throwing dice, drawing names out of a hat, and lotteries. In each case there is no predicting what specific names or numbers will be sampled. You may control how many names or numbers will be selected, but you cannot control what each specific name or number will be. Random sampling removes the researcher as the agent of selection and replaces him or her with "luck of the draw."

For example, Elizabeth may be able to obtain a list of all students signed up for the campus meal plan. To get a genuinely random sample of students that will represent all participants in the meal plan, she would typically assign each student a number beginning at "1," with each person numbered systematically. Then she would use a table of randomly generated numbers or a random numbers generator such as http://randomizer.org/ to generate the list of students who would form her sample. We will discuss how big a sample she needs later in this chapter.

Random number generators allow you to specify how big you want your sample to be and how you want your sample numbers computed and presented. You can have the generator pull numbers randomly, pull every 5th or every 10th number (see "Systematic Sampling" below), and/or begin sampling at a number you define. For example, to randomly generate a series of phone numbers for the 212 area code, you can instruct the generator to randomly produce a series of 10-digit numbers beginning with 212.

The sampling units may be individual people but could be couples or athletic teams, phone numbers, episodes of *Star Wars*, or editorials from the *Chicago Sun-Times*.

A common misconception of random sampling is that it will produce a sample that is diverse. This is not automatically so. For example, married Asian women over the age of 40 who are living in Arizona with two children and a household income of between $100,000 and $150,000 would be a very homogeneous population demographically. Random sampling from a population of such women would produce an equally homogeneous sample; we would not expect the sample to be diverse.

STRATIFIED RANDOM SAMPLING

One problem with purely random samples is that they may or may not reflect the population they are drawn from. Because "anything can happen" with random sampling there is always a possibility that an important subgroup will be entirely missed or overrepresented. For example, Elizabeth may have decided that she needs vegetarians in her survey sample, but a random sample of all students in the meal plan may have the effect of selecting this group out, not in.

Randomness does not respect the fact that all categories of people may need to be in your sample or that the process of random sampling might eliminate some categories. The result is that some categories may not be represented. **Stratified random sampling** is a way to "force" such groups into your sample.

To ensure that all the groups of interest are proportionately represented in a sample, you set aside a number of places in your sample relative to the size of the group in the population you are drawing from. Then you fill those places by random sampling from that specific subgroup.

For example, if Elizabeth needs both resident and nonresident students in her sample and knows that nonresident students make up 20% of the student population, she needs to ensure that 20% of her sample consists of such students. Suppose she decides on a final survey sample size of 100 students. She would then randomly select 20 nonresident students from a list of such students and randomly select 80 from a list of resident students.

Stratified random sampling is diagrammed in Exhibit 7.3.

EXHIBIT 7.3   Stratified Random Sample

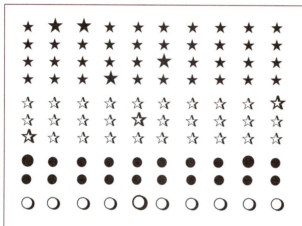

In this example the selected units are the large ones.

40% of the sample is set aside for ★
30% of the sample is set aside for ☆
20% of the sample is set aside for ●
10% of the sample is set aside for ○

The percentage of each group in the sample is the same as the percentage of that group in the original population. Within each of these groups random sampling takes place to select individuals for the overall sample.

SYSTEMATIC SAMPLING

Systematic sampling means sampling every *n*th person on a list, for example taking every 10th or every 100th person listed in a phone book. The interval that you select (10, 100, etc.) is the **sampling interval**. The method involves random sampling because typically you use a random number or random numbers to locate a starting point. For example, if you were sampling from a telephone directory, you might generate a random number to decide which page to start sampling at and then another random number to decide which name on that page to start at. Having identified a starting point you then take every *n*th name until you have the sample size you need. The random starting point means that you have no control over which names get selected and any human bias in who gets selected is therefore avoided.

Systematic sampling is diagrammed in Exhibit 7.4.

EXHIBIT 7.4   Systematic Sample

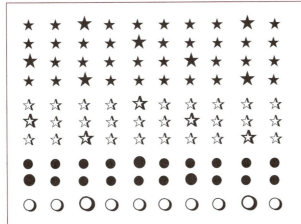

In this example the selected units are the large ones. A random starting point is selected (in this case, top row; third unit); then every *n*th individual is selected, in this case every 6th.

One problem with systematic sampling is that if a pattern in the original population matches the sampling interval you can get an overweighted or underweighted sample. For example, you might want to interview residents of a dormitory on their attitudes toward safety and security. You pick a dorm room at random and sample every 10th room after that. It so happens that every 10th room selected has an emergency alarm button outside it that residents cannot help but see as they enter and leave their rooms. It is possible then that your findings will be biased because every student in your sample will have a greater sense of security than others in the same dorm.

MULTISTAGE CLUSTER SAMPLING

Suppose you wanted a representative sample of a country's population. In practice this would mean trying to sample from a list of every resident of that country, assuming in the first place that you could get such a thing. There has to be an easier way, and there is. **Multistage cluster sampling** works by first sampling larger units such as states, provinces, or counties.

Towns and cities are then sampled from the state, province, or county sample. City blocks are then sampled from the town or city sample, and finally individual addresses are sampled from city blocks.

At the campus level, Elizabeth might consider multistage cluster sampling if she is unable to obtain a student directory from which to sample. In that case, she might randomly select housing units, then floors within the selected units, and then rooms within the randomly selected floors.

The advantage of this method is the relative ease of identifying people, or at least households. It is much easier to go state–city–city block–household than it is to find a comprehensive listing of millions of people. The catch is that at every stage of sampling the potential for bias in the final sample increases. No two states are identical, so any sample of states will have some attributes missing or underrepresented. For example, there are some states where same-sex unions are legal, and in those states there are communities where same-sex couples are more likely to be found. Multistage cluster sampling has the potential to completely eliminate same-sex couples from a sample or to overrepresent them depending on the states, towns, and perhaps even city blocks selected.

How Big a Sample Do I Need?

Two things govern sample size if you are attempting to make generalizations from your sample to the wider population you sampled from. These are the homogeneity of the population and level of statistical error you are prepared to live with in your results.

In the unlikely event that every unit in a population is identical, you would obviously need a sample size of only one! A simple example is surveying people on their intention to vote for a political candidate. If 100% of the population plans to vote for him, the population is 100% homogeneous in this regard. If the figure is 75%, the population is less homogeneous. If the figure is 50%, the population has minimal homogeneity. (If the figure is 40%, the population starts becoming more homogeneous again because a majority—60%—plans to not vote for the candidate.) Reasonably, the less homogeneous a population, the more likely it is you will need a bigger sample to ensure that its full range of diversity is captured.

The second influence on sample size is the level of statistical error you are prepared to live with. Intuitively, the larger the sample, the more likely it is to reflect the wider population from which it was drawn. You will recall from Chapter 6 that if our results are normally distributed, 68% of them will lie within plus or minus one standard deviation of the true mean, 95% will lie within two standard deviations of the true mean, and 99% will lie within three standard deviations of the true mean.

Therefore, if we want to report results at the 99% confidence level, we have to in effect examine three standard deviations' worth of data; if we want to report results at the 68% confidence level, we need to examine only one standard deviation's worth of data. In other words, higher confidence levels demand larger sample sizes.

Chapter 6 also reminds us that larger sample sizes are also required to reduce the standard error.

Standard error, homogeneity of the population, and sample size are related. If you know or assume two of these, statistical tables, software, or a relatively simple calculation will tell you the third.

Methods and Method Issues in Sampling

In principle, sampling is easy. In the case of nonprobability sampling the researcher makes sampling decisions based on some professional judgment. In the case of probability sampling a random selection process determines what individual units will be in the sample, and a sample size formula determines the number of units the sample should include. In the case of a census everyone is in by definition.

The basis of almost every study is a good sampling frame—the full list of individuals, groups, or media content from which the sample will be drawn. However, for survey research in particular the method selected may constrain your ability to develop an appropriate sampling frame, as discussed below.

POSTAL SAMPLING

Sampling postal addresses has an inbuilt problem because mail presupposes a postal address, which presupposes a residence, which not everybody has. Sampling postal addresses, even randomly, eliminates the homeless and the transient from the sample. Furthermore as people move, we may find that we are not reaching the individuals we intended to reach. This is not a problem if you intended only to reach "the household," but it is a problem if you attended to reach Jane Smith, who has now moved and is untraceable.

PHONE SAMPLING

Phone surveys became attractive to survey organizations and researchers once the majority of U.S. households had a phone. The ease of dialing a number relative to having to knock on doors or mail out surveys and wait for a response is obvious—and autodialing technology made it even easier. Sampling phone directories, however, is problematic because many phone numbers are unlisted and the owners of these numbers will not get into your sample.

Survey researchers attempt to overcome this problem with **random digit dialing**, a procedure that involves dialing computer-generated random numbers in the hopes of reaching unlisted numbers. Typically researchers decide on area codes and local exchanges they want to sample. This provides the first six digits of a phone number. Then computers are used to randomly generate the remaining four digits, the theory being that this will generate phone numbers that are in use but unlisted. This technique also has its problems because many sequences of numbers are not put into use by phone companies. The issue becomes even more problematic as phone users abandon traditional phones and cell phones in favor of Internet telephony services such as Skype and may not have accessible phone numbers at all.

Having a telephone account requires the means to pay for it, so sampling phone directories tends to sample out lower-income households. Conversely, many households have more than one phone number, so sampling these numbers will get those homes disproportionately represented. Phone numbers for traditional phones identified the owners' area code and exchange and therefore their geographic location. With cell phones this is not necessarily the case, so some information about an owner's location may be lost or he or she will not be included in the sampling for a specific area code.

A potential problem with phone surveys is the increasing number of people giving up traditional landline phones in favor of mobile phones. "Cell-only" Americans are more likely to be younger, less affluent, single, and more liberal. However, research (The Pew Research Center for the People and the Press, 2006) indicates that the absence of this group from traditional phone polls affects the results of asking questions on politics by less than 1%.

With phone surveys, there is a problem of nonresponse even if your phone call reaches a working number. Many people use caller ID and voice mail to filter out incoming marketing and research calls, and some even put their names on "do not call" lists. Even if you reach a working number, people may decline to participate in your survey simply because they don't like phone surveys. Also you have no guarantee that the individual answering the phone is the person you are trying to reach. (You want the owner but get the house sitter while the owner is vacationing in Switzerland.)

INTERNET SAMPLING

Despite the fact that the Internet is increasingly accessible, Internet users overall are different from the general population in three regards: the use of Internet technology, demographics, and geographic location.

Fricker, Galesic, Tourangeau, and Tan (2005) suggest that the Web user population has a different kind or level of knowledge than the general population and are specific that "for many researchers, the inability to select probability samples of Internet users eliminates Web surveys from serious consideration as a stand-alone method of data collection" (p. 373).

Furthermore, because there is no comprehensive directory of or standard format for e-mail addresses, not every e-mail user has an equal chance of being selected.

As a result of such issues, findings from Web-based surveys may not be generalizable to your study population.

For example, Horrigan (2007) found that only 51% of the U.S. population comprises "middle of the road" or advanced users of the Internet. The remaining 49% are basically low-level users of technology. Demographically, those "off the network" are more likely to be in their 60s, to be female, and to have lower levels of education and income.

That said, a 2009 survey by Horrigan found that home broadband adoption stood at 63% of adult Americans, a percentage that seems likely to increase. The greatest increase in adoption was among senior citizens, low-income Americans, and rural Americans, suggesting that Internet users will increasingly reflect the U.S. population as a whole as time goes by.

You may need to develop your own study population of known characteristics by building a list from information provided by visitors to a Web site as they respond to a survey, sign an online guestbook, or provide information about themselves during an online purchase. You may also need to use traditional mail appeals and publicity to drive individuals with known attributes to the Web site where you are hosting your survey. Clearly this alone will bias your survey results, but if you want to reach a population interested in your survey topic, then that may be a benefit rather than a liability.

SPECIAL POPULATION SAMPLING

Sampling or even accessing special populations such as military families, prisoners, or people with a particular medical condition can be tricky. Listings of special populations, such as people with a specific medical condition, often exist, but typically and with good reason organizations will not release members' names and contact information. On the other hand organizations that see a potential benefit to your research and consider it legitimate may be happy to cooperate once they have approved your research design and been assured of protections such as confidentiality that you have in place for the participants.

As an alternate, the list rental industry can provide mailing lists, often developed from information about magazine subscribers. People subscribing to special interest magazines are committed enough to their interests to pay for a subscription. Renting subscriber mailing lists is therefore one way to reach groups of people with a common interest. Renting the mailing list for readers of *Hydroponic Gardener* will allow you to reach hydroponic gardeners, but not all readers will be gardeners and of course not all such gardeners will subscribe to the magazine. Nevertheless, it may be worth the expense.

In the event that membership lists or subscription lists do not exist, personal networking, Web-based detective work, and building your own contacts from people who visit your Web site may be the only starting points you have available.

Ethics Panel: Checking the Ethics of Survey Research

Just as statistics can be used to misrepresent as well as to represent, so too abuses of sampling or shoddy sampling can contribute to misrepresentation.

First there is the issue of convenience. Under pressure of time, researchers may sample a student class, friends, or local media. Such sampling may be defensible, but generalizations from such samples probably are not.

Second, there is the pressure to get results. In applied fields such as audience research, marketing, and political communication, research companies can come under client pressure to get the "right answer." This can lead to sample selections that give clients the results they want to hear. If the research results get further summarized by news media doing "get to the point" writing, the research data can become further simplified and overgeneralized.

Check local and national newspapers for reports of public opinion polls. What populations can you detect were sampled? How were the samples obtained? What sampling procedures, if any, raise any ethical questions with respect to representing the original population?

Chapter Summary

- A census is a study of an entire population.

- A sample is a part of a wider population selected for study.

- There are two major categories of sampling—probability and nonprobability.

- Probability sampling includes random, stratified random, systematic, and multistage cluster.

- Nonprobability sampling includes convenience, purposive or judgmental, quota, network or snowball, and volunteer.

- Probability sampling is required in order to make generalizations to a population from a sample.

- Larger sample sizes reduce sampling error, but the extent to which they do so depends on the homogeneity of the sample.

- Statistical formulae allow us to calculate the ideal sample size for a given margin of error, or vice versa; and make generalizations from a sample to a larger population, if the sample has been randomly drawn from a population whose attributes have a normal distribution.

Recommended Reading

Crespi, I. (1998). Ethical considerations when establishing survey standards. *International Journal of Public Opinion Research, 10*(1), 75–83. Discusses the tension between ethical and practical considerations in survey design.

Sudman, S., & Blair, E. (1999). Sampling in the twenty-first century. *Journal of the Academy of Marketing Science, 27*(2), 269–277. An overview of issues and problems in sampling.

Recommended Web Resources

Council of American Survey Research Organizations (CASRO): http://www.casro.org. Provides basic information on surveys and survey sampling.

Research Randomizer: http://randomizer.org. One online site for generating random numbers.

StatPac: http://www.statpac.com/surveys/sampling.htm. A commercial survey software site with tutorials on sampling and other survey procedures.

Survey Sampling International: http://www.surveysampling.com. A commercial site providing sampling services internationally.

WebSM: http://www.websm.org. A European site on Web survey methods and sampling.

World Association for Public Opinion Research (WAPOR): http://www.unl.edu/wapor. Provides a code of professional ethics and practices at http://www.unl.edu/wapor/ethics.html.

References

Fricker, S., Galesic, M., Tourangeau, R., & Tan, T. (2005). An experimental comparison of Web and telephone surveys. *Public Opinion Quarterly, 69*(3), 370–392.

Horrigan, J. B. (2007, May 6). *A typology of information and communication technology users.* Washington, DC: Pew Internet and American Life Project. Retrieved February 1, 2009, from http://www.pewinternet.org/PPF/r/213/report_display.asp

Horrigan, J. B. (2009, June 17). *Home broadband adoption 2009.* Washington, DC: Pew Internet and American Life Project. Retrieved August 1, 2009, from http://pewinternet.org/Reports/2009/10-Home-Broadband-Adoption-2009.aspx

The Pew Research Center for the People and the Press. (2006, May 15). *The cell phone challenge to survey research: National polls not undermined by growing cell-only population.* Retrieved June 25, 2009, from http://people-press.org/report/276/

Student Study Site

Visit the study site at www.sagepub.com/treadwellicr for e-flashcards, web resources, and additional study materials.

Surveys

Putting Numbers on Opinions

Surveys are a way to portray
What people are thinking today.
They're a way with some speed
To get answers, you need
But poorly done lead you astray.

Chapter Overview

Surveys are frequently used in communication research for reasons of speed and cost-effectiveness.

A **survey** is a series of formatted questions delivered to a defined sample of people with the expectation that their responses will be returned somewhere between immediately and within a few days. The survey process starts with theoretically derived research questions or hypotheses and continues through question design and ordering, delivering questions to respondents, and obtaining their answers and analyzing them. A **questionnaire** is the specific set of questions that respondents answer.

This chapter discusses the advantages and disadvantages of surveys, different types of surveys, methods for delivering survey questions, and the important issue of wording survey questions.

Starter Questions

- I want to get the opinions of just 10 people; can I use a survey?

- I want people to respond to questions in their own words; will a survey let them do this?

- I need to ask some very personal questions; is a survey the best way to get such information?

- I mailed out a lot of surveys, but very few came back. What could I have done to increase the response rate?

- Don't people just ignore most surveys?

Advantages and Disadvantages of Surveys

One advantage of surveys is that respondents can answer large numbers of questions rapidly. Think of how many more questions there are in a one-hour multiple-choice quiz than in a one-hour essay exam. Typically this is because surveys rely on formatted questions such as yes–no questions, multiple-choice questions, and those in the Likert and semantic differential formats discussed in Chapter 5.

A second advantage is that many people can be surveyed rapidly. Phone, mail, and Internet technologies allow us to distribute surveys and collect answers rapidly from large numbers of people. Phone surveys with computer processing of data permit a national survey of 1,500 people to be run, analyzed, and reported within hours of the questions being finalized.

A third advantage is that with appropriate sampling and the assumption of normally distributed attributes in the sampled population, you can make generalizations with a known level of confidence from your sample to a wider population.

The major problem with surveys stems from the question format. Questions with limited response options such as yes and no or selecting a point on a Likert scale will give you numbers but no understanding of the "why" behind those numbers. For example, you may discover from a public opinion survey that 78% of voters would vote for candidate X, but this gives you little if any understanding of why they prefer candidate X. Even if you provided a series of possible answers such as "position on the environment" or "economic policy," you will have captured responses to ideas that you have defined as important. You cannot be sure that you have captured all the reasons that your respondents think are important.

A second weakness is that most survey designs do not allow us to assess causal relationships. For example, survey data indicating that overweight individuals are more likely to watch television does not permit us to conclude either that watching television causes obesity or the reverse. Correlation is not causality, as you will hear repeatedly in communication research. To make with confidence the statement that A causes B requires the experimental designs discussed in Chapter 9.

Another disadvantage of survey research is the increasing unwillingness of consumers to participate in them, at least via phone or mail. Because consumer-marketing communications via phone and mail often have the appearance of consumer research, consumers have grown increasingly resistant to anything resembling surveys. They use voice mail and caller ID to filter out phone surveys and may trash mail surveys, unopened, as "junk."

Another problem with surveys, though not unique to them, is having to decide whether the responses you received are valid or not; that is, do respondents' answers really match their behavior? People may report eating nutritionally balanced meals but may not do so, or they may provide researchers with answers they think the researcher is looking for. Especially for questions targeting personal behaviors and beliefs, researchers may find a gap between what they are told and what is going on in practice.

In this chapter we will follow the use of surveys in the context of a campus controversy—the proposed demolition of a historic building. At our hypothetical campus, the administration is proposing to demolish the "Hunter" building in order to expand parking spaces on campus. The Hunter building, beloved by generations of students for its "24/7" snack bar, idiosyncratic architecture, and sweeping campus views from the bell tower, has no special historic-site protections. Its fate therefore may well be decided in the court of campus opinion, on the basis of public opinion data from demolition proponents and opponents.

Types of Surveys

CROSS-SECTIONAL

Cross-sectional surveys are typically "a slice of life" or a cross section of life in that they capture what is going on at one point in time. A public opinion poll capturing attitudes toward a consumer product one day may produce remarkably different results the next day if in between there is a product recall, the launch of a better product, or adverse publicity about the product. Generally, there are two responses to this problem. The first is to decide that survey data from one point in time—a "snapshot"—are all that is needed because people's attitudes or behaviors are unlikely to change much. The second is to use a series of longitudinal studies, which track people's changes in knowledge, attitude, or behavior over time. Some types of longitudinal study are outlined below.

TREND

Trend studies measure the same items over time but draw different samples from the population each time. The questions remain the same—for example attitudes toward the Hunter building, handgun control, or recycling—but different individuals are sampled each time to answer the questions. A researcher can maintain sample size by replacing people as they move or drop out of the study, but there is no assurance that the new people will not differ in some way from the people they replaced.

PANEL

In **panel** studies, a group of individuals is sampled and recruited, and the same individuals are retained to answer questions over time. The advantage of a panel is that there is no variation in the composition of the sample over time. The disadvantage is that because people die, move, or decide not to participate, panels can have a high attrition rate. Predictably, the number of individuals in a panel generally declines over time.

COHORT

Cohorts are groups of people defined, most typically, by having an event in common. Thus all female corporate executives born in 1980 would be a cohort, as would the graduating class of 2011. Researchers study cohorts to see how, for example, career paths develop or, in the case of medical research, how the health status of a particular age group changes over time.

CROSS-LAGGED

Cross-lagged surveys measure a dependent variable and an independent variable at two points in time and thus allow us to draw conclusions about the causality. This is the only survey design that permits us to assess causality. More typically, we would use experimental designs (Chapter 9) for this.

In the case of our campus building controversy, proponents and opponents would run standard cross-sectional surveys to determine how different campus groups feel about the proposed demolition and what these groups might be prepared to do in terms of supporting or defeating the proposal. **Longitudinal surveys** over time are less likely, but cohorts of alumni by decade might well be surveyed to determine where the strongest support or opposition to the proposal lies, and trend studies to track changes in campus opinion over time might happen if the debate looks to be a long-term one.

Writing Questions

Developing a successful survey—by which we mean one that captures what you want to capture from a maximum number of respondents—requires more than just sitting at a keyboard and typing questions. The question format, question wording, and question order can all influence respondents' answers and the results you get, so time developing and pretesting questions is time well spent.

Most surveys seek to find out four things about respondents. These are demographic data such as age, sex, religion, and marital status; knowledge; attitudes; and behavior.

In the case of our campus controversy, advocacy groups on both sides would be interested to know student and alumni demographics such as class year and residence status, whether respondents are aware of the issue, how they feel about it, and what actions they might be prepared to take to defeat or support the proposal.

The function of question formats is to clarify both the question and the response options as far as possible for respondents while giving researchers relevant categories of answers that will help them analyze results.

Some questions are easier than others for respondents and researchers alike. Demographic questions for example can be relatively simple and simply formatted, as shown below.

Sex (check one)
___ Male
___ Female

Residence status (check one)
___ Resident
___ Commuter

However, consider how even a simple question such as "What is your age?" could be misinterpreted.

A respondent counting down the days to his 21st birthday could write in "as of today I am 20 years, 11 months, and 18 days old." Another respondent a day short of her 23rd birthday might conscientiously reply "22" when "23" would be more accurate. And because there's always someone out there with a sense of humor, you might get "3—in dog years."

We can clarify this question in two ways. First, we can change the instruction to "What is your age as of your last birthday?" Second, we can reformat the question. Generally, we don't need to know what age people are to the nearest year (although a specific age as it relates to driving, smoking, or voting might be an exception). In most cases, categories of age will suffice, such as the following:

____ 15–19
____ 20–24
____ 25–29

In this option respondents don't have to think about how exactly to define their age, and for those who are reluctant to give a specific age, providing them with an age range may help them feel more comfortable answering the question.

Question Formats

This section outlines typical question formats, some of which will be familiar from Chapter 5.

OPEN-ENDED QUESTIONS

Examples:

- In what building do you take most of your classes? _____
- How do you feel about the proposed demolition of the Hunter building? _____

Open-ended questions allow respondents to answer in their own words. The advantage of this is you may get insights that you could not get with highly structured questions such as those shown below. Open-ended questions are generally avoided in survey research because they are time-consuming to code and analyze relative to multiple-choice and **scaled questions**. For survey research, the first question above may be appropriate because it will generate relatively simple, brief responses. The second question, however, may elicit responses ranging from "OK" to a fulsome five-page essay and is more appropriately used as a focus group or interview question rather than a survey question.

DICHOTOMOUS QUESTIONS

Examples:

- What is your residence status?

    ___ Resident

    ___ Commuter

- Have you read the statistics chapter in this text?

    ___ Yes

    ___ No

- Are you in favor of demolishing the Hunter building to increase parking space on campus?

    ___ Yes

    ___ No

Dichotomous questions force respondents to choose one of two possible answers. This has the advantage of simplifying data coding and analysis. The problem with such questions is that life is rarely yes–no simple. For example, the above residence status question can be answered, but the second and third questions are problematic. For a student who has read only part of the statistics chapter, neither "yes" nor "no" is an accurate answer. Many people would have a problem with the "demolition" question above because major decisions are rarely that simple. Most people are likely to have an "it depends" answer, and the question provides no way to capture that sentiment.

Our interest groups on campus may provide some dichotomous response options such as "resident or commuter," "graduate or undergraduate," and "yes or no," but dichotomous questions are appropriate only where they provide a clear "either–or" option that makes sense to respondents.

When we can see other possible responses, two other question formats become appropriate. The first format is "additional categories," where respondents are given more than two possible answers. The second is the "intermediate categories" type, where respondents are able to check intermediate positions on a scale.

ADDITIONAL-CATEGORY QUESTIONS

Multiple-Choice Questions

Multiple-choice questions provide respondents with several possible answers and, depending on the precise question format, ask them to select one or more answers or to rank order them.

> Example:
>
> I am willing to help the "Save the Hunter Building" campaign by
>
> ___ Picketing the building
>
> ___ Contributing money
>
> ___ Working on a publicity campaign
>
> ___ Phoning alumni
>
> ___ Other (please identify)_____

This basic format may be used with different instructions, for example "please check one option," "please check as many answers as apply," or "please rank order your choices by writing '1' after your first choice, '2' after your second choice, and so on."

The difference between "select one" and "select as many as apply" is the level of information the researcher needs. "Select one" questions force respondents to a single choice. This question format may be appropriate in political polling where a voter can vote only for one candidate and that one candidate may be all the researcher is interested in knowing about. On the other hand the researcher may be interested in looking for patterns of response. Responses to the above question, for example, may tell the researcher whether or not the students who are most willing to donate money are also willing to be campus activists and join a picket line.

Rank order questions get around the problem of respondents checking every possible answer. If this happens, the researcher will have no understanding of which items are most important to respondents. With a rank order format, respondents are asked to assign each answer a score. The researcher adds the scores assigned to each question to get the overall ranking of each answer by respondents.

INTERMEDIATE-CATEGORY QUESTIONS

Likert Scale

Recall from Chapter 5 that Likert scales are statements with which respondents are asked to locate their level of agreement somewhere between "strongly agree" and "strongly disagree."

Examples:

Please rank your level of agreement with each of the following statements by marking one point between "strongly agree" and "strongly disagree."

	Strongly Agree	Agree	Neutral	Disagree	Strongly Disagree
1. The Hunter building should be demolished.	___	___	___	___	___
2. I know the rules of plagiarism.	___	___	___	___	___
3. I have never plagiarized.	___	___	___	___	___
4. I would never copy others' work without their permission.	___	___	___	___	___

Likert scales are always presented as statements, never questions. The response options usually run between "strongly agree" and "strongly disagree" on a 5-point scale, though 7-point and, infrequently, 3-point scales may be used.

Note that in the above examples, the last three statements appear similar. Here's why we might run all three of the above plagiarism-related statements. Comparing the answers to statements 2 and 3 lets us see if there is a difference between knowing and doing. Comparing the answers to statements 3 and 4 lets us understand whether respondents have understood the term *plagiarism*. If we get wildly different responses to statements 3 and 4, we can assume that the term *plagiarism* is not being understood in the same way as "copying others' work without their permission."

Semantic Differential Scale

Semantic differential scales present a topic or concept followed by scales anchored at each end by words that have opposite meaning. Respondents express their opinions of that topic by marking their positions between these word pairs.

Example:

The Hunter Building

Value for Money	___	___	___	___	___	Waste of Money
Expensive	___	___	___	___	___	Inexpensive
Friendly	___	___	___	___	___	Unfriendly
Warm	___	___	___	___	___	Cold
Ugly	___	___	___	___	___	Beautiful

A semantic differential scale is always anchored by bipolar adjectives or terms, such as *strong* and *weak*. As in the example above, campus advocacy groups may use semantic differential scales to assess how campus members see the Hunter building in terms of its "personality."

While these scales appear superficially easy to construct, considerable work can be involved in ensuring that the words do capture the concepts that you want to capture (i.e., the scales have high validity). Related, it is also important to ensure that the word pairs chosen do represent true opposites. For example, which best captures the opposite of "works hard"—"plays hard" or "lazy"?

Survey Wording

If it can be misinterpreted, it will be.

As noted, even a simple question such as asking a respondent's age can be misinterpreted. Misinterpretation occurs primarily because the question has been poorly worded and/or has not been pretested to see what misinterpretations are possible. To minimize the possibilities for misinterpretation, check your questions at draft stage and then pretest them with a sample of the people you will be surveying.

COMMON PROBLEMS WITH WORDING

Leading Questions

Leading questions force the respondent into an assumption that may not be true; they "lead" the respondent to a particular answer rather than letting respondents respond in their own terms.

Examples:

Why do you think the campus administration is unethical?

When did you first start plagiarizing your research papers?

The above examples force respondents to assume that the campus administration is unethical and that the respondent is plagiarizing. Neither is necessarily true, but by answering the question, regardless of their answer, respondents acknowledge that it is.

Check for leading questions and avoid them. For example, the above questions can be reworked in several ways as follows:

- Describe the ethical standards of the campus administration.

_____

- The campus administration is ethical.

Strongly Agree	Agree	Neutral	Disagree	Strongly Disagree
_____	_____	_____	_____	_____

- What position on the following scale best describes your view of the campus administration?

Completely ethical						Completely unethical
	_____	_____	_____	_____	_____	

Double-Barreled Questions

Double-barreled questions ask two questions simultaneously but allow for only one answer.

Examples:

- Do you think the Hunter building is an asset to the campus, or should it be demolished?
- Will you vote against the Hunter building demolition, or aren't you going to vote?

There is no way anyone can answer these questions logically because they are not either–or situations. Deal with them by splitting each question into two. In the case of the above two questions, make four questions:

- Do you think the Hunter building is an asset to the campus?
- Do you think the Hunter building should be demolished?
- Will you vote against the Hunter building demolition?
- Are you planning to vote?

Each of the above questions can be formatted as either a yes–no question or a Likert statement.

Negative Wording

Whenever possible avoid phrasing survey questions or statements as negatives. **Negative wording** may be simple and clear but still misunderstood by people reading in a hurry or misheard over the phone. For example, a simple question or statement such as "A course in statistics should not be required as part of the communication major" may be misread or misheard as "should be required." The solution is to phrase the question in the positive "should be required."

The Double Negative

A combination of negative wording and a double-barreled question results in the **double negative**. As Rosenthal (2006) reported, a classic "double negative" in a 1992 Roper poll asked, "Does it seem possible or does it seem impossible to you that the Nazi extermination of the Jews never happened?" What does this mean? What would you answer?

In a follow-up survey, Roper asked a clearer question, and the percentage of respondents expressing doubt that the Holocaust happened (which was the crux of the question) dropped from the original 22% to 1%.

LANGUAGE

In a global world, languages and dialects are inevitably a consideration in question design. Whether it is a local social services agency researching the health care status of immigrant communities or a multinational company researching consumer opinion in Lithuania, language use can make the difference between a successful survey and an unsuccessful one. For example, the word *program* will be met with puzzlement in countries that have "programmes." You would be well advised to seek a local consultant to ensure that subtle shades of meaning are translated successfully, for example that the word *family* means the nuclear family living under one roof and not the extended family.

GUIDING RESPONDENTS THROUGH SURVEYS

Generally, researchers use either a "**funnel**" or an "**inverted funnel**" format for overall questionnaire design. The funnel design starts with broad questions that a respondent will be comfortable with and progresses to specific questions. The inverted funnel takes the reverse approach by starting with specific questions and then moving to broader ones. For example, a funnel format may be used to first establish where respondents are on a broad liberal–conservative scale before moving to very specific questions that ask about the relationship of their political views to broadcast regulation or abortion. An inverted funnel format might start, for example, by asking respondents very specifically how many times a week they dine out; this would then be followed by broader questions focusing on why respondents dine out and their attitudes toward dining.

Mail surveys of course allow respondents to answer questions in any order. However, in phone surveys and face-to-face surveys the question order is determined by the researcher. This suggests that mail surveys need to begin with relevant questions that will hold the reader's attention. Phone surveys on the other hand may be best begun with relatively easy questions, such as "How many television sets are in your household?" This gives respondents a comfort level that may predispose them to answer more difficult questions.

Generally, questions related to the same theme should be grouped together, but sometimes a question may be "sandwiched" between unrelated questions as a check that all questions on the same topic are being answered consistently. Sensitive questions related to alcohol or drug use, sexual activity, or criminal background, for example, may be placed among questions with which respondents have a comfort level so that they are less resistant to answering them.

FILTER QUESTIONS AND INSTRUCTIONS

You may have some questions that some respondents cannot or should not answer because they are irrelevant to those people. For example, you may be studying how contemporary families get their news of the world.

One obvious source of news is the Internet, but not all households have access to the Internet, so you should route the respondents from such households past your Internet questions and on to the next set of questions related to radio, television, or newspapers.

This can be done with a simple instruction:

- If this home has an Internet connection, please continue with question 6. If it has no Internet connection, please go to question 18.

Alternately, you might use a filter question followed by an instruction:

- Does this home have an Internet connection?

___ Yes

___ No

If you answered "yes," please continue with question 6. If you answered "no," please go to question 18.

Such questions are called **filter questions** because they filter out respondents who cannot or should not answer specific questions.

Advantages and Disadvantages of Specific Survey Methods

The "Methods and Method Issues in Sampling" section in Chapter 7 introduced some of the advantages and disadvantages of different survey methods with respect to sampling. Exhibit 8.1 summarizes some of the considerations with respect to designing and running surveys.

EXHIBIT 8.1   Advantages and Disadvantages of Specific Survey Methods

Method	Advantages	Disadvantages
Phone	• Can survey large samples in a short time. • Most households have phones.	• Typically limited to a few short questions. • Consumer resistance. • "Barriers" of voice mail, caller ID, and "do not call" lists. • "Cell-only" users differ demographically from traditional landline users.

Method	Advantages	Disadvantages
Mail	• Give respondents time to consider questions and the ability to answer questions in any order. • Good for delivering questions on complex issues that require thought. • Suited to addressing personal lifestyle questions especially if respondents are guaranteed confidentiality and the questions are seen to come from a reputable source.	• Low response rate. • No way of knowing who completed the survey. • Can target only respondents who are literate.
Internet	• Can be administered quickly, flexibly, and inexpensively. • Asynchronous (can be done in respondents' own time). • Can target special interest groups. • Can present audio, video, or graphics. • Can engage respondents in real-time "chat" or video conferencing. • May elicit sensitive information that respondents would not provide face-to-face to an interviewer. • Results can be analyzed in real time as respondent data come in. • Surveys can be e-mailed to respondents or posted to a Web site.	• Results reflect the views of those who choose to respond and may not be scientifically valid. • Results can be assumed to represent the opinions of neither Internet users in general nor the public as a whole. • Cannot control the survey presentation because different browsers may display the survey differently. • May need mail, e-mail, or phone to drive respondents to your survey's Web site. • May not know who completed the survey.

Time, budget, and the size of the survey in terms of both number of questions and number of respondents will influence your method decision. Ultimately, there is no substitute for pretesting to ensure that wording, question formats, and question order do not present a problem for respondents.

Improving Survey Response Rates

The main problem with mail surveys is that potential respondents may see mail surveys as "junk mail" and trash them without opening them or just not get around to responding. To improve response rates, use a preliminary postcard, letter, or phone call to tell respondents about the survey and ask for their participation. Include a phone number that respondents can call to verify the legitimacy of the survey and ask any questions they may have. Follow-up reminder postcards and phone calls can also increase the response rate, as can small gifts, vouchers, free product samples, or a donation to charity in the respondent's name. Reply-paid envelopes are a must if you want mail questionnaires returned.

Similarly, phone survey response rates may be increased by using a letter or postcard to let respondents know that a research phone call will be made to them on a certain date at a certain time and to offer a 1-800 number they can call for further information. Restaurants and other consumer outlets that use phone surveys to assess consumer satisfaction may entice and reward respondents with a code number good for a discount on their next purchase. As De Leeuw and Hox (2004) discovered, if there is one "magic bullet" to improve the level of consumer participation, it may be your opening words—"I'm not selling anything."

Web-based surveys may also need conventional publicity methods to drive individuals to the Web site where you have your survey questions.

Capturing and Processing Survey Data

Data processing is the next step after you have obtained survey data from respondents. While you might use a calculator to analyze data from a small survey, it is more common to enter survey data into proprietary data-processing software such as SPSS (Statistical Package for the Social Sciences) or spreadsheets such as Excel.

There are several ways of entering raw data into a format suitable for data processing. Data can be typed directly into the statistical software. If the survey uses op-scan (fill in the bubbles) forms, the forms can be read by optical scanners, and the data can be formatted for processing. Proprietary software packages allow you to custom-design your own op-scan forms for surveys and to then scan the completed forms and get a compilation of survey results question by question.

Such software can also be used to produce Web-based surveys. Web-based surveys of course mean that the respondents enter the data themselves. There is no intermediate process such as scanning forms or hand-entering data by the researcher. Respondents essentially do the data entry themselves by keying in answers to questions. Web-based software such as *SurveyMonkey* and *Zoomerang* will analyze the survey data and display summary results at the push of a button.

"Hybrid" versions of phone surveys exist, in which people are invited by mail to take a phone survey by dialing a special phone number. The number uses voice mail technology to capture respondents' answers as they move from question to question. Although the technology allows for capturing spoken comments, it typically captures answers of the "push 1 if you agree; push 2 if you disagree" type. In this case the respondents are doing the data entry, directly into a computer for subsequent data analysis.

Using Other People's Surveys

If you are seeking public opinion data, for example, the information you need may be publicly available and reported by national media or available from any number of public opinion pollsters. There are three potential problems with such data. First, they may be proprietary, and you may not be able to access or use them without permission. Second, they may be from a source that has an agenda in conducting research; you will need to carefully evaluate the questions and how they were worded and the sample and how it was obtained. Third, you may not be able to process the data to meet your own needs. For example, answers may be broken down by gender but not by ethnicity.

An intermediate step between using publicly available information and designing and running your own surveys is to hire a professional survey firm to do the work for you. Such firms will work with you to develop and test the questions and will analyze the results for you and help you interpret them. The cost may be less than that of doing the entire project on your own, especially if your questions can be "piggybacked" onto other surveys targeted at the sample that interests you.

Ethics Panel: Clients and Methods as Ethical Decisions

I. Crespi (1998) distinguishes between professional standards and ethical standards in survey research. Professional standards are the standards of competence that govern sampling, survey design, and implementation. Ethical standards are the standards of responsibility to all parties affected by your research—clients, participants, those who will read your research reports, and society more generally. The two sets of standards are not necessarily related. For example, a professionally perfect survey may be ethically suspect. Or an ethically defensible survey may be professionally unsound as in the case where a judgment is made to provide a needed low-budget survey rather than no survey at all.

Professional researchers have ethical and professional responsibilities to their clients and ethical obligations to respondents, their profession, and society.

Thinking of a survey you might design for a commercial client such as a software company or a restaurant, would you

• use the survey results to publicize your own research firm?

(Continued)

(Continued)

- control how your client reports the survey results you obtained?
- recommend that a client with a limited budget prefer (probably cheaper) convenience sampling over probability sampling?
- refer the client to a competitor who you believe can do a better job than you can?

II. Surveys must not be morally objectionable, says Crespi (1998). He finds it morally unacceptable to do surveys for a tobacco company, a right-wing racist political party, or a military dictatorship.

Is Crespi's position defensible? Or are researchers, be they academic or commercial, obligated to do the most professional research they can, regardless of client or topic?

On what bases would you decline a potential client or research topic?

Refresh your ethics thinking with a visit to Chapter 3. The following two Web sites—which provide the codes of ethics for two areas of applied communication, public opinion research and direct marketing—will give you some more specific help:

- American Association for Public Opinion Research Code of Professional Ethics and Practices: http://www.aapor.org/AAPOR_Code.htm
- Direct Marketing Association Ethical Guidelines: http://www.dmaresponsibility.org

Research in Practice

With this chapter, we begin a series of case studies showing how communication research is used to help solve problems in communication practice. Our first case study involves using telephone surveys to assess the image of a hospital.

RESEARCH IN PRACTICE

Using Telephone Surveys to Assess the Image of a Hospital

Central Valley Hospital (the hospital's name has been changed for this case study) is a hospital located in an affluent suburban area in New England. A number of years ago, the hospital received extensive press coverage about whether the deaths of some patients at Central Valley Hospital were due to negligence. The press coverage continued over a number of years due to legal action relating to the deaths.

Prior to this press coverage, marketing research consistently showed that Central Valley Hospital had a very strong reputation in its market area, with area residents perceiving it as providing high-quality care in a community setting. Hospital administrators thought that the hospital's reputation would return to its previous level after the negative press about the hospital stopped.

Four years after the deaths occurred, Market Street Research, Inc. (MSR) conducted a telephone survey of 500 residents of Central Valley Hospital's market area, in order to assess residents' image of the hospital. The phone numbers for the study were generated using a random-digit dialing process, in which the three-digit prefixes of the telephone numbers in the communities that were targeted for the study were identified and the last four numbers were randomly generated. For each household, MSR confirmed that the residents lived in the area targeted for the study and identified and interviewed the person most responsible for making health care decisions. Households with residents who worked in health care or marketing were screened from participation. The response rate for the survey was 35.5%. The sample is a scientific sample, with an error rate of ±4.2 percentage points.

The survey results indicated that Central Valley Hospital's image had suffered as a result of the negative press. While the hospital's reputation had been superior to that of other community hospitals in the region, it was now not seen as distinctive. About one half of area residents could recall negative press about the hospital, including stories about the deaths and the malpractice suits, and those articles had clearly affected the confidence some area residents had in Central Valley Hospital.

In the telephone survey, MSR tested a number of positioning statements, to see which would have the most positive impact on area residents' perceptions of Central Valley Hospital. These statements included descriptions of actions the hospital had taken to improve its quality, the positive results of an accreditation process completed by a national accreditation agency, a partnership Central Valley Hospital had entered into with a major teaching hospital, and the high-quality ratings Central Valley Hospital's physicians had received from a large HMO (health maintenance organization). The findings indicated that the partnership between Central Valley Hospital and the major teaching hospital had the greatest impact on area residents in terms of their stated likelihood of using Central Valley Hospital in the future.

Central Valley Hospital worked with its advertising agency to develop an advertising campaign that focused on the partnership between Central Valley Hospital and the major teaching hospital.

After the campaign had run for 9 months, Market Street Research conducted a postcampaign telephone survey of 500 area residents in order to assess whether there had been any significant changes in area residents' perceptions of the hospital. MSR repeated the methodology it had used for the baseline survey.

The survey results were very positive. About one fourth of the respondents recalled seeing or hearing the ad campaign, and residents who recalled the campaign were significantly more likely than those who did not to be aware of Central Valley Hospital's areas of strengths, to have a more positive image of the hospital, and to prefer using the hospital for a range of services. In addition, the survey results as a whole showed a significant improvement over the baseline survey in terms of Central Valley Hospital's name recognition and image. The survey results clearly demonstrated that the ad campaign was highly successful at restoring Central Valley Hospital's reputation in its market area.

Contributed by Julie Pokela, PhD
President
Market Street Research, Inc.

Market Street Research, Inc., based in Northampton, Massachusetts, provides quantitative and qualitative marketing research and analysis services for health care, finance, technology, manufacturing, and education clients.

Chapter Summary

- Surveys are a "mainstream" method for capturing public opinion at a point in time.

- Surveys commonly use formatted questions such as multiple-choice checklists and scaled questions.

- Survey questions may be delivered to respondents by phone, mail, e-mail, Web site, or personal interview.

- Survey questions must be carefully written and pretested to ensure that they are not misunderstood.

- With proper sampling procedures, survey results can be generalized to a wider population with a known level of statistical confidence.

- Surveys can be fast and cost-effective.

- Most survey designs cannot assess causal relationships between variables.

- Survey results are "true" only as of the time the survey was done; there is no guarantee that the results will be true tomorrow.

Recommended Reading

Cobanoglu, C., Warde, B., & Morco, P. J. (2001). A comparison of mail, fax and Web-based survey methods. *International Journal of Market Research, 434*(4), 441–452. Compares three survey methods for response rate, response time, and cost.

Rosenthal, J. (2006, August 27). Precisely false vs. approximately right: A reader's guide to polls. *New York Times* Public Editor. Retrieved March 20, 2009, from http://www.nytimes.com/2006/08/27/opinion/27pubed.html. Discusses the problem of bad polls, reporting and misreporting bad polls, and how bad polls can undermine confidence in good polls.

Recommended Web Resources

Cool Surveys: http://www.coolsurveys.com/

Zoomerang: http://www.zoomerang.com/

The above two sites give you the ability to run online surveys at no cost.

Council of American Survey Research Organizations (CASRO): http://www.casro.org. This site has links to industry groups, colleges and universities doing research and research databases, and a code of ethics.

The National Opinion Research Center (NORC) at the University of Chicago: http://www.norc.org. Known for its national surveys of public opinion. See also the NORC-produced online booklet explaining surveys at http://www.whatisasurvey.info/

Survey Research Laboratory (SRL) of the University of Illinois at Chicago: http://www.srl
.uic.edu. The SRL links page at http://www.srl.uic.edu/Srllink/srllink.htm provides links
to research organizations, research ethics codes, sampling, and data analysis.

World Association for Public Opinion Research (WAPOR): http://www.unl.edu/wapor. See
especially the WAPOR Code of Professional Ethics and Practices at http://www
.unl.edu/wapor/ethics.html

References

Crespi, I. (1998). Ethical considerations when establishing survey standards. *International Journal of
Public Opinion Research, 10*(1), 75–82.

De Leeuw, E. D., & Hox, J. J. (2004). I am not selling anything: 29 experiments in telephone intro-
ductions. *International Journal of Public Opinion Research, 16*(4), 464–473.

Rosenthal, J. (2006, August 27). Precisely false vs. approximately right: A reader's guide to polls. *New York
Times* Public Editor. Retrieved March 20, 2009, from http://www.nytimes.com/2006/08/27/
opinion/27pubed.html

Student Study Site

Visit the study site at www.sagepub.com/treadwellicr for e-flashcards, web resources, and additional
study materials.

CHAPTER

Experiments

Researching Cause and Effect

Experiments' basic design
Starts with two groups of people defined.
If group A gets treatment
Not given to B
The effect of the treatment you'll find.

Chapter Overview

If the guiding thought for surveys is "let's ask people," the guiding thought for experimental methods is "let's do something and see what happens."

This chapter introduces the principles of experimental method. All experimental designs have one thing in common. They focus on manipulating one variable to see what will happen to another variable as a result. In practice, experiments range from simple field observations that lack rigor to sophisticated designs in which all variables are rigorously controlled and measurable.

The major contribution of experimental method to communication research is its potential to identify variables that have a significant effect on other variables and to determine whether such variables have a causal relationship to others.

Starter Questions

- Why would I prefer an experiment to other research methods?

- Do I need large numbers of people for an experimental design?

- Must I have a specific hypothesis before I design an experiment?

- Can experiments replicate real-world conditions?

- Do experiments need sophisticated statistical analysis?

142

Advantages and Disadvantages of Experiments

Stereotypical images of white-coated scientists manipulating "high tech" gadgetry notwithstanding, experimentation means nothing more than manipulating one variable to see if another variable changes as a result. In the context of communication research this might mean exposing consumers to different versions of an advertisement to see which version is the most persuasive, asking Web users to use different Web sites to see which site is the most easily navigable, or asking groups to solve problems under different conditions of group size or leadership style to see which type of group performs most effectively.

In all such cases, the experimenters are doing something to see what happens rather than just asking people questions. The basic rationale for experimental design is summarized by Gilbert, Light, and Mosteller (1975): "We will not know how things will work in practice until we try them *in practice*" (p. 46).

Causality

One purpose of experimental design is to determine which variables have an authentically **causal relationship**.

Causality can be the focus of intense political, regulatory, industry, and academic interest. Parents and politicians want to know whether exposure to video games, television, or violent or explicit sexual content causes some undesirable effect in children or adolescents. Educators want to know if using a particular teaching method will cause an improvement in student performance. Marketers want to know if a particular marketing strategy will cause an increase in sales. The answers to such questions feed into debates about media regulation, investments in educational technology, or where advertising dollars should best be spent respectively.

As researchers, we might be interested in knowing whether heavy use of the Internet causes a change in the nature or frequency of interpersonal communication. As policymakers, we might want to know whether exposure to alcohol advertising causes adolescents to drink more or to start drinking at a younger age than they might otherwise.

Generically, all such questions ask the generic question "Does A cause B?"

To be satisfied that A (the **independent variable**) does cause B (the **dependent variable**) to change we need to be assured of three things:

- A must precede B in time.
- A and B must vary together (**covariance**).
- B must demonstrably be caused by A and not by something else.

A must precede B if we are to argue that A causes B. We cannot argue that a new monthly newsletter for employees improved their morale if the only observed jump in morale occurred before the newsletter was launched. To measure change in the variables we are interested in we must measure them at "time 1" and then later at "time 2." This is a major weakness of surveys, which typically measure variables only once, at "time 1."

Also, A and B must vary together if we are to demonstrate causality. If we introduce our new employee newsletter into an organization and employee morale remains unchanged, we cannot argue that the newsletter had any effect on morale. We must be able to demonstrate that as the nature or frequency of communication with employees changed, so too did their level of morale.

However, knowing that A and B vary together is not in itself evidence of causality. We also need to eliminate the possibility that other variables might explain the effect(s) we see. For example, a human resources manager might observe that employee morale is indeed rising after the launch of a new newsletter and therefore conclude that the newsletter caused the increase in morale. Suppose, however, the newsletter had been launched as part of a package of employee benefits that included salary increases, profit sharing, and additional benefits. In this case there is an observable relationship between the introduction of the newsletter and the increase in morale, but it may not be a causal relationship. If we investigate further, we might find that the improvement in morale is explained by the salary increases and not at all by the newsletter. The relationship between A and B has been caused by a third variable that influenced them both.

The particular strength of experimental method is its potential to identify variables that have significant causal relationships and to assess the direction of causality.

The main problem with experimental methods is the artificiality of the experimental conditions. Typically participants in an experiment are invited into a lab or room to watch videos, to try a new product, or to read a message of some kind. The researcher may be trying to study how people watch television, shop for products, or understand newspaper news, but experimental designs rarely capture the natural environment in which people use the media, shop, or make decisions with work colleagues. This problem is referred to as a lack of **ecological isomorphism**. The experimental condition is not the same as the outside world it seeks to replicate and therefore may have a questionable validity.

As we will see, a further problem with experiments is that the more sophisticated designs may require large numbers of people who are willing to become experimental participants perhaps for extended periods of time.

In the rest of this chapter we will follow professor Tom, who hypothesizes that peer interaction among students influences academic performance. We will see professor Tom move from basic to more and more sophisticated experimental designs as his thinking about this relationship develops.

The different levels of experimental design are diagrammed as follows:

X = manipulation of a variable; what is done to the experimental groups.

R = random assignment of individuals to groups, a key concept in experimental design.

O_1, O_2, etc. = observation 1, observation 2, etc.

Field Experiments and Ex Post Facto Designs

As can happen, professor Tom's interest in the relationship between group interaction and academic performance is sparked by a casual observation. His students come together for a test after a widespread power outage, and he happens to notice that their test results indicate that on-campus students overall performed better than commuter students. "Why might this be?" he asks, and discovers that as a result of the power outage and loss of such distractions as television and Internet access, many of the resident students in his class got together and studied for the test. The commuter students did not.

Professor Tom is getting the benefit of what we might call a natural experiment or **ex post facto design** because he did not design an experiment but merely took the opportunity to observe "after the fact" that a temporary change in study conditions seems to have affected test results.

Intrigued, he decides to run a simple experiment to test his initial observation. Prior to the next test, he asks some student volunteers to form a study group and study for the test together. This basic design is a **field experiment** or observation. Here, he is manipulating a variable (study conditions) and observing the results (test scores) for the study group versus the rest of the class.

This level of design is diagrammed as follows:

$$X \quad O_1$$

Field experiments and ex post facto designs have limited value when it comes to deciding whether X caused O. In both cases, measurements or observations take place only after the experiment has happened. Because we have no observations beforehand there is no baseline from which to measure change in test scores, and so we cannot determine how much change has occurred, if it has occurred at all. We cannot rule out the possibility that variables other than the conditions of study influenced the test results. There is no assurance that the study-group students are the same as the non-study-group students, and we cannot be confident about the direction of causality. For example, is it possible that the higher test scores are explained not by the group study experience as such but by the fact that students who typically score high on tests anyway prefer to study in groups?

At this point in the research process, professor Tom is refining both his research question and his experimental design. Basically, he has started with a broad research question:

> *RQ:* Is there a relationship between how students study for tests and test performance?

His simple field experiment suggests that this might be the case, and it is now time to review the relevant scholarly literature and arrive, if possible, at a more specific hypothesis.

His reading of the literature suggests that studying as a member of a group can mean getting instant answers to questions, group support, shared resources, help from knowledgeable colleagues, and perhaps peer pressure to succeed. On the other hand, he suspects that study groups also may have the potential to degenerate into uncontrolled socializing and that studying alone offers unique advantages such as no interruptions and the potential to study at any time and for as long as the student needs to. He decides that the evidence is inconclusive; obviously much depends on the nature of the study group and the individual student.

He decides that he now has enough evidence to propose a two-tailed hypothesis:

> *H₁:* There is a relationship between studying in groups and test performance.

(Remember from Chapter 2 that a one-tailed hypothesis would propose a specific direction, for example that there is a positive relationship between studying in groups and test performance.)

What experimental design should he use to establish that there is such a relationship?

Basic Experimental Design

ONE-GROUP PRETEST–POSTTEST DESIGN

A basic experimental design consists of a baseline observation (O_1) followed by exposure to an experimental condition (X), followed by postexperimental observation (O_2) to see if any change has occurred in the experimental group. It is diagrammed as follows:

$$O_1 \quad X \quad O_2$$

With this design we can see any changes that might occur as a result of variable X. In the case of our example, professor Tom would get a baseline measure (O_1) of test performance of a group of students, place them in a group study session (X), and then measure their test performance again (O_2).

If he found a difference between the "before" and "after" measures (O_1 and O_2), he might propose that the group study sessions are what caused it, but this is not a rigorous enough design to answer the causality question.

To be certain that he has found a causal relationship, he needs to rule out two possibilities—first that any observed improvement in test scores might have occurred anyway for some reason and second that some influence other than the group study sessions caused the improvement.

The problem with the one-group pretest–posttest design is that many other variables not formally considered in the experimental design might also be playing a part. For example, if "study alone" students study in the library and the "study together" students study in a dorm room, the study location may explain the difference in test scores. (Hypothetically, the "study alone" individuals may have easier access to library reference resources.)

We need to be sure that we have ruled out all other possible explanations before deciding that study conditions, and only study conditions, explain the difference in test scores. This means designing a level of control into experiments.

Designing for Control

Control in experimental design has two meanings. In a general sense, control means to remove all other possible variables from the experimental design so that we can be sure that our treatment variable and only our treatment variable is causing any changes we see. **Control groups** are groups not exposed to any experimental variable. As shown in the following example, they are used as a baseline against which to measure any changes in groups that are exposed to experimental variables.

TWO-GROUP PRETEST–POSTTEST DESIGN

One way to be more certain that group study sessions have an effect on test scores is to use two groups of students and to place only one group into group study sessions. If the students in the group study sessions show a measurable change in test scores and the second group (the control group) does not, we can be more confident that the group study sessions had an effect.

This design is diagrammed as follows:

$$O_1 \quad X \quad O_2$$
$$O_1 \qquad \quad O_2$$

Here, both groups' test scores are measured before and after one group has been placed in the group study sessions. Because the second group (the control group) has no exposure to these sessions we would expect to find improved academic performance only in the group that was placed in the group study sessions (X). If we find a change in the control group, we have to accept that something other than the group study sessions is causing the observed changes in test scores.

If professor Tom determines that the group study students had significantly higher test scores, he might conclude that studying together explains these test scores. Unfortunately, he could be wrong. A yet more sophisticated experimental design is needed if he is to have full confidence in his results.

Designing for Random Assignment

If we have more of one characteristic in a group than in another group, it may be that characteristic and not the experimental variable that is explaining the results. For example, variables that might influence test scores could include an individual's age, number of years at college, work commitments, presence or absence of first-year orientation to campus life, level of Internet access, attitudes toward education, and so on. We cannot remove all such variables from our experimental design because we do not necessarily know what they are.

This is where **random assignment** comes in. With random assignment into groups, we can assume that the probability of some peculiarity occurring in one group is no greater or less than the probability of it occurring in another group. Any difference we observe between groups then should be due to the variable we are manipulating and not to something unique to one group.

Random assignment means, for example, that individuals with a particularly high IQ would be randomly assigned across both groups. The probability then is that the effect of IQ is equalized across both groups and IQ can be eliminated as an explanation because in principle it affects both groups equally.

TWO-GROUP RANDOM ASSIGNMENT PRETEST–POSTTEST DESIGN

The following design is essentially the same as a two-group pretest–posttest design but with the very important distinction that individuals are now randomly assigned to groups, as shown below. *R* denotes random assignment to groups.

$$R \quad O_1 \quad X \quad O_2$$
$$R \quad O_1 \qquad O_2$$

Professor Tom is no longer asking students to volunteer to study in a group; he is using a random numbers mechanism (see Chapter 7) to assign students to a group. It is always possible that as a result of random assignment he may end up, unknowingly, with Republicans, Rastafarians, or Rotarians overrepresented in one group. But random assignment allows him to argue that all such attributes have the same probability of occurring in each group. If his experiment shows changes in one group, then, he can reasonably assume that the change is due to the experimental variable.

With random assignment, a control group, and a pretest–posttest design, professor Tom is well on the way to answering the causality question, but now this design has itself created a problem. What is the possibility that the pretest or baseline measurement itself had some effect on participants?

If professor Tom wants to measure change in test scores against a baseline test, he might ask some questions a second time to find out if students score more highly on them after the group study experience. Obviously, students already exposed to these questions may find them easier to answer. What may explain the change in test scores then is not the group study experience but the previous exposure to the questions. In other words the pretest itself has affected test performance.

To eliminate this possibility, professor Tom needs yet another group that has not been exposed to the pretest. This group will, however, participate in group study sessions prior to the posttest.

The experimental design for this group would look like this:

$$R \quad X \quad O_2$$

To eliminate the possible influence of the pretest, there is no O_1.

Finally, to ensure that the experimental variable and only the experimental variable explains his results, he adds one further group to the design. It is a group of randomly assigned individuals to whom absolutely nothing happens except the final posttest. In the unlikely event that this group's posttest results are the same as for other groups, he would be forced to the conclusion that something other than the experimental variable is at work. This group's design is as follows:

$$R \qquad O_2$$

THE SOLOMON FOUR-GROUP DESIGN

Adding the above two groups to the experimental design results in a four-group design known as the Solomon Four-Group Design, as shown in Exhibit 9.1.

Exhibit 9.1   **Solomon Four-Group Design**

Diagram				Explanation
R	O_1	X	O_2	Random selection, pretesting, and posttesting, subject to experimental variable. This is the "test group."
R	O_1		O_2	Random selection, pretesting, and posttesting, *not* subject to experimental variable. This control group shows what would have happened without the experimental variable.
R		X	O_2	Random selection, posttesting only, subject to experimental variable. This control group checks that the pretest is not influencing the results.
R			O_2	Random selection, posttesting only, *not* subject to experimental variable. This control group checks that nothing other than the pretest and the experimental condition is influencing the experiment.

With this design we can compare pretest with posttest results, compare control groups with experimental groups, and take a look at a group to which nothing has happened except for a final test. Now we can be assured that the experimental variable preceded the posttest and that no other variable explains the changes we have observed.

We have now met two of the conditions needed to establish causality—**temporal ordering** (the causal variable must precede in time any effect) and the elimination of any other variables that might have caused the observed effect. If we can demonstrate that the independent variable and the dependent variable vary together (covariation), we will have met the third condition for demonstrating a causal relationship between them.

Covariation is usually expressed as a **correlation coefficient**. Revisit Chapter 6 for further discussion of correlation.

Time Series Analysis

Even though experiments run over a period of time, that time typically is short and we cannot know if the results obtained at the end of the experiment will still be true at some point in the future. We can address that problem with a procedure called **time series analysis**.

Time series analysis, as the name implies, is a series of observations made over time. Instead of the classic experimental O_1 and O_2 observations, time series analyses require a repeated series of observations at times O_1, O_2, O_3, O_4, and so on. Done before an experimental manipulation, these observations can check for the stability of the preexperimental condition. Done after an experimental manipulation, they can check whether an experimental result is stable over time.

Time series analyses can be diagrammed as follows:

$$O_1, O_2, O_3, O_4 \ldots X, O_5, O_6, O_7 \ldots$$

Factorial Designs

The experimental designs described so far in this chapter assess the relationship between two variables—study conditions and test scores. Analyses that examine the relationship among three or more variables are referred to as **multivariate analyses**, and experimental designs that manipulate three or more variables are referred to as **factorial designs**.

Professor Tom gets interested in a multivariate design as the next step in his research because intuition, observation, and his literature review all tell him that the relationship between studying in groups and test performance must be influenced by other factors—gender for example. Is it possible that men and women differ in their study preferences? His readings suggest that men and women may differ in their communication styles and preferences, so could it be that study groups have a greater effect on test scores for one gender than for another?

He formulates another hypothesis (two-tailed because he has no evidence to suggest that males will show a greater effect than females or vice versa), as follows:

H_2: The effect of study condition on test scores will differ between men and women.

His experimental design to test this hypothesis now requires four groups of participants, as shown in Exhibit 9.2, along with some hypothetical experimental results.

Because there are two categories of gender (male and female) and two types of study style (group and individual), the design is referred to as a 2 × 2 design. If there were three types of study style such as group, individual, and online, the design would be a 2 × 3.

Suppose the initial (bivariate) study showed that the average test scores for group study students were not statistically significant compared with the scores for other students. Professor Tom might conclude that group study sessions do not improve test scores, but suppose he runs the experiment as a 2 × 2 design and gets the results shown in Exhibit 9.2.

Exhibit 9.2 Two-by-Two, Three-Variable Factorial Design, Gender by Study Condition Showing Hypothetical Results

	Average Score on 10-Point Performance Test	
	Male	Female
Individual Study	10	5
Group Study	5	10

The pattern here suggests that male students score better under individual study conditions and that female students do better under group study conditions. In other words, there is an interaction between gender and study condition that influences test scores. The scores shown in Exhibit 9.2 mean that the average scores for the individual study and group study students would be the same. It is only when the study is run as a 2 × 2 design, with gender as an additional variable, that we can see that the group study condition does have an effect but that it varies according to gender.

We can add more variables to the experiment at a cost of ever more complex experimental design. Suppose professor Tom's review of the literature leads him to hypothesize that residence status may also have an effect on test scores. (Intuitively, commuter students may be less able than resident students to socialize with peers and to access library and academic advising services.) He proposes two hypotheses and from his reading and experimental work to date is now prepared to make them one-tailed, directional hypotheses as follows:

H_3: On-campus residence status will be associated with improvement in test scores for both male and female students.

H_4: On-campus residence status will be associated with improvement in test scores for both group study and individual study students.

How can he examine the interaction among residence status, gender, and study conditions as they relate to test scores? Basically by expanding the number of cells in the experimental design. Let's assume that Exhibit 9.2 represents the results for resident students. The same experimental design is repeated with male and female groups consisting of commuter students. Overall, this is now a $2 \times 2 \times 2$ design: two levels of residence status by two types of study condition by two categories of gender.

The design now has eight experimental groups ($2 \times 2 \times 2 = 8$). Hypothetical results from this design are shown in Exhibit 9.3.

EXHIBIT 9.3   Hypothetical Results From Two-by-Two-by-Two, Four-Variable Design

	Average Score on 10-Point Performance Test	
	Male	Female
Resident Students		
Individual Study	10	5
Group Study	5	10
Commuter Students		
Individual Study	1	6
Group Study	6	1

Looking for the effect of residence, we can see that the average test score for resident males studying individually (10) is much higher than for their commuter counterparts (1) and resident females in a study group score much higher (10) than their commuter counterparts (1). On the other hand, male commuters in a study group scored somewhat better (6) than their resident counterparts (5) and female commuter students studying individually score somewhat better (6) than their resident counterparts (5).

It appears that the above hypotheses are only partially supported. On-campus residence status is clearly associated with improved test scores only for male students studying individually and for female students studying as a group. So while professor Tom can conclude that residence status does have an effect on test scores, the effect is mediated by gender and conditions of study.

Between-Subjects and Within-Subjects Design

One problem with experimental design is the number of people that can be required to run an experiment. The $2 \times 2 \times 2$ experimental design discussed above would require 80 people if we had 10 subjects of each type in each cell. Where each person participates under only one set of conditions, such as "female, group study, and resident," the design is called a **between-subjects design**. One way to reduce the number of participants required is to in effect use them twice or expose them to more than one experimental condition, for example to both group and individual study conditions. This is called a **within-subjects design**.

One problem with within-subjects design obviously is that one experimental condition may have an effect on another condition. Participants already exposed to a group study condition, for example, may have a different reaction to an individual condition than they would have if they had not been exposed to a group study condition. A second problem is that for some conditions, a within-subjects design is simply not possible. In our example, we cannot ask males to be females or resident students to suddenly become commuter students.

Validity and Experimental Design

As you will recall from Chapter 5, it is important to develop measures that are valid—that is, that do capture the concepts that the researcher intends to capture.

In the example discussed in this chapter, there are four variables of interest— gender, residence status, test scores, and study conditions. Of these, gender and residence status can be operationalized simply by asking students to identify themselves as male or female and as resident or commuter.

More tricky are study conditions and test scores. Study condition at one level is simple; students are either in a study group or not. However, student behavior within a study group can vary widely in terms both of attendance and of participation. Conversely, students categorized as studying individually may well be studying as members of a group by virtue of their participation in online discussions. Defining them as not being in an experimental study group does not mean they are not in an informal study group. The biggest question may be test scores. We would like to be able to make some general statements about academic performance as a result of our experiments, but we have operationalized academic performance as "test scores," which may or may not capture academic performance at a more general level outside of the classes we are studying.

A further issue is that the experimental design requires a sufficient number of participants assigned randomly to each of the cells. Typically, we would be thinking of 10 to 15 participants per cell, with no fewer than 5 per cell. The design shown in Exhibit 9.3 has eight cells. At 5 to 15 participants per cell, this design would require 40 to 120 participants.

Professor Tom pours himself a cup of coffee, reviews his research, and decides that he has made a good start untangling the relationship among some of the variables that might influence his students' academic performance. Certainly, he has been able to do this with a level of certainty beyond that which a survey would have provided. As he contemplates the logistics of finding at least 40 students who can be randomly assigned to experimental groups on the basis of gender, residence status, and study conditions, he starts to wonder if perhaps a good, in-depth interview with 1 or 2 students might not give him just as much understanding of the variables that influence academic performance.

Chapter 10 addresses such qualitative techniques as interviews and focus groups.

Ethics Panel: Two Famous and Controversial Experiments

Chapter 3 discusses codes of ethical behavior for human communication research. The many different codes discussed converge on some important ideas about the treatment of research participants. These include:

- Participants must be given the opportunity to choose what shall or shall not happen to them.

- Subjects must be fully informed, comprehend the study, and volunteer to be in the study.

- Participants should not be harmed.

- The research should maximize possible benefits and minimize possible harm.

- The researcher should systematically assess the risks and benefits from the study.

- The selection of research subjects should be fair and equitable; subjects ought not to be recruited simply on the basis of accessibility or manipulability.

Stanley Milgram's Experiments on Authority

As noted in Chapter 3, in the 1960s Yale University researcher Stanley Milgram found that most of his subjects were willing to give apparently harmful electric shocks to another person simply because a scientific "authority" told them to do so. Even though the other person was apparently in pain, many, though not all, participants continued to increase the level of shock at the command of the researcher. The overall objective of these experiments was to explain the conditions of obedience to authority. The "victim" was, in fact, an actor, and the "pain" was simulated, and this information was revealed to participants at the end of the experiment.

Philip Zimbardo's Stanford Prison Experiment

In 1971 professor Philip Zimbardo randomly assigned 23 male student volunteers to two experimental groups. One group was to act as prisoners and the other group as guards in a simulated prison environment that was to run for 2 weeks. Over the next few days the "guards" became increasingly sadistic to the point that on Day 5 Zimbardo felt obliged to

(Continued)

(Continued)

discontinue the experiment. Zimbardo argues that such behaviors were born of boredom and that under such conditions good people are capable of turning bad.

See the "Recommended Reading" section of this chapter for more information about both these studies.

Based on the principles summarized above, how would you assess the ethical standards of these two controversial series of experiments?

RESEARCH IN PRACTICE

After-School Activities

Providence, Rhode Island, has the third-highest child poverty rate for cities of its size in the United States, with about 40% of its children living in poverty. As is the case in many cities across the United States, Providence is looking to after-school programs as a way of improving students' academic performance and future success by tying academic objectives to fun activities, as well as to provide enrichment programs like art and music that have been cut from the curriculum of many schools. Providence targeted middle school students for these programs, because middle school is seen as a critical transition time for student success and engagement.

Market Street Research, Inc. (MSR) conducted pre- and poststudies of middle school students and their parents in order to assess attitudes toward after-school programs, barriers to participation in those programs, and changes in those attitudes following the development of a pilot after-school program.

In terms of the prestudy, MSR conducted six focus groups and a quantitative survey of students and parents. Three of the focus groups were held with middle school students and three with middle school student parents. The focus groups were recruited through outreach in Providence middle schools. MSR obtained phone numbers of the parents and called them to get their permission for their children to participate, as well as to recruit the parents to the groups.

In terms of the quantitative research, MSR conducted 200 face-to-face interviews with middle school students during their lunch periods. MSR also obtained telephone numbers for parents from students during the lunch periods and completed 200 telephone interviews with parents of middle school students. The sample of students and parents is a convenience sample, since not all students and parents had an equal opportunity to participate in the study.

In terms of the poststudy, MSR conducted a telephone survey of 304 respondents, split almost equally between middle school students and parents. MSR obtained a list of parents of all middle school students in Providence from the survey sponsor, and respondents were randomly selected for the study. The sample is a scientific sample, with an error rate of ±5.3 percentage points.

The presurvey results clearly demonstrated that middle school students' low levels of participation in after-school programs were the direct result of concerns about safety. Even though parents and students clearly preferred that students participate in after-school programs, both groups were concerned about the safety of doing so. They were worried about getting to the programs and back home afterward on streets that they saw as unsafe, particularly in winter when the programs end after dark. They were concerned about safety in the programs, worrying that students were not adequately supervised and could bully or hurt others. As a result of safety concerns, parents had invested in computer games, preferring that their children spend their after-school hours at home on the computer rather than face potential danger elsewhere.

This information was surprising to officials in Providence. They thought safety would be a concern but did not realize it was the major barrier to participation in after-school programs. The Providence After School Alliance (PASA) used the research findings to develop a new pilot after-school program and made addressing safety concerns a focus of the design. For example, PASA has concentrated its after- school programs around a number of hubs in targeted neighborhoods, which it calls AfterZones. The hubs have been strategically placed in order to minimize the need for transportation to and from after-school programs, in order to enhance perceptions of safety among parents and students. PASA also moved from drop-in programs to programs with set enrollments and hours and communicates with parents if students don't attend the programs.

In addition to dealing with safety issues, PASA was concerned that the students who could most benefit from after-school programs would not participate because they wouldn't see the programs as "cool." PASA addressed this concern by developing a branding strategy for its after-school programs designed to appeal to middle school students. It worked with a marketing firm to develop a brand that fused urban and Latino hip-hop culture and communicated that brand through all communication materials related to the AfterZones, including PASA's Web site (see a PASA registration form at http://www.mypasa.org/failid/ESAZ_Registration_Form2.pdf).

The poststudy survey of parents and students indicated that safety had disappeared as an issue—the majority of parents and students thought the AfterZone programs were much safer than prior after-school programs. In terms of the appeal of the programs, students were asked to imagine that PASA was a person and to think about how they would respond to that person. The majority of the students perceived PASA as a person they would want to be friends with and hang out with regularly, clearly showing that the branding strategy was effective.

Contributed by Julie Pokela, PhD
President
Market Street Research, Inc.

Market Street Research, Inc., based in Northampton, Massachusetts, provides quantitative and qualitative marketing research and analysis services for health care, finance, technology, manufacturing, and education clients.

Chapter Summary

- Experimental methods range from simple observation to sophisticated factorial designs.
- Experimental methods involve exposing participants to controlled conditions such as different versions of a persuasive message or different instructions for a group project.
- Experimental methods can determine whether there is a causal relationship between variables.
- Experimental methods can isolate the effect of different variables on a variable of interest.
- Good experimental design requires random assignment of participants to experimental and to control groups.

- To determine the specific influence of a variable, sophisticated experimental designs such as the Solomon Four-Group Design may be required.

- Factorial designs examine the interaction among three or more variables.

- The basic weakness of experimental design is that experimental conditions rarely resemble real-life situations.

Recommended Reading

Dreifus, C. (2007, April 3). A conversation with Philip G. Zimbardo: Finding hope in knowing the universal capacity for evil. *New York Times*. Retrieved April 18, 2009, from http://www.nytimes.com. An interview with professor Zimbardo, in which he discusses both his Stanford Prison Experiment and Stanley Milgram's experiments. See also: Haney, C., Banks, W. C., & Zimbardo, P. G. (1973). Interpersonal dynamics in a simulated prison. *International Journal of Criminology and Penology, 1*, 69–97.

Field, A., & Hole, G. J. (2003). *How to design and report experiments.* Thousand Oaks, CA: Sage. This book takes you through the entire research process including getting ideas about research, refining your research question(s), designing the experiment, statistical analysis, and writing up results.

Milgram, S. (2009). *Obedience to authority: An experimental view.* New York: HarperCollins. This reprint of Milgram's 1974 book provides a good explanation of Milgram's obedience experiments and his findings.

Recommended Web Resources

Dr. Philip Zimbardo's Stanford Prison Experiment: http://www.prisonexp.org. Contains a slide show presentation on the Stanford Prison Experiment and a link to Dr. Zimbardo's Web site.

Dr. Thomas Blass's Stanley Milgram Web site: http://www.stanleymilgram.com. This site provides information on the social psychologist Stanley Milgram and his controversial studies.

Web Center for Social Research Methods: http://www.socialresearchmethods.net. This site provides an overview of social research methods, including experimental design.

Reference

Gilbert, J., Light, R. J., & Mosteller, F. (1975). Assessing social innovations: An empirical base for policy. In C. A. Bennett and A. A. Lumsdaine (Eds.), *Evaluation and experiment: Some critical issues in assessing social programs* (pp. 39–193). New York: Academic Press.

Student Study Site

Visit the study site at www.sagepub.com/treadwellicr for e-flashcards, web resources, and additional study materials.

10 Observation

Watching and Listening for In-Depth Understanding

You can observe a lot by watching.

Chapter Overview

Not all human communication can be summarized satisfactorily as a "6" on a 7-point scale. Intuitively, watching and talking to people sometimes feel preferable to measurement as research methods, and comprehension and understanding often seem preferable as research goals to merely being informed.

As the above quote, attributed to Yogi Berra, suggests, watching, listening, and interpretation are important approaches to understanding human communication. The main methods discussed here—interviews, focus groups, and observation—are all essentially qualitative methods, but more important they share a common goal of trying to understand and interpret human behavior. Excellent listening, interviewing, and observational skills are needed to obtain valid understandings of human communication, and excellent writing skills are needed to capture and convey to readers what your research participants have told you.

Starter Questions

- Why would I prefer observation to measurement?

- Can I make generalizations to a wider population from observational studies?

- Must I have a specific hypothesis before I design an observational study?

- How valid are the findings from observational studies?

- Can observational studies be free of bias?

Advantages and Disadvantages of Watching and Listening

Superficially, the difference between the methods discussed in this chapter and the surveys and experiments of previous chapters is the difference between qualitative and quantitative. But more important differences underlie the approaches.

Survey and experimental methods are based on the assumption that the researcher will determine the basic research question, how specific questions or instructions will be phrased and formatted, and how they will be delivered to respondents. These methods also typically assume that the individuals in a survey or an experimental group are similar. Additional individuals are added to a sample not so much to get new and different perspectives as to get a sample size from which generalizations can be made with confidence.

By contrast, the approaches in this chapter generally have the researcher taking more interest in what the participants themselves think are the important issues and in capturing their perspectives and explanations in their own language. A key assumption behind this research is the individuality and subjectivity of each participant. Adding additional people to a sample provides not "more of the same" but rather new and different data.

In further contrast, watching and listening approaches may not even begin with a specific research question or hypothesis. Instead, theories about human communication may emerge as the research data are analyzed. Often the research "spark" is a simple "What's going on here? I don't understand."

As cultural anthropologist Clifford Geertz (1973) phrased it, the difference is between an experimental science in search of law and an interpretive one in search of meaning.

Interviews and focus groups are particularly well suited to capturing people's opinions in their own words. Participant observations can capture behavior and the explanations and interpretations of that behavior and can provide a check on the relationship between people's views and their behaviors.

Because many qualitative approaches emphasize working with research participants in real-life settings, their findings are likely to have a much higher validity compared to the results of experimental research, which typically takes place in artificial settings. On the other hand, the variability of human behavior over time can put a question mark over the reliability of findings. Because the participants in an interview or a discussion are typically selected on the basis of a judgment by the researcher rather than by random selection, there can be questions about the validity of the selection and the extent to which participants represent a broader population. (See Chapter 7.) As noted below, the act of observation itself affects what we are observing and reporting, and so how to account for the researcher's own influence on the outcome of an interview or discussion becomes an issue.

Getting Started

Many varieties of watching and listening research take place under the "umbrella" of ethnography. **Ethnography** is basically the study of human social behavior or cultures. The term *ethnography* (from the Greek— *ethnos* = people; *graphein* = writing) suggests that we are observing, describing, and interpreting people's behavior. How we do that and with what level of involvement are the focus of this chapter.

In this chapter we will follow a hypothetical research project focusing on students' use of new media. We will see how thinking about communication theory and the relationship between researchers and their research participants can shape the nature of the research and the interpretation of research results.

Some principles of ethnographic research (adapted from Kirsch, 2001) are

- conduct research primarily in natural settings;
- combine direct observation with interviews;
- focus on local, subjective knowledge and categories; and
- engage directly with the community's members.

As Kirsch (2001) points out, a number of important decisions must precede ethnographic research. These include selecting informants, deciding whether to interview people individually or in groups, choosing between structured and unstructured interviews, and deciding how to analyze the data from the research.

Let's assume we have an interest in student use of new media such as social networking sites, online movie sites, collaborative media such as wikis, and such processes as blogging, texting, and tweeting. We are interested in how and why such media are used, what explains their adoption, and how students see them as differing from conventional media such as broadcast television, newspapers, and widescreen cinema.

Our research has two possible starting points. First, we could develop theoretically informed hypotheses based on, for example, the concept of parasocial interaction or of uses and gratifications theory. Parasocial interaction theory proposes that a bond of familiarity or intimacy develops between real or fictitious media characters and their readers, viewers, or listeners, who come to believe that media characters have a special relationship with them (Horton & Wohl, 1956). Uses and gratifications theory proposes that media audiences, rather than being passive consumers, actively use media content to help them achieve specific goals (Blumler & Katz, 1974). Either or both theories could help us develop specific ideas about new media use that we could test using interviews, focus groups, or observations of students using new media.

On the other hand, some of these media seem to have important new characteristics such as mobility and interactivity that we do not see in traditional media. Perhaps we would be better to listen, observe, and be open to the possibility of new theories about communication technology and its uses rather than having our research framed, and perhaps constrained, by old theoretical models. In this case we would do research with a view to developing new ideas rather than testing existing ones. This will be the bias running through the examples in this chapter.

Basic Researcher-Participant Relationships

One basic decision is the level at which we engage with the people whose communication behavior we seek to understand. Too remote and we may not discern important details and subtleties; too close and we may develop biases toward our participants that will affect our observation and reporting, or possibly even the answers we get or the behavior we are observing.

As physicists remind us, the act of observation itself affects what we are observing and reporting. We can strive for distance and an impartial relationship with our informants, or we can decide that close personal involvement will produce more accurate accounts of our informants' lives, framed though they may be by our own subjectivity.

Gold (1958) described four "classic" relationships between researcher and informants as follows:

- Complete observer
- Observer as participant
- Participant as observer
- Complete participant

The complete observer has no interaction with informants; they are not aware that they are being observed. This does not mean that the researcher has no contact with informants.

The observer-as-participant role is, according to Gold (1958), used in one-visit scenarios. The researcher has to decide what to observe and what questions to ask, now that he or she is interacting with informants. Because the level of involvement is low, potentially working with a lot of people in a short time, researchers face the risk of inadequate understanding or of misunderstanding their informants' answers.

The participant-as-observer role occurs typically in studies of communities, where the researcher may spend some time. Over time, mutual trust may develop between researcher and research participants, and within this mutual trust lie potential problems. For example, as the relationship approaches friendship, one or both parties may be reluctant to ask or answer questions in a way that will hurt the friendship. Obviously this may bias both the observations the researcher is trying to make and the answers he or she receives to questions.

In the complete-participant role, the researcher participates so closely in informants' lives that his or her research role may be unknown to them. Researchers are in effect masquerading—pretending to be other than what they really are. They adopt the role of cocktail waitress or college student (see the ethics panel in this chapter) to gain insight into such lifestyles but remain researchers at heart. The potential problem with this role is that researchers may become so involved in their participant role that they cannot function well as observers, or vice versa.

If we are to understand the role of new media in the student lifestyle, we have some choices to make about our level of involvement with students. As complete observers, we might try to unobtrusively observe in some campus setting how and why cell phones and laptops are used. As observers-as-participants, we might do "one-time" interviews with students. In the participant-as-observer role, we might try to get invited to a dorm room movie viewing or join an online social networking group and participate and report on our findings. In the complete-participant role, we might join and participate in, for example, the online community "Second Life," with other members of the community being unaware of our primary role as researchers.

The precise balance between participant and observer is a function of how best to study the communication phenomena you are interested in, how each of the above roles might shape the nature of the data you gather and your reporting, and ethical standards related to your relationship(s) with research participants.

The Terminology of Research

As noted in Chapter 1, participants in research projects can attract a variety of labels, such as *subject, participant, informant, respondent,* or *interviewee.* Some of these words have a specific meaning in research.

For example informants are people selected because they can talk about others as well as themselves. Respondents on the other hand are basically defined as speaking for themselves. Interviewees are, self-apparently, people who are interviewed; they may be informants or respondents. All the above are obviously part of a research project and therefore also may be known as participants. The term subject is less likely to be used, as that term is associated primarily with experimental method.

The terminology can suggest the researcher's basic orientation toward research. "Subjects" implicitly are subject to direction in some way by the researcher; "participants" on the other hand are part of a research project and at some level may shape its progress and outcome. In this chapter the terms are used somewhat interchangeably to remind you of the diversity of terms in use.

Interviews

Interviews consist of a series of questions designed to elicit information the researcher is interested in. At one extreme are specific questions designed to test a research hypothesis. In this first case, the researcher may be able to use very specific questions with limited response options such as "yes" and "no." At the other extreme are questions based on a researcher's assumption that he or she does not necessarily know what is going on and therefore must take an open-minded, exploratory approach. This case calls for generic, open-ended questions, starting perhaps with something like "I'm new to this; can you explain to me what's going on here?"

Effective interviews require practice, preparation, and attention to each of the following issues.

SETTING

Just as a laboratory setting may influence the results of experimental research, so too can the interview setting affect the nature of the interview. You may have interviewees come to your workplace, or you may need to conduct the interview at your interviewees' workplace. Each setting has advantages and disadvantages. Workplace interviews will require the permission of management, and the workplace setting may constrain what employees feel they can tell you. If you are trying to understand the role of "texting" in a student's social life, you may have little choice but to follow students around as they do this. Interviews in your office or room may liberate interviewees from any feelings of peer pressure but may have them feeling pressured to provide answers they think you, the researcher, are looking for.

SENSITIVITIES

Consider religious, cultural, and technology sensitivities when arranging interviews. For cross-cultural interviews in particular, dress, language, body language, vocabulary, and status and gender relations all need to be considered. For example, first-name relationships may be inappropriate. Intermediaries may be needed to set up interviews or to conduct them on your behalf. Xerri (2005) for example reports how he used his sisters to set up interviews with women who would have otherwise been reluctant to be interviewed by a male.

Audio- or video-recording interviews can save you from taking notes and allow you to focus on the interview. However, people may "clam up" in front of a camera, may be nervous about what will happen to the recorded interview, or perhaps, most important, may decide to "talk for the record." In other words what they want recorded may differ from what they might have told you "off the record." You have an ethical obligation to disclose that the interview will be recorded, if that is your plan, and you may have to negotiate with informants whether recording will happen or not.

STRUCTURE

Fully structured interviews mean that the interviewer becomes not much more than a recording device. In this type of interview the researcher has determined what questions are important, their format, and the order in which they will be asked. The interviewer merely records the answers provided.

Semistructured interviews dictate the broad questions to be asked, but the interviewer has discretion in how the questions will be asked. The interviewer may even drop some questions to allow respondents to respond fully to more important (to the researcher) questions. The interviewer might also ask additional questions, with the aim of eliciting full and responsive answers.

Unstructured interviews come from the researcher's decision that he or she needs to understand communication phenomena in the informants' own terms. In this situation, interviews will at least begin with very broad, open-ended "Tell me about . . ." questions, although as the interview progresses it is likely that the questions: will become more focused and tuned to the researcher's basic interests.

Which structure we choose for our research project will be determined largely by our theoretical starting point. Specific hypotheses we might have developed based on our reading of, say, uses and gratifications theory will probably generate very specific questions, perhaps even scaled or ranking questions that we will want answered. If our research objective is to obtain new insights, then we will prefer unstructured interviews that maximize the opportunity for students to talk and free-associate about texting, online movies, and why they "tweet" their friends but not their parents.

SEQUENCE

Sequence refers to the order in which questions occur. You will recall from Chapter 8 that often a "funnel" metaphor is used to describe question order. In a "funnel format" questions move from broad and general to narrow and specific. An "inverted funnel" sequence means that the interview starts with specific questions and moves to broader questions.

For example, a funnel sequence of questions on social networking technology might begin with "How would you describe the relationships you have with your Facebook friends?" An inverted funnel sequence might begin with "How many times a day do you text other people in your classes?" In the first case, the informant's answers provide the interviewer with a launch pad for further questions exploring social networking. In the latter case, informants are presented with a specific question that should be easy to answer and as a result should give them a level of confidence about answering further questions.

As with surveys, sensitive personal questions that interviewees might be reluctant to answer may be "sandwiched" in the middle of a series of questions with which they will have a comfort level. Placing such questions in the middle implies that the sensitive questions are "just questions," and the interview moves on. The technique is useful where personal lifestyle questions related to sexual behavior, drug use, and the like need to be asked.

Most interviews begin with personal questions such as name, class year, or job title that most informants can easily handle. Note though that seemingly harmless questions such as age and religion or even names may be intensely personal and emotional to interviewees and not a good starting point for an interview. If you sense that these questions might affect the substantive aspects of the interview, it may be wise to consider whether they are necessary.

QUESTION TYPES

You need different types of questions to fully elicit, probe, and interpret informants' understandings of phenomena you are interested in. Anthropology professor James Spradley (1979) developed a series of question categories that can be summarized as follows:

Descriptive questions ask informants to describe the phenomena. "Mini-tour" questions are one type of descriptive question that asks for an overview of everyday occurrences, for example, "How do you use your social networking sites in a typical day?'

Structural questions explore the relationships among the terms informants use. For example, "Would you describe text messaging as part of your social networking?"

Contrast questions help the researcher understand similarities, differences, and relative importance of informants' concepts. For example, "You talk about watching online movies and watching online movies with your friends. Could you explain the difference between 'watching online movies' and 'watching online movies with your friends'?" Another type of contrast question is a rating or **ranking question**. For example, "You talk about watching online movies, watching online movies with your friends, and relaxing with online movies. Which two of these three are most similar? Which one differs most from the other two? Why?"

If you use all the above question types you can have some confidence that you have thoroughly explored your interviewees' view of their worlds and that you have a true in-depth understanding of them.

Focus Groups

Another way of eliciting opinions is to bring small groups of people together in a focus group to discuss a topic of interest. Focus groups typically consist of 6 to 12 people in a discussion setting led by a moderator. Focus groups can be used to explore such pragmatic issues as how people interpret and respond to political campaign messages or to help researchers operationalize theoretical constructs and hypotheses. They are often used before surveys to pretest survey questions and may be used after surveys to help researchers understand the survey answers.

Focus groups are based on the assumption that the ideas that emerge from several people discussing a topic can provide greater quality, diversity, and insight than the ideas generated by the same people interviewed separately as individuals.

For our new media research, we might consider using focus groups for several reasons. In this fast-moving field, we may pick up new "buzzwords" and terminology that we need to understand. The group should in principle generate new ideas that we have not thought of, and its discussions should also show us areas of agreement and disagreement about new media and their use.

Focus group moderators need good interview and discussion skills to encourage reticent members to speak and to control the more verbose members. They also need to take a middle ground between allowing group members free expression and limiting discussion to the topic at hand. To keep the discussion on track and to maintain order, it is a good idea to prepare in advance a discussion guide that lists key questions and the question order.

Obviously, we would need to select appropriate group members. Often, they will consist of one demographic group (students, in our case) but be recruited to maximize the diversity of opinion within that group (for example "high tech" innovators and those who have yet to join a social networking site).

Typically, the group's discussion will be audio- or video-recorded to provide transcripts for subsequent analysis.

Successful focus groups have clear objectives, good recruiting so that there is an appropriate group composition, preparation of both questions and facilities, and a moderator who listens and maintains a free-flowing discussion focused on the topic (Axelrod, 1975).

Unobtrusive Watching

As a conscientious, skeptical researcher, one question at least will occur to you as you think about what people are telling you. "Does what they are telling me match their behavior?" There is no necessary connection between the two. For example, many people express the belief that democracy is important but do not vote. Others may say good health is important but do nothing about diet and exercise. Is there a way to get a direct check on people's behavior and relate it to what they may be telling you? The answer is yes. Participant observation, discussed above, is one way, but our presence as observers may affect the observation.

Unobtrusive measures, on the other hand, document people's behavior without their being aware of it. Unobtrusive measures provide a check on what informants may have told you about their behavior. This can be important with respect to personal health and safety behaviors where there may be a gap between word and action. Suppose all of our respondents assure us that they would never "text" while driving. Take a look at campus traffic to see the extent to which that is happening. Unobtrusive measures typically do not provide a direct check on any one individual's self-report. They should, however, provide a general sense of whether the self-reports you get of people's behaviors are credible.

Other Methods

There are many research methods based on observation and listening. For example, **conversation analysis** is a method for analyzing how people negotiate understanding and the rules for understanding. For example, if a question is posed during a conversation or discussion, what are the rules of conversation that determine whether it gets an answer or not? If the question does not get an answer from somebody, how does the conversation then change? As conversation analysis is, in practice, an analysis of transcripts of recorded conversations, it is described in Chapter 11, "Content Analysis."

Interviews, focus groups, observation, and surveys may all be used to develop a case study. A **case study** can be summarized as bringing together all relevant information to write an informative story that will help readers learn how other organizations or individuals managed a project or responded to a problem or crisis. The purpose of the story is usually to provide a history and/or an analysis that will help readers learn how (or how not) to manage a similar situation in their own organization.

Making Sense of Qualitative Data

When you gather data on people's communication behavior by watching and listening you end up with words rather than numbers. The question then becomes how to establish a sense of order and interpret what may be hours of audio or video recordings or page after page of notes, transcripts, or observations.

The basis of almost all analyses of qualitative data is **categorization**—that is, identifying each piece of data as belonging to a particular category predetermined by the researcher or generated from the data themselves. By analyzing these categories and the relationships between categories, researchers are able to see patterns of behavior or thinking that shed light on their research interests. Fundamentally, there are three ways of categorizing qualitative information. The first is to assign items to specific unchanging, preassigned categories. The second is to start with theoretically informed categories that may change as new data come in. The third is to start with no preconceived categories and to allow categories and theories to emerge as data analysis progresses.

FIXED CODING

Coding typically means assigning units of information to a category and then counting the frequency with which these different units occur. Suppose, for example, we are questioning students in an attempt to understand their use of online movie sites. With fixed coding, we might, for example, hypothesize from our review of the uses and gratifications literature that there will be four important factors that explain use of online movies—convenience, relaxation, escape, and the opportunity for social viewing with friends. We would then develop a simple record sheet that records the number of times we find each of these mentioned in our data. Such a coding sheet would look like Exhibit 10.1.

Exhibit 10.1   Sample Analysis Sheet for Qualitative Data: Predetermined Categories

Understanding Student Use of Online Movie Sites—I		
Categories Derived From Theory	**Number of Mentions**	**Reasons Item Is Considered Important**
Convenience		
Relaxation		
Escape		
Social Viewing		

FLEXIBLE CODING

A problem with such fixed coding is that it provides no room for the inevitable "other" categories that will emerge as we read through our interview or focus group transcripts. Furthermore, one of the reasons we listen to people in the first place is to gain new insights. For this reason, we need flexible coding that allows for new categories to emerge rather than forcing every piece of information into our four preconceived categories and perhaps one additional and overgeneral "other" category.

For example, as we read though people's answers about online movies, it appears that there are two broad reasons for watching online movies—convenience and the opportunity to socialize. As we examine the explanations we have been given about convenience, we see that several different notions of "convenience" emerge—geographic (I can stay home and watch movies), scheduling (I can watch movies anytime), portability (I can watch on my cell phone or laptop), and cost (I am not inconvenienced by needing money to go to the movies). All of these ideas seem to fit under the umbrella of "convenience," so we decide to set up four subcategories, as shown in Exhibit 10.2. Similarly, "socializing" turns out to have three components. Two are perhaps predictable: "relaxation" and "social viewing." On the other hand, it appears that online movie time is also a social learning opportunity in the sense that students learn about careers and career behavior in criminal justice, health care, business, and entertainment and may even change courses or majors on the basis of what they learn from the movies. This is clearly a new concept, and it would be reasonable to set up a new "social learning" category. For the moment, it appears to be seen as part of socializing, but as our analysis progresses, we may decide that this is a major new concept related to career development and that we will be able to rationalize setting it up as a third major category, alongside "convenience" and "socializing."

Many qualitative analyses of human behavior are grounded in an approach developed by Glaser and Strauss (1967) that considers theory as "grounded in data." That is to say rather than using data to test a theory or hypothesis, the theory itself emerges as the data analysis proceeds.

A basic of the **grounded theory** approach is the "constant comparative method." In this technique, we would look at statements and ideas that emerge from our observations and assign each statement to a category. The constant comparative method consists of testing each new statement or idea against the categories we have developed and reworking categories as necessary as our data analysis proceeds. We in effect did this in previous paragraphs when we analyzed the data students provided on their use of online movies and developed the summary table shown as Exhibit 10.2.

EXHIBIT 10.2   **Sample Analysis Sheet for Qualitative Data: Categories Emerge From Data**

Understanding Student Use of Online Movie Sites—II			
Categories Emerge From Data			**Working Notes**
Convenience	geographic		1. Which of these are most used as a reason to watch online movies?
	scheduling		
	portability of medium		2. Is there a difference between weeknight relaxation and weekend relaxation?
	cost	money time	3. Am I hearing different words for the same concept?
Socializing	relaxation	food social planning	4. Are residents and commuters telling me the same thing?
	social viewing	topicality academic work networking	5. Note: Need to be able to write an account that student would recognize as authentic.
	social learning	careers work behaviors	

Drowning in Data? A NUD*IST to the Rescue

Just as there are statistical programs to handle numeric data, there are computer programs that handle qualitative data—for example, NUD*IST. NUD*IST stands for Non-numerical, Unstructured Data: Indexing, Searching, and Theorizing. This program was developed to search for words and phrases and to pull together items that you have flagged as belonging to a particular category. NUD*IST and its more contemporary equivalents allow new coding categories to be created as new ideas emerge from your data. The end result is a "tree structure" showing how concepts relate and how they each feed in to the three or four major dimensions that typically will be the outcome of the study.

Ethics Panel: A Professor Becomes a Student

Nathan, R. (2005). *My freshman year: What a professor learned by becoming a student.* Ithaca, NY: Cornell University Press.

"Rebekah Nathan," a "50-something" professor of anthropology, decided that she needed to better understand her students and their lives. She took a sabbatical leave and, on the basis of her high school transcript, enrolled as a freshman student at her own university for a semester. She moved into a dorm, took on a full course load, ate in the student cafeteria, joined student clubs, played volleyball and tag football, and, of course, attended class and completed (most) assignments.

To understand student life, she drew on interviews and conversations with classmates and observations and interactions with professors and university staff. The issues she explored included friendships, race relations and social life, classroom participation, eating and sleeping in class, plagiarism, scheduling conflicts, dropping readings and assignments, holding down a job, not holding down food, and relations with faculty.

Nathan did not volunteer that she was a professor, nor did she lie if anyone specifically asked her. In day-to-day interactions, she allowed students to assume she was one of them. When conducting formal interviews she identified herself as a researcher, explained her study, and obtained written permission to publish informants' words. She did reveal her identity to some students with whom she developed a close relationship.

Nathan has been on one hand criticized for enhancing her own academic career at the expense of students and on the other hand commended for following approved procedures such as obtaining informed consent and clearing her study through her university's institutional review board.

Academic opinion on the need for such "undercover" studies is mixed.

Review Chapter 3, "Ethics: Your Responsibilities as a Researcher," and answer the following questions.

1. Why would "Ms. Nathan" not want to be open about her status, occupation, and reason for being on campus?

2. Do you feel that students involved in this study were exploited in any way?

3. Do any aspects of this study strike you as ethically suspect? Why or why not?

4. Nathan's research was approved by the campus institutional review board. Do you agree or disagree with the board's decision? Why?

Resources:

American Psychological Association Ethical Principles of Psychologists and Code of Conduct: http://www.apa.org/ethics/

National Communication Association Code of Professional Ethics for the Communication Scholar/Teacher: http://www.natcom.org/index.asp?bid=13592

RESEARCH IN PRACTICE

Promoting Clean Energy

I estimate that I must have stared through the one-way mirror at a focus group over 500 times during my 30-year career in advertising. Despite the familiarity of the routine, I'm never bored. In fact, I never fail to learn something surprising!

An example of this occurred in 2003, when some clients I was consulting for, the Clean Energy States Alliance and SmartPower, needed more insight on a perplexing situation:

Clean Energy suppliers had gone into a number of markets to try to get consumers to switch to a renewable energy company as their electric power supplier, for a surcharge of $6 to $10 a month on their electric bill. An encouraging number of consumers had told them: "I love the idea of clean energy, and I'd pay a little more each month to support it." Yet, when they'd go into a market, despite running a lot of advertising showing belching smokestacks and coughing children, very few people signed up. We needed to identify the disconnect between what consumers told us and what they did. We had hired a small, bright New York City agency, Gardner Nelson, to execute a campaign for us. The agency urged us to conduct some focus groups.

So we recruited six groups in Connecticut and Massachusetts from among consumers, business, and "opinion leaders." Operating on the theory that "if you want to find out how people feel about something, take it away from them," we gave each participant a pencil and paper and asked them to imagine fossil fuels on Earth have died. Their task was to write an obituary.

What we found was surprisingly counterintuitive: People were far less critical of fossil fuels than we had imagined. While they recognized the problems of pollution, they saw fossil fuel as a necessary evil because it can be relied on to power our world.

Here's a sample excerpt:

Fossil fuel died after a long, slow illness called greed.... Currently, the world is adjusting ... to solar and wind mill sources. These are several kinks to be worked out and roadblocks to conquer. Will we ever be warm again? Miss you fossil fuel.

–Massachusetts Opinion Leader

Surprisingly, in every obituary, fossil fuels had died because we used them up. Not a single respondent said fossil fuels died because they were bad or because people figured out better energy solutions.

We also discovered that our respondents were unexpectedly knowledgeable about clean energy. They knew how it was made *but* didn't see it as being up to the job. It was seen as "eccentric," with "kinks to work out."

One way to encourage people to react at an emotional level is to take away their rational tool kit: their vocabulary. So we next asked respondents to imagine that all the energy used to power their world is clean, gave them paper and colored pencils, and had them draw what a "clean energy world" would look like and date the pictures.

(Continued)

(Continued)

In almost all the drawings, clean energy was seen as "weak" and not capable of powering our world. Everyone drew multiple types of clean energy: solar panels, hydro, even sail-powered cars! The dates on the drawings were revealing: Their worlds were either in the past (1700s) or decades away (2050, 3000).

We also learned that people thought of clean energy as science fiction. The crux of the respondent attitude: Clean energy wasn't seen as ready. Respondents believed clean energy would require huge sacrifices. They didn't think it was strong enough or could be harnessed in sufficient quantity to replace fossil fuels.

Another important theme to emerge from the discussion was self-sufficiency. It was clearly present in probing what would cause our respondents to "act." And dependency on foreign sources was an underlying fear.

Our conclusions based on these focus groups were that our campaign needed to be built around two key ideas: (1) Clean energy is more real and more powerful than we think, and (2) it can help make us self-sufficient for our energy needs.

The agency developed a creative brief based on this research that was quite different from the previous "good for the environment" efforts. Self-sufficiency was developed in the longer copy units. But we also devised a series of single-minded 15-second TV spots to express the first idea. Each started out with a surprising statistic: "America now makes enough clean energy to power every home in 11 states," "America now makes enough clean energy to power every factory in New York, New Jersey, Pennsylvania, Massachusetts, Connecticut, and Rhode Island." Each ended with the line: "It's real. It's here. It's working." Our logo then appeared with the words: "Clean Energy. Let's Make More."

Without the innovative design of our focus groups, we never would have arrived at that campaign. And by the way, today, that advertising is real, it's here, and it's working!

Contributed by Richard Earle

Richard Earle had a 30-year advertising career at six New York agencies, the most recent being Saatchi & Saatchi, where he was the executive vice president and group creative director. During this time he supervised major campaigns for Procter & Gamble and Johnson & Johnson and worked on over 50 national brands. Currently he consults on branding and social marketing as a senior associate at The Regis Group in Leesburg, Virginia, and is an instructor at the Harvard School of Public Health. He is the author of The Art of Cause Marketing: How to Use Advertising to Change Personal Behavior and Public Policy *(McGraw-Hill, 2002).*

Chapter Summary

- Qualitative methods are generally based on the assumption that people are idiosyncratic and have unique and subjective views of their world. The inability to generalize to a larger population is not therefore regarded as a problem.

- Qualitative research may begin with theoretically derived hypotheses, or it may develop theories from research data as they are analyzed.

- Qualitative methods are generally preferred over surveys and experiments because they are better able to elicit people's views in their own words.

- Qualitative research may be structured and focus on questions predetermined by the researcher or be open-ended and elicit ideas that informants volunteer.

- The results of qualitative research are typically written up in the participants' own language.

- Participant or unobtrusive observation provides a check on whether people's words match their behavior.

Recommended Reading

Denzin, N. K., & Lincoln, Y. S. (Eds.). (2005). *The SAGE handbook of qualitative research* (3rd ed.). Thousand Oaks, CA: Sage. A summary volume on qualitative research.

Krueger, R. A., & Casey, M. A. (2000). *Focus groups: A practical guide for applied research* (3rd ed.). Thousand Oaks, CA: Sage. Covers all the practicalities of planning and running a focus group and analyzing and reporting results.

Lindlof, T. R., & Taylor, B. C. (2002). *Qualitative communication research methods* (2nd ed.). Thousand Oaks, CA: Sage. Shows with examples how qualitative studies are designed, conducted, and written.

Morgan, G., & Smircich, L. (1980). The case for qualitative research. *Academy of Management Review, 5*(4), 491–502. The authors argue that qualitative research is a way of thinking rather than a set of specific techniques. Its appropriateness depends on the type of phenomena to be studied.

Spradley, J. P. (1979). *The ethnographic interview.* New York: Holt, Rinehart & Winston. Describes 12 steps for developing an ethnographic study. For a sense of how "readable" such studies can be see also Spradley's *You Owe Yourself a Drunk: Adaptive Strategies of Urban Nomads* (1970), *The Cocktail Waitress: Woman's Work in a Man's World* (1975, with Mann, B. J.), and *Participant Observation* (1980).

Recommended Web Resources

Forum: Qualitative Social Research: http://www.qualitative-research.net/index.php/fqs. An open-access online academic journal of qualitative social research.

Qualitative Research Consultants Association: http://www.qrca.org. Links to qualitative research practitioners.

University of Surrey, social research update: http://sru.soc.surrey.ac.uk/. A resource for interviewing, focus groups, study design and analysis, and more.

References

Axelrod, M. D. (1975). Ten essentials for good qualitative research. *Marketing News, 8*(17), 10–11.

Blumler, J. G., & Katz, E. (1974). *The uses of mass communications: Current perspectives on gratifications research.* Beverly Hills, CA: Sage.

Geertz, C. (1973). *The interpretation of cultures.* New York: Basic Books.

Glaser, B. G., & Strauss, A. L. (1967). *The discovery of grounded theory: Strategies for qualitative research.* Chicago: Aldine.

Gold, R. L. (1958). Roles in sociological field observations. *Social Forces, 36*(3), 217–223.

Horton, D. R., & Wohl, R. (1956). Mass communication and para-social interaction: Observations on intimacy at a distance. *Psychiatry, 19*(3), 215–229.

Kirsch, S. (2001). Ethnographic methods: concepts and field techniques. In R. A. Krueger, M. A. Casey, J. Donner, S. Kirsch, & J. N. Maack (Eds.), *Social development paper #36. Social analysis. Selected tools and techniques*. Washington, DC: The World Bank. Retrieved July 4, 2008 from www.worldbank.org/reference

Spradley, J. P. (1979). *The ethnographic interview.* New York: Holt, Rinehart & Winston.

Xerri, R. C. (2005). *Gozitan crossings: The impact of migration and return migration on an island community.* Qala, Malta: A&M Printing Ltd.

Student Study Site

Visit the study site at www.sagepub.com/treadwellicr for e-flashcards, web resources, and additional study materials.

11

Content Analysis

Understanding Text and Image

Content analysis means
Counting what can be seen.
Use counting and categories
For basic analyses
And insights on speech, text, or screen.

Chapter Overview

Media for content analysis can include any recorded communication from papyrus to podcast, published or unpublished. Approaches to studying media content are almost as diverse as the approaches to studying human communication behavior. In a general sense, any study of media content is a content analysis, but in communication research the term usually implies a quantitative approach and a series of specific steps aimed at ensuring systematic sampling, coding, and counting of media content.

This chapter provides an overview of content analysis procedures. We will also visit other approaches, primarily qualitative. These include rhetorical analyses—the analysis of argumentation and persuasion—and semiotics—the study of interpretation and meaning.

Starter Questions

- Why would I want to analyze text?
- How does analyzing texts differ from analyzing human behavior?
- Why would I prefer analyzing texts to analyzing human behavior?
- Can textual studies be done with any level of accuracy?
- Can textual studies be free of bias?

Advantages and Disadvantages of Content Analysis

In the context of communication research, content analysis is a quantitative, systematic, and objective technique for describing the manifest content of communications (Berelson, 1952).

- *Quantitative* means that we count occurrences of whatever we are interested in.

- *Systematic* means that we count all relevant aspects of the sample. We cannot arbitrarily pick what aspects get analyzed.

- *Objective* means that we select units for analysis and categorize them using clearly defined criteria.

- **Manifest** means that we count what is tangible and observable. For example, we cannot count patriotism in consumer advertising because patriotism is ultimately an abstract or **latent** (hidden) notion. What we can count is the frequency with which the word *patriotism* occurs, the frequency with which a national flag appears, or perhaps the number of minutes music defined as patriotic is played in the background.

Some researchers argue that latent content can be studied. The difference between the perspectives of latent content and manifest content is essentially the difference between trying to measure a concept (such as patriotism) and measuring the variables that operationalize that concept (such as number of occurrences of the national flag). You can revisit this discussion in Chapter 5, "Measurement."

By systematically sampling, coding, and counting media content it is possible to make discoveries related to almost any form of content. What adjectives distinguish left-wing politicians' descriptions of global warming from those of right-wing politicians? How do rock 'n' roll lyrics from the 1950s differ from millennium rock in their treatment of love? Are minorities depicted in advertising over- or underrepresented with respect to their numbers in the population? Which political candidates do the bumper stickers on campus vehicles mostly endorse? How does the language differ when people in an intimate relationship communicate by e-mail rather than phone?

It is possible to analyze the content of almost any recorded medium—press, radio, or Web content but also billboards, T-shirts, license plates, lawn signs, photographs, love letters, or "tweets."

A strength of content analysis is its emphasis on the systematic coding, counting, and analysis of content. The procedures of any content analysis study should be explicit, precise, and replicable so that other researchers can verify the results of the research. Usually, the raw material of content analysis is readily accessible, be it presidential speeches, advertisements for liquid soap or lingerie, BBC foreign news coverage, comic strips, or *New York Times* editorials. Content analysis can be done anytime at low cost, and human-research approvals are not required.

Content analysis addresses only questions of content. For example, "Have representations of the military on television changed since 9/11?" is an appropriate question for content analysis. "Are media representations of the military causing more people to enlist?" is not a question content analysis can answer (though it may contribute to an answer).

A limitation of the method is that it really only has application if used for comparisons. A "one-shot" survey indicating that 72% of voters would vote for candidate X if the election were held tomorrow produces a finding that is useful to a campaign manager. However, a content analysis indicating that candidate X used the term *patriotism* 17 times in the course of a campaign is not inherently useful information unless it has some point of reference. What we are interested in as content analysts are questions such as "How does the frequency of the term *patriotism* in candidate X's speeches compare with that of candidate Y?" "How does the use of the term *patriotism* compare with the candidate's use of the term *environment*?" or "Has the frequency of use of the term *patriotism* increased or decreased over the course of the campaign?"

A further issue, if not a weakness, is the issue of interpretation. Traditional perspectives on content analysis insist on counting manifest or observable content. As in the example above, we might count the frequency with which the word *patriotism* appears in a politician's speeches over time and detect an overall increase. However, that does not necessarily entitle us to assume that the politician has become more patriotic over time; it entitles us to assume only that his use of the term has become more frequent.

An Exercise in Content Analysis

Generally, because content analysts seek to make generalizations from communication content, they take a scientific approach. Systematic sampling, clear definition of units, and unambiguous categories are important aspects of any content analysis study.

A content analysis study typically has seven parts:

- Develop a hypothesis or research question about communication content.

- Define the content to be analyzed.

- Sample the **universe** of content. "Universe" has the same meaning for media content as "population" does for people.

- Select units for coding.

- Develop a coding scheme.

- Assign each occurrence of a unit in the sample to a code in the coding scheme.

- Count occurrences of the coded units and report their frequencies.

Let's look at a brief example using the above steps.

For our example, we come full-circle back to the pharmaceutical advertising discussed in Chapter 1. There are many content analysis studies of pharmaceutical advertising, but many related questions can be asked. For example, do newspaper medical columns even-handedly report the failures as well as the successes of new pharmaceuticals? What pharmaceutical products feature most prominently in daytime television soap operas? What is the relative frequency with which we see prescription pharmaceuticals and over-the-counter pharmaceuticals in the news coverage of major metropolitan newspapers?

Let's go down a relatively untraveled road—the representations of pharmaceuticals and their use in contemporary comic strips. Our rationale for this study is that comic strips may be promoting an image of pharmaceutical use to comic strip readers, just as much as pharmaceutical advertising promotes this product category to consumers. We decide to expand the study to include alcohol and tobacco because our overall interest is in how comic strips portray substance use and because we want a point of reference against which to assess our findings about pharmaceuticals. Our hypothesis is that the two types of substance will differ in frequency of occurrence. This is a two-tailed hypothesis because we have no evidence that one type of substance is more likely to appear than another.

HYPOTHESIS

H_1: Alcohol and tobacco products will differ from pharmaceuticals in frequency of occurrence in comic strips.

DEFINE THE UNIVERSE OF CONTENT TO BE ANALYZED

The content to be analyzed is comic strips. We decide that our interest is in current content and opt for the last full calendar year because we want to capture a full year of seasons and events that may be associated with drinking, smoking, and pharmaceuticals.

We could look at all comics sold over the counter in book form, or we could go to a site such as www.comics.com, which boasts of having over 90 comic strips. We could look at newspaper editorial cartoons or animated television cartoons, but we decide on a universe of comic strip pages from the Sunday edition of our major local newspaper because the Sunday comics reach a large national audience and are therefore important because of their potential impact on a wide variety of readers. We decide that because so many strips are syndicated our major local paper will represent most other major papers nationally in terms of comic strip content.

We narrow the universe by deciding that we will sample only comic strips that regularly show human characters. We know from casual observation that cartoon animals might smoke, drink, and pop pills, but we decide that our theoretical interest is in humans. That gets our universe down to, say, 20 weekly strips or a total of 1,040 over the course of a year.

SAMPLE THE UNIVERSE OF CONTENT

We now have a sampling frame, the list from which specific samples will be drawn, of 1,040 comic strips.

We decide to systematically sample the first Sunday of every month. If we randomly sampled the year we might sample out some important seasons altogether. We want to capture all the seasons, so systematic monthly sampling is appropriate. That gives us a manageable sample of $12 \times 20 = 240$ comic strips.

SELECT UNITS FOR CODING

Having selected a universe from which to sample and developed a sampling frame, we are now faced with the question of what units we will sample. Krippendorf (1980) identifies five possible types of units:

- Physical units occupy an observable space in print media or time in audiovisual media. An example in our case would be an entire comic strip or the individual panels within each strip.

- Syntactical units are units of language, such as words or sentences.

- Referential units refer to a person or an event, for example a specific cartoon character or an event such as drinking coffee.

- Propositional units are structures such as stories or dramas.

- Thematic units are broad topics within a structure, such as relationships with the boss or peers.

As we progress from physical units to thematic units we face an increasing difficulty making decisions about them. Physical units such as photographs are apparent whereas themes such as "environment" or concepts such as "ethos" may appear only in the eye of the researcher.

Because we are looking at substance use in the broad setting of people's lives, we decide to examine entire comic strips rather than each panel within them for instances of substance use. Because we are analyzing comic strips, we have a further decision to make. Should we look at visual content only, words only, or both? We decide that portrayal of substance use implies visual portrayal and that therefore we will analyze the visual content. As a further analysis, though, we will also analyze the strips for wording, as a check on what we are seeing as visuals.

DEVELOP A CODING SCHEME

Because our interest focuses on the frequency with which substances are referenced in comic strips, we develop a coding scheme as shown in column 1 of Exhibit 11.1. The coding sheet will record the number of times we find a mention or depiction of the substances we are interested in.

EXHIBIT 11.1   **Sample Coding Sheet for Content Analysis**

| Substance | Frequencies of Appearance | | | | |
| | User | | | Setting | |
	Overall	Male	Female	Work	Home
Tobacco					
Visuals					
Words					
Alcohol					
Visuals					
Words					
Prescription Drugs					
Visuals					
Words					
Over-the-Counter Drugs					
Visuals					
Words					
Illegal Drugs					
Visuals					
Words					
Generic Reference to Drugs					
Visuals					
Words					

A simple study might compare the relative frequency of appearance of different drug categories, as shown in column 2. A more complex study might look at the relative frequency by, for example, the type of person using the substance or the setting (columns 3 through 6). Ground rules for content analysis are that categories must not overlap, and no unit can be coded twice. "Substance X" if shown or the word *aspirin* if found must fit one and only one of our categories. We don't expect the characters in the Sunday supplement cartoons to be doing illegal drugs, but if we have made a decision to search for all forms of mind- or body-altering substances, we need a coding scheme that allows for that possibility. Another issue arises. How do we handle occurrences of generic words such as *drug(s)*, *pharmaceutical(s)*, or *medicine(s)*? We can't ignore a reference to a substance simply because it is generic, so we add another category—"generic"—to our coding scheme.

ASSIGN EACH OCCURRENCE OF A UNIT TO A CODE IN THE CODING SCHEME

Identifying word references should be easy; we are looking for specific names such as *beer, cigar, latte,* or *aspirin* that clearly identify a substance. With visual occurrences we have more of a judgment call. What *is* that character ingesting? Where more than one interpretation is possible it is usual to form a panel of judges who will vote on how to code an item. This is likely to be necessary in our study.

For any analysis involving multiple coders, it is usual to ask them to code a number of units as a trial run. Formulas are available to help calculate the degree to which the coders are in agreement. If they are in agreement we can have some confidence that our criteria for coding are clear; if not it is time to revisit our criteria and redefine them so they are clear.

COUNT OCCURRENCES OF THE CODED UNITS AND REPORT THEIR FREQUENCIES

The results of a study like this will be reported as the number of occurrences recorded for each of our substance categories.

We would report and discuss the relative frequency of the substances shown in our coding sheet. This gives us the basic comparison that content analysis does well and helps us decide whether our initial hypothesis is supported or not.

Our study thus far has done little more than help us decide the relative occurrence of substances by category. For a more detailed study, we could break our substance categories down further. For example "tobacco" could be broken down into the categories of "cigarettes," "pipes," and "cigars." Alcohol could be broken down into "beer," "wine," and "liquor." Similarly, the drug categories could be broken down into more specific categories.

Also, it would be much more informative if we could assess the conditions under which these substances appear and perhaps the types of people using them. A further level of analysis then would be to categorize substance use according to type of user—for example male or female, blue collar or white collar—or conditions of use—for example home or work. Our coding sheet would then include the columns shown on the right-hand side of Exhibit 11.1. A chi-square test (Chapter 6) would tell us overall whether the distribution of occurrences varies significantly by type of user or by setting.

Content analysis of language can be automated and expedited with any one of the many content analysis software packages available. Such software needs "training" if the results are to be valid. The software needs to know, for example, whether the word *right* is being used in the sense of "not wrong," "not left," or the verb form "to correct." (If word frequency is your only interest, you have a crude content analysis device in the form of your word processing software. Simply use your software's "find" command to find how many occurrences of a word a document has.)

Content analysis's principal use is in analyzing media content such as news, entertainment, or advertising (in part because of the ready availability of media content), but it can also be applied in such areas as organizational communication and interpersonal communication. For example, transcripts of interactions between people constitute texts and are open to content analysis just as much as television advertising, newspaper editorials, or State of the Union addresses.

Interaction Analysis

Interaction analysis, pioneered by group dynamics scholar Robert Bales (1950), seeks to capture and understand interactions among members of a group and the different roles that group members play. Three broad categories of group behavior are task-oriented, group-oriented, and self-centered. Task-oriented individuals focus on the group's work, for example asking if the group has all the information it needs or assigning specific tasks to members of the group. Group-oriented individuals work to ensure that the group remains cohesive, for example by making jokes to relieve tension or by showing supportiveness for other members' ideas. Self-centered individuals may refuse to participate or may dominate discussions.

Suppose we are looking at the transcripts or a video recording of a corporate team trying to develop a marketing strategy for a new product. The flow of discussion over the weeks leading up to the group's final decision can be coded using Bales's (1950) categories or subcategories as shown in Exhibit 11.2. Here, the group is the unit of analysis, and we are coding observed behaviors for three different meetings at Time 1, Time 2, and Time 3.

EXHIBIT 11.2   **Sample Coding Sheet for Group Behaviors Over Time**

Behavior	Frequencies of Appearance		
	Time 1	Time 2	Time 3
Task-Oriented			
Reminds group members of deadlines			
Proposes solutions to problems			
Group-Oriented			
Makes statements supporting a group's idea			
Makes statements approving of group's progress			
Self-Centered			
Refuses assignments			
Makes antagonistic statements			

We could use the results of such an analysis to test a hypothesis that group behaviors change over time, for example that group-oriented behaviors occur more frequently in the preliminary stages as group members clarify their roles and relationships before moving on to task-oriented behaviors. We could compare the results of such analyses for two different groups, one known to produce excellent decisions and the other known to produce mediocre decisions. This might then allow us to identify the characteristics of high-performing groups and provide a basis for training low-performing groups to do better. We could also use exactly the same criteria to analyze individual behaviors. For example, if we were to replace "Time 1," "Time 2," and "Time 3" in the chart with people (Mick, Keith, and Charlie) we could record, analyze, and compare the behaviors of individuals. We could of course combine both approaches and record individual behavior over time.

Conversation Analysis

Conversation analysts look for the rules governing social acts. They study the mechanisms that allow conversations to happen successfully as opposed to degenerating into chaos. The analyst's interest is in the mechanisms that ensure that a conversation takes place successfully rather than the content of interpersonal conversation. Conversation analysts examine documents, in this case transcripts of conversations, for such occurrences as

- turn taking—the point at which "speaking rights" are handed from one person to another,

- adjacency pairs—units of speech that occur together such as questions and answers, and

- repair mechanisms—actions that restore a conversation when it is in danger of breaking down.

Conversation analysis involves recording and transcribing conversations, looking for occurrences of such mechanisms, and examining specific examples for insight on the dynamics of conversation. A major difference between conversation analysis and content analysis is that conversation analysts add to the conversation's transcript a standardized series of codes that mark particular aspects of the conversation, such as the time between a speaker's utterances or the volume of an utterance.

Rhetorical and Dramatistic Analyses

The Greek philosopher Aristotle defined rhetoric as the study in any given case of the available means of persuasion. In this context, rhetorical analysis means examining texts to identify and assess their persuasive strategies.

It is unfair to distil the breadth and richness of Aristotle's writings down to three concepts, but his identification of **ethos**, **pathos**, and **logos** as keys to successful persuasion remains an enduring contribution to communication research in the 21st century.

- Ethos addresses the nature or character of the speaker.
- Pathos addresses the use of emotion.
- Logos addresses the use of fact and logic.

Analyzing the use of these three factors gives us insight on whether a speech, an opinion piece, or a television advertisement might or might not be effective. With pharmaceutical advertisements as but one example, we might examine for persuasive effect the nature and character of product spokespersons, the use of fact and logic (specifics of how the product works, for example) and emotion (the pleasure you will feel as product X frees you of pain or immobility, for example).

Kenneth Burke (1945), a 20th-century literary theorist, devised a dramatistic approach to communication behavior. He regarded communication essentially as performance, as actors acting out a drama against a particular background or scenario.

Burke's (1945) dramatistic pentad (five-part) analysis asks the following questions:

- **Act**—what act is taking place?
- **Agent**—who is taking this action?
- **Agency**—how or by what means did the act take place?
- **Scene**—where and when did the act take place?
- **Purpose**—why was the act done?

Burke (1945) believed that by examining the first four components of the pentad, one could obtain an answer to the question posed by the fifth—what was the purpose or motivation of the act?

For example, our hypothetical study of substance use in comic strips could be analyzed using Burke's (1945) pentad. If we identify an act (smoking), an agent (employee), an agency (offering a cigarette to the boss), and a scene (work), we might infer a purpose or motivation of the employee trying to ingratiate himself with the boss.

Burke (1945) proposed that information about the dynamics and motivations of communication could be obtained by "ratio analysis." **Ratio analysis** means examining the relative significance of each pentad unit in any given situation, for example act-scene, act-agent, act-agency, act-purpose, agent-agency, agent-scene, and so on. By examining these ratios, we can gain insight into the motives behind the communication or reveal inconsistencies between elements.

Semiotics

At heart, **semiotics** is concerned with the relationship between language, and especially signs, and meaning.

For example, stop signs have a commonly accepted meaning of "Stop—and then proceed when safe to do so." Taken literally, a stop sign says "Stop!" It does not say "and then proceed when safe to do," so where did the "and then proceed" meaning come from, and why do most of us agree to accept that meaning?

Semiotic analysis means exploring the relationships between signs and their meanings. It helps us understand how messages might be interpreted and misinterpreted. Note the plurals. If the relationships between signs and meanings are arbitrary, then multiple interpretations of the relationships are always possible. There are drivers who, at least by their behavior, appear to interpret a stop sign as saying "Slow down a bit . . . if you feel like it and you do not see a patrol car."

Much applied semiotic research centers around consumer products and the meanings that attach to them (Mick, Burroughs, Hetzel, & Brannen, 2004). The value of semiotic analysis is that the researcher explores the multiple possibilities for (mis)interpretation and so becomes alert to all the nuances and possibilities of interpretation associated with a product. Predictably, consumers vary in their interpretations, so one purpose of such research is to see how interpretations of logos, product design, or the product experience vary by type of consumer.

The appeal of semiotic analyses is the vast range of situations in which they can be applied. Semiotic researchers have studied how the shapes of vehicles affect memorability of the car brands, the relationship between self-image and the shape of the perfume bottle a woman is likely to buy, and the images conveyed by corporate logos.

Narrative, Discourse, and Critical Analyses

This chapter has focused on content analysis primarily, but many other approaches to text analysis are possible and are well documented in book and journal articles that your academic library will have. The following approaches will give you further insight on approaches you might consider. Use the bold-type terms as search terms in your scholarly databases to get descriptions, examples, and the advantages and disadvantages of these approaches.

Narrative analysis analyzes the formal properties of stories that people tell. It generally attempts to identify a plot, a setting, characters, and an order of events in people's accounts of their lives. Narrative analysis pays specific attention to how stories play out over time.

Discourse analysis focuses on systems of meaning and how particular labels or concepts ("freedom," "gay," "green,") are developed and made powerful by the use of language.

Critical analyses explore the way in which communication establishes, reinforces, and maintains power structures in society. Two major approaches are **Marxist criticism** and **feminist criticism**. Marxist critics examine communication content for the (often hidden) messages that reinforce the ideology of "the system," or those in power. A critical organizational scholar might, for example, content-analyze employee newsletters to determine the extent to which a management "party line" dominates the content. Feminist criticism generally seeks to assess communication content from a woman's perspective. Approaches may range from determining the relative dominance of male versus female "voices" in a text to identifying sexism in language to developing new analytic methods that challenge such perceived masculine concepts as hierarchy.

Purposes and methods for analyzing media content often overlap. For example, content analysis may be used to obtain a critical reading of pharmaceutical advertising, and critical methods may be used to assess the effectiveness of advertising.

Ethics Panel: Could Analyzing Media Content Result in Harm?

A literature search using the terms *content analysis* and *ethics* will show you any number of studies focused on the content analysis of codes of ethics. This panel addresses a different issue—the ethical implications of content analysis and textual analyses more generally. Such analyses focus on text and do not involve human participants directly. Why therefore would any of these methods have any impact on individuals that would give rise to ethical concerns?

Consider the applications, overt or covert, of content analysis in the world of electronic communication.

"Pop-up" advertisements on your Web browser are based on an analysis of the Web sites you visit.

Postini, a Google subsidiary, offers e-mail administrators a way of monitoring e-mails for compliance with company policy (Google, 2007). Postini clients can set up e-mail monitoring to analyze content and prevent sensitive content from leaving an organization or to identify potential policy violations and thus protect intellectual property, company reputation, and business relationships. Content analysis of employee e-mail is routine in many corporations for all the reasons noted above.

While we can all be thankful for e-mail spam filters that themselves are based on analysis of incoming e-mail message content, we might see applications such as Postini as an invasion of privacy if applied to our e-mail.

Questions

- Could the knowledge that one's business or personal communications are being monitored and analyzed cause psychological distress?

- If so, should the institutional review boards responsible for human subjects' safety be required to review such studies, even if no human participants are studied directly? Revisit Chapter 3 for more detail on these review boards (IRBs).

- Should the content analyst treat personal or business e-mails, Internet discussion content, and letters and phone calls in the same way as television commercials or newspaper pages in terms of permissions and releases?

RESEARCH IN PRACTICE

Reaching Out to Hispanics Living With Paralysis

In late 2006, Vanguard Communications began work with the Christopher and Dana Reeve Foundation's Paralysis Resource Center (PRC) to educate Hispanics about the wealth of information, resources, and services available for people with mobility-related disabilities, as Hispanics were generally underrepresented in the PRC's call volume. After conducting a series of communications research activities including focus groups and a media analysis, Vanguard and the PRC collaborated to develop the *Vivir Sin Límites* (meaning "limit-free living") Hispanic outreach campaign.

As the team began its work to design a campaign that would reach Hispanics, it was clear that a few key research questions needed answers. How are people living with paralysis

(Continued)

(Continued)

portrayed in the U.S. Hispanic media? Where do Hispanics living in the United States get their health information? What resonates with these audiences, and what would motivate them to call the PRC? To answer these questions the team conducted a two-pronged research effort consisting of a comprehensive media content analysis and focus group testing.

The media analysis helped establish a baseline from which to compare future media coverage and determine effective strategies for positioning the PRC as the premier source of information about paralysis. The analysis focused on the way people living with paralysis are portrayed in the nation's top English- and Spanish-language print publications including newspapers and Hispanic-focused magazines.

A major finding of the media analysis was that paralysis was rarely discussed in depth. Coverage usually focused on paralysis as a result of a violent crime or an accident. The reality of what it's like to live with paralysis was never discussed, and portrayals of those with paralysis were rarely inspiring or hopeful. Based on these articles, it was clear that readers were provided with little information about the realities of paralysis, including that people with paralysis live healthy, productive lives. To educate Hispanics about the many ways people with paralysis can be independent, productive, and active, the images and messages selected for the campaign needed to showcase diverse personal stories of those who are living independent, productive, and active lives with paralysis.

To ensure that this message and image concept would resonate with Hispanics, draft themes, messages, slogans, and images were tested in a series of focus groups with Hispanics living with paralysis and with Hispanic women who are close friends with or family of a person living with paralysis. Focus group participants had highly positive reactions to messages and images that showcased a life that is not limited by a person's physical disability. In particular, visual images such as a person with paralysis engaged in educational pursuits or sports best supported the *Vivir Sin Límites* message. The focus groups also indicated that Hispanics seek their health information in Spanish-language magazines and newspapers, on health Web sites, and in radio and television programming.

Based on the outcomes of this research, the team conceptualized a positive *Vivir Sin Límites* campaign, incorporating inspiring accounts of people with paralysis living highly productive lives. The campaign was kicked off at a national media event in Washington, DC, featuring Hispanic individuals with paralysis who shared personal stories of how the PRC helped them live independent and productive lives. The launch highlighted an array of materials available to Hispanics in English and Spanish, including a comprehensive Web site and a toll-free, bilingual help line. Other campaign materials included a brochure, fact sheets, a bookmark, and a bilingual resource guide about living with paralysis.

To promote the campaign launch and the PRC as the premier source of information for Hispanics on paralysis, outreach was conducted to Hispanic print publications, television and radio outlets, and online resources. Media outreach efforts produced more than 3 million audience impressions, including an interview on the top national Spanish-language morning television program, Univision's *Despierta América*. The PRC also experienced increased call volume, achieving one of the primary objectives of the outreach campaign.

Contributed by Vanguard Communications

Vanguard Communications is a public relations and social marketing firm based in Washington, DC.

Chapter Summary

- Content analysts measure communication content quantitatively.
- Content analysis is a process of systematically sampling, coding, and analyzing media content.
- Interaction analysis examines groups for the behaviors that hinder or facilitate group processes.
- Conversation analysis examines records of conversations to determine the rules that govern interaction between people.
- Rhetorical analyses examine content to understand the nature of persuasion.
- Semiotic analyses focus on the (usually multiple) meanings of texts and signs.
- Critical analyses focus on the use of language as it promotes and maintains power in organizations and societies.

Recommended Reading

Bailey, A. A. (2006). A year in the life of the African-American male in advertising. *Journal of Advertising, 35*(1), 83–104. A contemporary example of content analysis of advertising.

Chandler, D. (2002). *Semiotics: The basics.* London: Routledge. An overview of semiotics. Shows how language and signs cannot be regarded as neutral carriers of meaning.

Hirokawa, A. Y. (1988). Group communication research: Considerations for the use of interaction analysis. In C. H. Tardy (Ed.), *A handbook for the study of human communication: Methods and instruments for observing, measuring, and assessing communication processes* (pp. 229–246). Norwood, NJ: Ablex. Shows ways of coding behaviors in groups.

Holsti, P. R. (1969). *Content analysis for the social sciences and humanities.* Reading, MA: Addison-Wesley. An introductory text on content analysis.

Neuendorf, K. A. (2002). *The content analysis guidebook.* Thousand Oaks, CA: Sage. A more recent book with step-by-step instructions and examples.

Richards, K., & Seedhouse, P. (2005). *Applying conversation analysis.* New York: Palgrave Macmillan. See in particular the chapter on conversation analysis as a research methodology.

Recommended Web Resources

Annenberg–Robert Wood Johnson Coding of Health and Media Project: www.youthmediarisk.org. An ongoing project analyzing media content for health-related behaviors. Look at the codebook and sampling procedures in particular.

Center for Media and Public Affairs: http://www.cmpa.com/about_methods.htm. An explanation of content analysis in practice.

Matthias Romppel's content analysis resources: http://www.content-analysis.de. Links to bibliographies, research, software, and text markup and encoding systems.

Resources on Kenneth Burke: http://www.comm.umn.edu/burke. A comprehensive listing of Kenneth Burke resources hosted by the Department of Communication Studies, University of Minnesota.

Umberto Eco Web site: http://www.umbertoeco.com. Eco is a semiotician, literary critic, and novelist, popularly known for his novel *The Name of the Rose*. Check out his Web site on semiotics.

References

Bales, R. (1950*). Interaction process analysis: A method for the study of small groups.* Reading, MA: Addison-Wesley.

Berelson, B. (1952). *Content analysis in communication research.* New York: Hafner.

Burke, K. (1945) *A grammar of motives.* New York: Prentice-Hall.

Google. (2007). *Postini introduces new email content policy management features.* Retrieved March 1, 2008, from http://www.google.com/intl/en/press/pressrel/20071113_postini.html

Krippendorf, K. (1980). *Content analysis: An introduction to its methodology.* Beverly Hills, CA: Sage.

Mick, D. G., Burroughs, J. E., Hetzel, P., & Brannen, M. Y. (2004). Pursuing the meaning of meaning in the commercial world: An international review of marketing and consumer research founded on semiotics. *Semiotica, 52*(1–4), 1–74.

Student Study Site

Visit the study site at www.sagepub.com/treadwellicr for e-flashcards, web resources, and additional study materials.

12 Writing Research

Sharing Your Results

The research report is a part
Of the research professional's art.
It may take awhile
But follow a style
If you want to be thought of as smart.

Chapter Overview

It would be inappropriate to conclude a book on communication research without discussing how the findings of communication research are communicated. Research cannot contribute to our wider knowledge unless people know about it. In this chapter we take a look at the writing process itself, scholarly writing and presentations, and ways to reach the many publics to whom your research may be relevant.

Starter Questions

- How can I best explain my research to other researchers in my interest area?
- How can I best explain my research to news media?
- Is there one best way to present my research results?
- What ethical implications might influence how and when I publish my research results?

Joining the Discussion

You have read all the relevant literature, reasoned through to hypotheses or research questions, identified an appropriate research method, and implemented it. Now comes your reward! You should have a keen sense of anticipation as your project data start to come in. Your data analyses will confirm or refute your hypotheses, lead you down new paths, or perhaps produce ambivalent results that lead you to a "definite maybe" conclusion and the beginnings of another round of research.

It would be nice if you could stop and relax at that point, but other vital steps await—publication and presentation.

This book began with a basic notion that the purpose of research is to contribute to knowledge; there can be no contribution unless your research is presented so that others come to know about it and understand it.

This chapter will be free of microlevel advice about subject-verb agreement, sentence fragments, and comma splices, but it will invite you to think strategically about the many potential audiences for your research report and how you will need to adapt your reporting to the needs of each.

First, some thoughts about writing in general.

The Writing Process

Most individuals write in one of two different ways.

The first is to envisage the entire "final product" in one's head and then simply write it down. In this view writing becomes little more than the mechanical act of transcribing your thoughts onto paper. The alternate view is that you cannot possibly know what you are writing until you have written it down and taken a look at it. In other words, it is only by writing a first draft, examining it critically, and reworking (and reworking and reworking) it that you can arrive at a polished, professional product.

Which approach you will prefer depends not only on your personal approach to writing but also on the type of research you do. Standard survey and experimental designs allow you to envisage and write a lot of your final paper before your research begins. Such research requires that you identify hypotheses or research questions, describe your research methods, identify the people or media that will be sampled and how, and of course review the published literature so that your questions, methods, and sampling can be fine-tuned and so you know that you are not duplicating research that has already been done. With this type of research it is possible, in principle, to write up almost all of your final paper before having even started your research. All that will be missing at this point will be your results and conclusions.

By contrast, you will recall from Chapter 2 that Evered and Reis (1981) described their research as having no initial hypotheses or specific research instruments. Rather they admitted to groping their way through the organizational realities they encountered until gradually they built up a picture that made sense to them. Their project undoubtedly involved writing copious notes and assembling the notes into categories or sequences that made sense to them as their research progressed. Clearly, in research like this where even the methods may evolve and change as the research progresses, the final paper cannot take shape until the researchers declare their research finished and have their raw data synthesized into a final shape that makes sense to them. In such cases, thinking and writing about the research as it progresses can obviously shape the research process as well as the final paper.

For most researchers, writing falls somewhere between these two extremes. Generally, before our research starts, we will be able to (and should) write a literature review, basic research questions, and a description of who or what will be sampled and how our data will be analyzed. It is a good idea to do this to maintain a framework and a focus for your research.

It is also a good idea, and for observational research an essential idea, to maintain notes of everything that happens during your research. These notes should include not only your observations, transcripts, and other data but also notes of your own thinking about your project. That way, when it is time to write your final paper, you will have both your data and different ways of thinking about your data. Note taking and recording are easily done with such tools as digital recorders and voice recognition software. The former devices are light and portable and let you record thoughts and interviews as your project progresses. Voice recognition software lets you dictate to your computer and converts your speech into text with surprising accuracy after some initial "training." Photographs and video may also complement your note taking.

If you are in an exploratory mode it becomes even more important to keep the transcripts of interviews, your observational notes, interpretations, and the like because one buried word, phrase, or metaphor may become the "trigger" for your understanding.

Writing for Scholarly Publics: The Importance of Style

Publication is the way scholars engage in informed conversation with each other. The best way to find out whether your research findings hold up is to publish them and in doing so invite others to examine your research, critique it, and perhaps replicate it to see if they get the same results.

One way to ensure that all relevant aspects of your research are appropriately reported is to follow a style guide such as APA (American Psychological Association), MLA (Modern Language Association), or Chicago (University of Chicago Press). Such guides provide specific instructions for formatting scholarly papers and for citing other authors' work. They provide an essential checklist for planning your research before you do it and a check that you have reported everything a scholarly audience will want to read once you have completed your research and written it up. Exhibit 12.1 shows a generic outline of a scholarly report.

EXHIBIT 12.1 **Generic Scholarly Report Format**

Title Page	
Abstract	
Introduction	Goal and Significance of Research Review of Literature Statement of Research Question(s) and/or Hypothesis(es)
Method	Participants, or Media Content, and How Selected Procedures Used Measures Used
Results	
Discussion	Significance of Results Limitations and Flaws of Study Conclusions Recommendations for Future Research
References	
Appendices	

Citations must be done accurately because scholarly readers, and especially newcomers to the field, will want to be able to access the same material you did. By accurately citing all the material you have drawn on, you help other scholars by identifying material you have found useful, you give the authors whose work has helped you the courtesy of public recognition, and you avoid potential issues of plagiarism.

Review Chapter 4 for the basics of APA citation style. Chicago and MLA also reference material by putting authors' names in the body of a paper and then listing the referenced material alphabetically by author at the end of the paper. However, the three styles differ in how exactly they do this. For example, Chicago and MLA styles use the authors' full first names; APA style uses initials only.

Chicago and other styles also permit the use of footnotes. With footnote style, a number in the body of the paper is used to refer to the publication details of a book or journal article placed at the bottom of the same page. Footnote style provides readers with the convenience of a full citation at the point where it is first referenced in the text but does not provide one convenient list of references.

Every scholarly journal has a specific style that you will be expected to follow, and you must follow that style consistently. Specific guidelines for scholarly styles are available in any academic library, online, and, of course, from the journal editors.

Presenting for Scholarly Publics: Papers and Panels

Published research reports are not the only way researchers "go public." A second major method is academic conferences. Communication associations such as the National Communication Association (www.natcom.org), the Canadian Communication Association (www.acc-cca.ca), and the International Communication Association (www.icahdq.org) all hold annual conferences at which scholarly research is presented.

Here, research presentations typically take two forms—panels and poster papers.

A panel consists of six or so scholars with common research interests presenting the results of their research. Typically, each panelist presents for 15 minutes or so, and there is additional time for discussion with each other and with audience members at the end of the presentations. The papers presented are often "works in progress." The feedback that presenters receive on their papers gives them ideas for improving their research or revising their papers before submitting them for publication.

Typically, the conference organizers will expect to get a full scholarly paper for review before the conference, but the presentation time of 15 minutes or so means that the authors will present only the key points of their research.

In poster sessions presenters have a display panel upon which they post a summary of their research along with any graphics they wish to display. There is no oral presentation, but people interested in a topic can meet researchers alongside their poster papers and discuss the research informally in a session lasting an hour or two. This gives a greater opportunity for discussion with the authors and gives the authors more feedback from a self-selected group of people who are specifically interested in their research.

Writing for Other Publics: Interest Groups and News Media

Communication research findings have relevance to corporations, non-profit organizations, interest groups, and government agencies. For example, a study giving new insights on how television advertising can influence the food preferences of children may interest parents, nutrition advocates, the food industry, the advertising industry, and regulatory agencies.

We will refer to the reports written for such interest groups as "professional" reports because typically they are written for professionals working in a particular sector. As a communication graduate, you may need to write research you have done or summarize the research of others in the form of a professional report for a client or employer.

Professional reports at their most basic level have a structure of introduction-body-conclusion. The introduction summarizes the research and its relevance. The body of the report summarizes the research method(s) and results. The conclusion summarizes the relevance of the results and proposes any action that might be required, based on the research findings. Typically, there will be no literature review and no list of references. The focus of the report is on helping readers understand the results and their relevance.

In the general scheme of things, the readers of *Text and Performance Quarterly, Communication Monographs, Feminist Media Studies,* and the many other scholarly communication journals are small and specialized audiences. Most people do not read such publications, and nonscholarly readers approaching such journals may well be intimidated by their level of detail and by terminology ranging from "multiple polynomial regression" to "phallocentric interpretive stances."

This does not mean that nonscholarly audiences will not be interested in your research. To the contrary, news media and their audiences may be very interested in your research. But if your research is to be understood and appreciated widely, then adapting scholarly writing to the interests, comprehension levels, and knowledge of news media audiences is clearly required.

News media editors look for stories that are relevant to their readers, viewers, or listeners. In terms of communication research, relevant stories might range from cross-cultural communication, if the results of a study in cross-cultural communication translate into a story on how to date someone from another culture, to technology impact, if the results of a study on families watching television translate into a story on how to organize a family TV viewing night.

Adapting scholarly research reports to the needs of news media implies two strategic tasks—answering the "What's in it for us?" question and writing to news media style, be it news or a feature for print, broadcast, or Web media.

Report writing and news writing are covered in many professional books, textbooks, and journals that will be available in your academic library.

Professor Tom Writes a Checklist

You will recall that in Chapter 9 we followed professor Tom as he ran a series of experiments aimed at studying the effects of group versus individual study conditions on academic performance. Now, as he thinks about sharing the results of his research, he recognizes that at the very least he will want to debrief his student participants (an ethical requirement, as you will recall from Chapter 3), write a scholarly paper for publication, and present his results at an academic conference. Because his research focuses on student learning, he can anticipate questions from his academic colleagues on campus. The student affairs office will be interested to know if his research has implications for the way it organizes student study sessions. His campus public relations office will want a summary of his research to do a news release, and the alumni office may be interested in doing a feature story.

He ponders some of the communication disasters he has experienced—the colleague whose presentation consisted of reading a 20-page paper for 35 minutes ("Why," professor Tom wondered, "could he not have just given us copies of the paper?"), for example, and the 30-slide PowerPoint presentation that sent him to sleep. Fortunately in the back row of a darkened auditorium nobody noticed, but he recalls knowing how his students feel at times. He wonders why his last interview with a local television reporter did not get on air and decides that his discussion of "variance attributable to exogenous variables" should have been much shorter, jargon-free, and to the point.

Professor Tom pours himself yet another cup of coffee and jots down what he needs to remember. His list is shown as Exhibit 12.2. Use the checklist as a guide for your own writing and presentations, always referring to a specific style guide such as APA, MLA, or Chicago for scholarly writing of course.

EXHIBIT 12.2   **Communication Checklist**

	Communication Checklist
Scholarly Paper	Abstract, literature review and references, rationale, research questions and/or hypotheses, description of method(s), sampling, measures used, results, conclusions, discussion, and list of references—accurately cited.
Panel Presentation	Brief notes on an index card or one page if necessary. Key points only. *(Continued)*

Exhibit 12.2 *(Continued)*

	Communication Checklist
Poster Paper	Title, summary of research questions/hypotheses, method(s), and results. Summary graphic(s) as necessary. Large type on poster-size paper so people can read the paper at a distance.
PowerPoint –Maybe	Plain background. Light type on dark background or dark type on light background. "Think six": no more than six words per line, six lines per slide, and six slides overall. Large type. Simple graphics. Simplify. Simplify. Simplify. Key points only. Use a handout for detail.
Professional Report	Executive summary; introduction/background. Body of report—method(s), sample, and results; conclusions; recommendations; and supplementary material.
For Campus News Office and Talking Points for Interview	One-page summary sheet. Key points: objective of study, method (brief), results, and conclusions/so what? Simple language that news audiences can understand.
"Tweet!"	In 140 characters or less, what have I discovered, and why is it important?

The Ethics of Style and Accuracy

Any research writing involves decisions about what is reported and how it is reported. Even when rigorously following APA, MLA, or Chicago style, every author decides what information will be reported, or not, and what specific words will describe a method, sample, result, or conclusion.

As Gusfield (1976) points out, language for the scientist is supposed to be a "windowpane"—a panel of clear glass through which the external world can be seen clearly and without distortion. But scholarly writing inescapably has its own tactics aimed at convincing readers that the author has made a significant contribution to our knowledge of human communication.

For example to establish objectivity, authors may "remove themselves" from the narrative by writing passively in the third person, as in "respondents were interviewed," rather than actively, as in "I interviewed the respondents."

At the other extreme, researchers may use what Van Maanen (1988) calls "impressionist writing," which uses a literary style to attract and engage the reader, and may sacrifice objectivity in the interests of reader understanding.

Somewhere between these two extremes, writers wittingly or unwittingly shape readers' interpretations of research simply by choice of words. For example, we discussed in Chapter 10 how terms such as *informant* or *subject* may shape both the researchers' and readers' attitudes toward participants in the research.

A problem with writing summary reports or writing for news media is that detail inevitably becomes lost and terminology that may have a specific meaning for scholars gets dropped in the interests of maximizing understanding for a wider audience.

The question arises of whether, as conscientious writers, we can achieve the goal of giving our readers an unbiased reporting of our research. Happily there are some answers to this question.

First, systematic reporting of research questions, literature review, method, and sampling decisions will help scholarly readers decide whether our results and conclusions are unbiased and defensible.

Second, the peer review process helps ensure that published papers meet scholarly standards and do not make unsubstantiated claims.

Third, we can aim not for the impossible goal of eliminating all our biases but for the goal of making any biases explicit so that readers will have as full an understanding of our research as possible.

Ethics Panel: Balancing Between Scholarly and Popular Writing

Accounts of communication research become less specific and more general as they "move" from the original scholarly journals to popular media. They may also get embellished with metaphors, analogies, and commentaries as journalists try to interpret the original research for lay audiences.

Based on your reading of this chapter and your own research writing,

- to what extent can writing a scholarly research paper limit the extent to which potentially interested publics will know about the research?

- to what extent is writing a news release or professional report on a research project an ethical decision about how well or how much your readers should be informed?

- do journalists have a responsibility to cite the original research paper they are reporting on so interested readers and viewers can find it? and

- do researchers have any responsibility for what journalists do in terms of interpreting an original research paper?

RESEARCH IN PRACTICE

An Analysis of Online Pressrooms in Leading Companies Around the World

Back in 1998, we started an ambitious project to implement a virtual pressroom at IBM Spain. In a few months, our pressroom on the Internet became a model to follow by many other companies in Spain, as well as a good reference for our IBM communication colleagues around the world. We began the site by providing plain information in text format to journalists. Later we added high-quality pictures, as well as some audio and video files for broadcast media. We also introduced feedback tools on our Web site to get journalists' comments and deployed an RSS tool in 2003. However, in 2004, we asked ourselves if we were really on the verge of innovation and if there were any good practices that we were missing with the progressive convergence of Internet, phone, and television technologies. So we decided to benchmark our virtual pressroom against those of the top European and U.S. companies.

First we tried to find information through secondary sources and read most academic studies that researched the way in which corporate communication departments were adapting to new technologies, but we could not find any studies that showed the degree to which corporate communication departments in different geographic regions use Internet technologies. So we decided to conduct our own research.

We wanted to find out specifically if Spain, the rest of Europe, and the United States differed in the way corporate newsrooms were used, to find out how newsrooms were used, and to identify future trends in Internet use. We did this by content-analyzing corporate Web sites from a number of different countries. We first did bibliographic research to find relevant studies; then we conducted a focus group with media representatives to find out about the use of newsrooms by communication professionals. We then selected 15 companies from those with the highest revenue in five European countries, 30 companies from Singapore (because of its high use of information technology), 30 companies from the United States, and 50 from our home country of Spain.

Once we selected the countries, we selected the companies within them by using information from primarily *Fortune* magazine. We designed and pretested a "questionnaire" to use on the Web sites, and then we visited the 170 company Web sites we had selected to gather answers to our "questionnaire."

We found that most companies had a Web site, targeted first at customers and second at the media. Most had a pressroom dedicated to information for the media. Most pressrooms were only one click away from the home page. Most sites did not require registration to access the pressroom. Press releases are the most common content in the pressrooms. The releases are classified, most commonly by date, indicating that most companies recognize the importance of organizing their information. Backgrounders or reports are more popular in the United States, the United Kingdom, and France than in the Nordic countries. Biographies of senior executives are found most frequently in the U.S. Web sites. The United States and Spain are most likely to provide financial data. The percent of companies providing a company history varies widely from country to country. Only half the companies have a photo archive, but these companies do provide high-resolution images in jpeg format. Charts or illustrations are very unusual, but half the companies offered corporate logos for downloading. Half the companies with photo archives provide a legal warning regarding use of their images. Video and audio resources are rare. Almost all sites provide a contact phone number and e-mail contacts for communication staff. Only 30% provide an inquiry form.

Two thirds of the companies took 3 or more days to reply to an e-mail query, and up to 70% did not answer journalists' queries. None of the companies offered interviews via the Web, and very few offered mobile phone news alerts. Only in the United States and the United Kingdom is the author of a press release commonly documented. Fewer than half the companies update their pressroom on a daily basis.

We concluded that large companies, independent of their country of origin or industry sector, recognize the importance of online tools for corporate communication. No one country stands out significantly from the rest although the Nordic corporate Web sites showed some notable deficiencies even though these countries are usually considered models for the penetration of new technologies. The development of online pressrooms does seem to be a function of the resources available for their development. Some sectors do appear to be more advanced than others.

Of course the other side of the story has yet to be researched—how do the media use these pressrooms?

Contributed by Alfonso González Herrero
Manager of External Communications
IBM Spain, Portugal, Greece, and Israel.
Madrid, Spain

Chapter Summary

- Scholarly research papers detail and discuss the theory behind the research, the research method(s), sampling, results, and conclusions.

- Style guides such as APA, MLA, and Chicago give guidance on how to report scholarly research.

- The exact style and format of your final paper will be determined by the scholarly association or journal you are writing for.

- Interest groups and news media will be interested in your research only if it is timely and relevant.

- You can make your research relevant to news media and their audiences by writing in the appropriate news format and style.

- Research reports written for interest groups emphasize results, conclusions, and relevance to the reader.

Recommended Reading

Gusfield, J. (1976). The literary rhetoric of science: Comedy and pathos in drinking driver research. *American Sociological Review, 41*(1), 16–34. A classic analysis of scientific writing as a persuasive literary form.

Herbers, J. M. (2006, March 24). The loaded language of science. *The Chronicle Review, The Chronicle of Higher Education,* pp. B5. A commentary by a scientist who argues for the power of language and that scientists have a responsibility for the rhetorical impact of their writing.

Lipson, C. (2006). *Cite right: A quick guide to citation styles—MLA, APA, Chicago, the sciences, professions, and more.* Chicago: University of Chicago Press. Important citation styles, all in one book.

Pacanowsky, M. (1983). A small-town cop: Communication in, out, and about a crisis. In L. Putnam & M. Pacanowsky (Eds.), *Communication and organizations: An interpretive approach* (pp. 261–282). Beverly Hills, CA: Sage. An example of research written in a narrative, literary style.

Recommended Web Resources

Citation Machine: http://citationmachine.net

EasyBib: http://www.easybib.com

EndNote: http://www.endnote.com

RefWorks: http://www.refworks.com

The above software is designed to help correctly format references. The Web sites are listed without criticism or endorsement, and no criticism of similar Web sites not listed is intended or implied.

APA's Online APA Style Tutorial: http://www.apastyle.org/learn

Chicago-Style Citation Quick Guide: http://www.chicagomanualofstyle.org/tools_citationguide.html

MLA Handbook Site: http://www.mlahandbook.org/fragment/public_index

The above three Web addresses are the "home" sites for the three style guides outlined in this chapter.

Web Journal of Mass Communication Research: http://www.scripps.ohiou.edu/wjmcr/policy.htm. This is a Web-published "e-journal," not a traditional print journal. Read the brief home page to see the procedures for manuscript submission and review. Note the "footnote" style. This journal does not use the more conventional APA style.

References

Evered, R., & Reis, M. (1981). Alternative perspectives in the organizational sciences: "Inquiry from the Inside" and "Inquiry from the Outside." *Academy of Management Review, 6*(3), 385–396.

Gusfield, J. (1976). The literary rhetoric of science: Comedy and pathos in drinking driver research. *American Sociological Review, 41*(1), 16–34.

Van Maanen, J. (1988). *Tales of the field: On writing ethnography.* Chicago: University of Chicago Press.

Student Study Site

Visit the study site at www.sagepub.com/treadwellicr for e-flashcards, web resources, and additional study materials.

Glossary

Abduction. Reasoning from an observed effect to possible causes.

Act. In Burke's **dramatistic analysis**, the behavior that is taking place.

Action research. Research engaging with groups or communities specifically to solve problems.

Agency. In Burke's **dramatistic analysis**, the means by which an act takes place.

Agent. In Burke's **dramatistic analysis**, the individual(s) taking the action.

Anonymity. A way of protecting research participants in that the data collected from them does not identify them in any way. Typically anonymity is ensured by instructing **respondents** not to put their name on any information they provide.

APA. American Psychological Association. APA is the standard style for many communication scholars when they reference other people's work. It uses an "author (date)" style in the body of the paper and places the full citations, alphabetized by author, at the end of the paper. APA is also relevant in terms of the American Psychological Association Ethical Principles of Psychologists and Code of Conduct.

Appeals. The bases of persuasion. For example sex appeal and fear appeal in advertising.

Authority. A way of knowing based on knowledge from a credible or respected source of information.

Between-subjects design. An experimental design in which participants are exposed to only one experimental condition.

Bivariate statistics. Statistics that describe the relationship between two variables.

Boolean operators. Terms such as *and*, *or*, and *not* that allow one to fine-tune a database search.

Case study. An informative narrative, history, or analysis to help readers' understanding or to provide them with theoretical insights.

Categorization. The process of identifying an item of data as belonging to a category predetermined by the researcher or generated from information provided by informants.

Causal relationship. A relationship between variables in which changes in one demonstrably result in changes in another.

Census. A study of every member of a population.

Chi-square (χ^2). A statistical test for determining whether two groups have a significantly different distribution of scores on the same variable.

Citations. The publication details of books, journal articles, or Web sites.

Closed-ended research questions. See **research question.**

Code/coding. The process of transforming data into a simplified form, usually for computer processing.

Cohort. A group of people defined, most typically, by having an event in common.

Concurrent validity. Demonstrated when a measure correlates highly with other measures designed to measure the same construct.

Confederates. Participants in a study who have been briefed by the researcher to behave in a particular way.

Confidence interval. A range of values, estimated from a **sample**, within which a value for a **population** is estimated to fall.

Confidence level. The calculated probability of a value being true. Typically for communication research a confidence level of 95 is used, meaning that a reported value is estimated to occur 95 times out of 100 if a population is repeatedly sampled.

Confidentiality. The assurance given to research participants that the researcher will not release information that will identify them. The researcher can link information that participants provide to the identity of the person providing it.

Construct. Idea or concept.

Construct validity. Occurs when the measures of one concept or **construct** agree with the measures of other related concepts.

Content analysis. A quantitative, systematic technique for categorizing and describing the manifest content of recorded communications.

Content validity: face and expert or panel. The extent to which a measure fully represents a given concept, typically as judged by a panel of experts. See also **face validity, expert validity**, and **panel validity**.

Contingency table. A table that shows how scores for two or more variables are related, for example gender by income. See also **cross-tabs.**

Contrast questions. Questions that ask **respondents** to explain the difference between two or more things or concepts.

Control. In experimental design *control* refers to an experimental group that does not receive any experimental treatment in order to provide a baseline for measuring changes that might occur in other groups. As a goal of research *control* refers to gaining information about human behavior in order to be able to control it.

Control group. Experimental group not exposed to any experimental variable.

Convenience sampling. Sample based on convenience to the researcher.

Convergent validity. Occurs where there is a demonstrable agreement between the concept or construct you are trying to measure and other related concepts.

Conversation analysis. A research approach that analyzes the rules governing conversational interactions.

Correlation. A statistical procedure for measuring the strength of association between two or more variables. More generally, the degree to which variables are related.

Correlation coefficients. Express the strength of the relationship between two variables.

Covariance/covariation. A relationship between variables in which the values of one variable change as the values of another variable change.

Criterion validity. Demonstrated when a test or measure correlates highly with some tangible, external criterion.

Critical analyses/criticism. Studies that explore the way in which communication establishes, reinforces, and maintains power structures in society.

Cross-lagged surveys. Surveys that measure the relationship between a **dependent variable** and an **independent variable** at two points in time.

Cross-sectional surveys. Surveys taken at one point in time, as opposed to **trend studies.**

Cross-tabs. (Short for *cross-tabulations.*) A table that shows how scores for two or more variables are related. See also **contingency table.**

Curvilinear relationship. A relationship between two variables, the strength and direction of which are variable. If plotted as a graph, the relationship will show as a curved (nonlinear) line.

Data reduction. A process of reducing "raw" data to a simpler form, using, for example, summary statistics such as **measures of central tendency**.

Data set. All the data from a research project.

Database. In the context of bibliographic research, a collection of (mostly) scholarly articles that can be searched electronically.

Deduction. Reasoning from a theory to define the observations you would make to test the theory.

Degrees of freedom. A measure of the number of ways data could be combined and still produce the same value for a statistic.

Dependent variable. A variable whose values change as a result of changes in another (**independent**) variable.

Description. An account or documentation of observed conditions. One basic goal of research is to describe communication phenomena in a way that others can understand it.

Descriptive questions. Questions that ask informants to describe a phenomenon.

Descriptive statistics. Statistics that describe and summarize the data for a sample.

Dichotomous questions. Force **respondents** to choose one of two possible answers, for example "yes" or "no."

Discourse analysis. Focuses on systems of meaning and how particular labels or concepts are developed and maintained by the use of language.

Divergent validity. Demonstrated when a measure of a construct or concept is shown to be unrelated to measures of unrelated concepts.

Double negative. A combination of **negative wording** with a **double-barreled question**, almost guaranteed to confuse **respondents**.

Double-barreled questions. Questions that ask two questions simultaneously but allow for only one answer.

Dramatism/dramatistic analysis. Analyzing communication as performance, as actors acting out a drama. For example, Burke's dramatistic pentad asks, What act is taking place? Who is taking this action? How or by what means did the act take place? Where and when did the act take place? Why was the act done?

Ecological isomorphism. The extent to which an experimental condition is similar to the real-world conditions it is attempting to simulate.

Empirical/empiricism. The view that knowledge should be based on experience and observation.

Epistemology. The study or theory of knowledge. Epistemology addresses such questions as "What is knowledge?" and "How do we know what we know?"

Ethnography/ethnographer. The study of human social behavior, typically with emphasis on description.

Ethnomethodology. The study of how people make sense of their culture and everyday activities and communicate that understanding to others.

Ethos. Aristotelian concept of source character or credibility in argumentation.

Ex post facto design. An "after the fact" experimental design in which there is no **control** over experimental conditions.

Experiment. A research design based on manipulating one variable in hopes of observing an effect on another variable. Typically an experimental condition is applied to one group and the results are compared with those from another group (**control group**), which has had no experimental treatment.

Expert validity. Validity as judged by relevant experts. See also **panel validity**.

Explanation. An attempt to account for the relationships observed among phenomena. A basic goal of research is to explain how and why communication phenomena occur.

Exploration. "Mapping out" a new area of research before proceeding to study it more specifically.

Face validity. A question or measure appears to capture the concept it is intended to capture. See also **expert validity** or **panel validity**.

Factorial designs. Experimental designs that manipulate multiple variables at a time.

Feminist criticism. Critical analysis of communication from women's perspectives.

Field experiment. A less sophisticated level of experimental design, where the effects of changes in one variable on another are observed under limited conditions of **control**.

Filter questions. Questions that determine whether a **respondent** is qualified to answer a question and that typically redirect the **respondent** to another question if not.

Focus group. Small group of people brought together to discuss a topic of interest to the researcher.

Frequency/ies. The number of times a particular score or result occurs. Commonly reported in the form of **frequency tables**.

Frequency table. A table showing the number of times that scores from a data set occur.

Fully structured interview. Interview in which the researcher has determined what questions are important, the order they will be asked in, and how they will be structured.

Funnel/inverted funnel. A set of questions that move from general to specific or vice versa.

Grounded theory. A research approach that argues that theories should emerge from data analysis, not prior to data analysis.

Hypothesis. A testable statement about the relationships expected among variables of interest. **Two-tailed hypotheses** predict a relationship between two variables but do not specify the direction of the relationship. **One-tailed hypotheses** specify the direction of a relationship between variables. A **null hypothesis** specifies that there is no relationship between variables.

Idiographic. A research approach with an emphasis on understanding the subjectivity and individuality of human communication, rather than universal laws.

Independent variable. A variable whose changes in values result in changes in another (**dependent**) variable.

Induction. Reasoning from observations to a theory that might explain the observations.

Inferential statistics. Statistics that estimate the values for a population from a sample of that population.

Informants. Interviewees considered capable of speaking on behalf of or about others.

Informed consent. The process by which potential research participants are informed of the nature of the research and given the opportunity to sign or not sign a voluntary agreement to participate.

Institutional review board (IRB). A panel established to review research proposals for their impact on human participants.

Interaction analysis. Research that seeks to document group roles and interactions among members of a group.

Intercoder or observer reliability. A measure of the extent to which two different coders code the same phenomenon the same way.

Interpretive perspective. A research approach that seeks to understand how humans interpret or make sense of events in their lives.

Interval. Generally, the distance between points on a scale. In research terms *interval* refers to a scale in which there is an assumption of equal intervals between points.

Interview. A question-and-answer session designed to elicit information the researcher is interested in.

Interviewees. Individuals who are interviewed.

Intuition. Refers to arriving at an answer without quite knowing how you arrived there; a hunch or "gut instinct."

Latent. Hidden or not apparent.

Leading questions. Questions worded to lead **respondents** to a particular answer rather than the one they might have genuinely given.

Likert scale. An interval scale on which **respondents** record their reaction to a statement by checking their level of agreement between "strongly agree" and "strongly disagree."

Logos. Aristotelian concept of logic in argumentation.

Longitudinal surveys/studies. Surveys/studies that capture data over a period of time.

Manifest. Apparent or observable.

Marxist criticism. The study of communication content aimed at assessing its political orientation or identifying messages that reinforce the ideology of "the system," or those in power.

Maximum. The highest value in a **data set.**

Mean. The average of a set of scores.

Measurement. The process of finding out whether people (or media content) have more or less of an attribute we are interested in. It is done by assigning numbers to the phenomena we are interested in.

Measures of central tendency—mean, median, and **mode**—describe the central features of a **data set** rather than its outlying values.

Measures of dispersion—range, variance, and **standard deviation**—describe the range and variability of values in a **data set.**

Median. The midpoint of a set of scores.

Metric. A unit of measurement.

Minimum. The lowest value in a **data set.**

Mode. The most frequent score in a set of scores.

Multiple-choice questions. Questions that offer **respondents** a selection of answers from which they are instructed to select one or more.

Multistage cluster sampling. Sampling based on first sampling large units such as states or provinces and then sampling smaller units such as towns, city blocks, and so on.

Multivariate analysis. An analysis that examines the relationship among three or more variables simultaneously.

Multivariate statistics. Statistics that describe the relationship among three or more variables.

Narrative analysis. The study of the formal properties of stories to identify such aspects as plot, setting, characters, and an order of events.

Negative wording. Questions phrased using a negative rather than a positive (e.g., "don't" rather than "do").

Network sampling. Sampling using members of a network to introduce you to other members of the network. Also known as **snowball sampling.**

Nominal. A system of classification based on names rather than scales or rank-ordering—for example press, radio, and television.

Nomothetic. A research approach with an emphasis on measurement with a view to making generalizations about human behavior.

Nonprobability sampling. Sampling based on a sampling judgment by the researcher.

Normal curve. Scores with a normal distribution form a symmetrical curve from lowest to highest value with the majority of scores "peaking" in the middle.

Null hypothesis. See **hypothesis.**

Numbers. Numbers assign value and relativity to phenomena. As contrasted with **numerals,** they can be calculated.

Numerals. Numerals are labels such as street numbers that cannot be computed.

Observer reliability. A measure of the extent to which observers are in agreement in their coding of observations.

One-tailed test. Proposing that any difference between two groups will be in one direction; that is, one group will score higher than another.

Ontology. The study of the nature of existence and what it is that language actually refers to.

Open-ended questions. Questions to which **respondents** can reply in their own words.

Operationalize. To define a concept in such a way that it can be measured.

Ordinal. Scales with some measure of progression such as "freshman, sophomore, junior, and senior."

Panel. A group of the same individuals retained to answer questions over time.

Panel validity. Validity as judged by a group of relevant experts. See also **expert validity**.

Participant. Any individual who has volunteered to be in a research project.

Pathos. Aristotelian concept of emotion in argumentation.

Peer review. The process of assessing scholarly research by others working in the same field.

Phenomenology/phenomenologist. A research approach that attempts to understand human behavior and consciousness from the individual subjective point of view.

Phrenologist. A practitioner of a now discredited "science" based on the assumption that people's personality could be assessed from the size and shape of their skulls.

Pilot. A prototype or pretest. A small study conducted prior to a full-scale study to ensure that the full-scale study will work successfully.

Popular articles. Articles published without a refereeing process, typically in newspapers and magazines, and targeted to a consumer public.

Population. Every individual or item of a type you want to study. The entire set of individuals or items from which a sample is drawn.

Positivism. The idea that phenomena are governed by, and can be explained by, rules based on objective observation and generalizations from those observations.

Prediction. One goal of research; understanding human behavior in order to forecast the conditions under which it will occur.

Predictive validity. Predictive validity occurs when a measure successfully predicts a tangible outcome. For example, GRE scores should predict success in graduate school. See also **criterion validity**.

Probability sampling. Sampling based on random selection of the sample units.

Proprietary information. Research data or methods that are privately owned and therefore may not be used without the owner's permission.

Purpose. In Burke's **dramatistic analysis,** the reason or motivation that explains an **act.**

Purposive/judgmental sampling. Sampling based on specific criteria the researcher may have.

Q Methodology. A research approach used to assess individuals' subjective understanding. Typically, participants rank a series of statements about a topic according to their perceived accuracy. Quantitative analysis of these rankings identifies a small number of factors that show the patterns of subjectivity within the participant group.

Qualitative. A research approach based on the use of language rather than numbers to report and interpret human behavior.

Quantitative. A research approach based on measurement, counting, and, typically, statistical analysis.

Questionnaire. A set of questions to which **respondents** reply.

Quota sampling. Sampling that attempts to replicate in a sample the features that the researcher thinks are important in the population.

Random assignment. The use of random selection to assign research participants to experimental groups.

Random digit dialing. A telephone survey method in which phone numbers are randomly dialed in hopes of reaching unlisted numbers.

Random sampling. Sampling in which every member of a population has an equal chance to be selected and in which selection is determined by "luck of the draw" rather than a decision by the researcher.

Range. The difference between the maximum value and the minimum value for a given variable.

Ranking questions. Survey questions that ask **respondents** to order items according to their perceived importance or preference.

Ratio. Ratio scales contain a "true" zero, for example zero speed on a speedometer.

Ratio analysis. In Burke's **dramatistic analyses**, this means examining the relative significance of each pentad unit (**act**, **scene**, **agent**, **agency**, **purpose**) in any given situation.

Rationalism. The view that knowledge is best acquired by reason and factual analysis rather than faith or emotion.

Refereeing/refereed. The process of having one's research reviewed by other researchers in the author's field. See also **peer review**.

Reification. Turning an abstract into a concrete thing. For example assuming that because there are measures of intelligence there is a unitary tangible entity called intelligence.

Reliability/reliability coefficients. A measure of the extent to which a test or measure performs consistently.

Research question. The basic research interest posed as a question. **Open-ended research questions** ask simply whether there is a relationship between variables. **Closed-ended research questions** ask about the direction of the relationship.

Respondents. Interviewees or survey participants considered capable of speaking only on behalf of themselves. The individuals responding to **survey** or interview questions.

Rhetoric. The study of the principles and means of persuasion and argumentation.

Rhetoricians. Those who study **rhetoric.**

Sample. A set of individuals or items selected from a wider population.

Sampling. The processes by which a specific number of people or items are selected to represent a wider population.

Sampling distribution. The distribution of values in a sample.

Sampling frame. The master list from which a sample is selected.

Sampling interval. The interval selected in **systematic sampling** (e.g., every 10th or 100th unit).

Sampling units. The units selected for study.

Scaled questions. Questions in which **respondents** are asked to mark their answer on a scale.

Scales. Measurement devices used to locate an individual's ranking on some attribute. Classic scales in communication research are the **Likert** and **semantic differential** scales.

Scatterplot. A graph showing the scores for one variable plotted against the scores for a second variable for each individual in a sample.

Scene. In Burke's **dramatistic analysis,** the location where an **act** takes place.

Scholarly articles. Research papers that have been **peer reviewed** and published in academic journals.

Scientific method. A research approach based on developing specific hypotheses or propositions that can then be tested using specific observations designed for that purpose.

Search engine. Device such as Google or Yahoo that retrieves information from the Web.

Search term. The words typed into a database or search engine when searching for information.

Semantic differential. A scale anchored at opposite ends by opposing words such as "strong–weak" or "hot–cold."

Semiotics. The study of the relationships between signs and their interpretation and meaning.

Semistructured interview. Interview in which questions and question order are largely predetermined but allow room for **interviewees** to add their own insights and views.

Serials. Regularly published scholarly publications such as journals.

Snowball sampling. See **network sampling**.

Social scientists. Researchers who share the assumption that the methods of science can be applied to researching and understanding human behavior.

Standard deviation. A measure of the extent to which scores vary on either side of their mean value. The square root of **variance**.

Standard error. For a **sampling distribution** (the distribution of scores for a **sample**), the standard deviation is called the *standard error*.

Stratified random sampling. Sampling in which randomly selected units from small or minority populations are forced into the sample to ensure that they are represented in proportion to their presence in the population.

Structural questions. Questions that ask **interviewees** to explain the relationships among different terms. For example, "Would you say that X is a part of Y?"

Subjects. Individuals who participate in an experiment.

Survey. A research method in which predetermined, formatted questions are distributed to relatively large numbers of people. Typically, **respondents** respond by phone, mail, e-mail, or Web site.

Systematic sampling. Sampling by selecting every nth unit from a population.

***t*-test**. A statistical test for assessing whether the mean scores for two groups are significantly different.

Temporal ordering. Ordering based on a time sequence. To determine that A causes B, A must precede B in time.

Tenacity. A way of knowing based on accepting knowledge, correctly or incorrectly, because it has stood the test of time.

Test-retest. To determine the reliability of a measure by testing and retesting it under the same conditions. If the measure is reliable, it will produce similar results each time.

Time series analysis. Analysis of a series of observations made over time.

Trade publication. A journal published for a particular industry. The articles are written by experts but not necessarily to the standards of an academic research publication.

Trend studies. Studies that measure the same items over time.

Triangulation. The use of two or more research methods to address the same research question. If results from different methods agree, researchers can have greater confidence in their findings.

Two-tailed test. Proposing simply that scores for two groups will differ. No direction is specified, as it is with a **one-tailed test**.

Univariate statistics. Statistics that describe only one variable.

Universe. In communication research, *universe* has the same meaning for items as **population** does for people. For example, survey researchers sample people from a population; content analysts sample media content from a universe.

Unobtrusive measures. Observations of people's behavior without them being aware of such observation.

Unstructured interview. An interview using broad questions and a loose schedule of questions so that **interviewees** have the freedom to volunteer information and to explain their responses.

Validity. A measure of whether a test measures what it is supposed to measure.

Variable. The aspects of a concept that are capable of being measured or taking on a value. The construct *academic performance* cannot be measured; the variable *grade point average* can.

Variance. A measure of the extent to which scores vary on either side of their mean value. The square root of **standard deviation**.

Volunteer sampling. Obtaining a sample by asking for volunteers.

Within-subjects design. An experimental design in which participants are exposed to more than one experimental condition.

Worldview. A major conceptual framework for understanding the world. For example, the view that humans are essentially similar and their behavior can be measured and predicted, versus the view that humans are individual and unpredictable and their behavior may be described but not predicted.

Z-score. The number of units of **standard deviation** any individual score is above or below the mean for the variable.

Index

About the Author

Donald Treadwell is a professor in the Department of Communication at Westfield State College. He teaches courses in communication research, organizational communication, public relations, and public relations writing. He is the communication internship program coordinator and graduate and continuing education advisor.

He has published in *Communication Monographs, Journal of Technical Writing and Communication, Public Relations Review, Journal of the Association for Communication Administration, Journal of Human Subjectivity,* and international health education journals.

He is a member of the National Communication Association, the International Society for the Scientific Study of Subjectivity, and the Communication Institute for Online Scholarship. He has international consulting experience in agricultural extension and health communication.

His graduate degrees are from Cornell University and Rensselaer Polytechnic Institute.